PATRIOTS PASSION

From Day One

By:
Michael A. King

To Ken,
Enjoy
Patriots #1, forever!!!
Best Wishes

Michael A King
1/20/11

Patriots Passion From Day One

© 2010 Michael A. King

UNOFFICIAL COMMEMORATIVE ISSUE Edition: December 2009OFFICIAL COMMEMORATIVE ISSUE Edition: October 2010

All rights reserved. No part of this book may be reproduced or transmitted in any form or by any means without written permission of the author.

ISBN 978-0-9820363-2-7

Read **U**s **F**or **F**un Publishing
P. O. Box 623
Dover, MA 02030
readusforfun.com

Read Us For Fun Logo designed by Heather Balchunas
www.hbillustrations.com

Dedicated to

Bill Lucy, a friend forever; a good man; and an everlasting presence in my life.

In Memory of
Josie, Mister and the Mrs., thank you for everything;
I'll always remember and love each of you forever.

In remembrance of
Ron Burton, Darryl Stingley, and John Tanner –
true Patriots heroes.

ACKNOWLEDGMENTS

To not show any favoritism, all names were drawn out of a hat for sequence. This hat, a Boston Patriots blue cap adorned with a *Pat the Patriot* logo, was with me for every moment of research, writing, re-working, and editing of this book. That said, here we go . . .

To Mr. Robert Kraft and the entire New England Patriots organization: thank you for producing a fun, interesting, and captivating subject to research, making this 14-month, 24/7 odyssey much more than just an unforgettable trip down memory lane. Mr. Kraft, we've never met, but thank you for having such classy people in your organization. Also, to you and Jonathan Kraft, thanks ever so much for passing my Red Sox book on to Fred; for this, thank you forever; it was the beginning of my once-in-a-lifetime journey.

To Greg: thank you. You're the best, and remember, always do the right thing. I love you – you're the light of my life and you just lost the game.

To Wendy: thank you. Every friendship and partnership has a defining moment. After sending out the S.O.S for an artist in the summer of 2008, now I realize why you answered the email within 30 seconds! Your support, ideas, creativity and dedication can't hold a candle to our friendship.

To Fred: thank you for . . . what can I say? Thanks for often providing the guiding light! You were 100 percent correct on the format, always had a "you're on the right track" for me during trying times, got me addicted to Patriots gamebooks, offered rock-solid advice, and mostly, are living proof that nice guys can finish first!

To Christy: thank you for the results in your quest for photos. You're professional, thorough, prompt, and courteous a reflection of the values in your organization. You're a true credit to the New England Patriots.

To Beth: thank you for your tireless and top-notch editing. Your efforts also earned me not just a new editor, even better, a good friend. To your assistant, thank you Greg – the help was greatly appreciated.

To Michelle: thank you for all your hard, accurate, and well-structured work. Just a small portion of research found the pages of the book; however, if the balance of the pages are as accurate, guess what? This book will be mistake-free!

To Liz and Jim: thank you for all your efforts. Everyone at Braintree Printing is always more than helpful.

To Cesar and the gang at Acapulco's in Needham the best Mexican food north of the border, thank you for use of the table/desk. Can't wait to see you, Felipe, Roberto, Isabella, Roberto, Jr., Susie & Samantha, and Laura & Kendra on my next visit.

To Ken Wadness and the Chickering School 4th grade class of 2008-09: thank you for the start; and remember, make studying fun, because it is!

To Kathy: thank you from the bottom of my heart. Thank you for completing my life with the best "better late than never" to ever happen to me.

To Mom and Dad: I love you. I'll never forgot your spirits, and your memories will live within me forever.

TABLE OF CONTENTS

Acknowledgments	iv
Foreword	vi
Introduction	1
The Team	2
The Coaches	14
The Offense	19
The Defense	31
The Special Teams	37
The Draft	43
The Stadiums	49
"Firsts" On The Field	55
Odds & Ends	59
Super Bowl Time	74
Patriots Anniversary Teams	90
The Opponents	95
Around Pro Football	108
Game by Game From Day One	116
Who Wore the Jersey First?	194
College Football Coaches' Quotable Quotes	197

FOREWORD

Forget about knowing trivia and other minutia, when it comes to the New England Patriots, there was a time when we didn't even know if their games would be on television.

We've come a long way from those days of broadcast blackouts, one-win seasons and aluminum bench seats. Since Robert Kraft bought the Patriots in 1994, saving them from a certain move to St. Louis, the Patriots have been to five Super Bowls with three rings to show for their efforts. Their success of this decade has captured the attention of football fans worldwide; over 160 separate fan clubs now exist in all corners of the globe. Ask most Patriots fans these days and they'll not only tell you Tom Brady's passer rating but also the stats of everyone else on his offense. The convergence of the Digital Age and the Patriots as the dominant team in the National Football League has created a volcano of information. Patriots trivia and minutia is now common knowledge.

That's why Patriots fans need to read this book.

This book is not the typical compilation of history, statistics and re-hashed stories now ingrained like rote in the Patriots section of our brains. (Remember the one about the snow plow that cleared the space for John Smith's winning field goal? Exactly.) Instead, Michael King, with his incredible memory and knack for details, offers us the kind of fun facts that can't be looked up in a media guide or the Internet. Call it trivia extrapolated, if you will. *Patriots Passion: From Day One* spans the history of the Patriots in a way no author has attempted thus far and succeeds in creating an entirely new compendium of Patriots information.

Enjoy this next level of Patriots knowledge!

Fred Kirsch
Publisher & Editor-in-Chief, Patriots Football Weekly

INTRODUCTION

On November 22, 1959, Boston was awarded the eighth and final franchise in the soon-to-be American Football League (AFL) – or so thought a Patriots ownership team led by former sportswriter and local businessman Billy Sullivan. Just a few days later, the group from Minneapolis-St. Paul withdrew from the AFL to accept the National Football League's (NFL) offer of a franchise to begin playing in 1961. The search began again for an eighth city, and on January 30, 1960, the city of Oakland, CA, was awarded the franchise. The Oakland Raiders – not the Oakland Señors, as they were originally named through a newspaper contest – took the last spot. The other six charter AFL teams were in Buffalo (Bills), Dallas (Texans), Denver (Broncos), Houston (Oilers), Los Angeles (Chargers), and New York (Titans). The AFL was ready to begin its inaugural season in the fall of 1960 and start a face-to-face competition with the NFL.

To an entire generation of gridiron fans, pro football made its debut in Boston on Friday, September 9, 1960. Not wanting to conflict with Sunday TV broadcasts of the already entrenched NFL games, and in an attempt to draw fans, the brand spanking new AFL scheduled Friday and Saturday night games in established NFL markets whenever possible. With a majority of the city caught up in the presidential election featuring Massachusetts native son Senator John F. Kennedy, the Boston Patriots still managed to draw some of their own attention. While the JFK camp was hoping to need a reason to make January 1961 inauguration plans, the second Friday in September belonged to the Patriots and the new upstart AFL. Boston was readying to square off against the Denver Broncos (1960/game 1) at Boston University's Nickerson Field for the official debut of a football league hoping to gain a foothold among football fans.

In their first 11 years, not having a stadium of their own, the Boston Patriots played in six different venues – including Fenway Park – before settling in the Boston exurb Foxboro in the cold and dismal Schaefer Stadium and changing their name to the New England Patriots we know today. Their first three decades were less than stellar, but they managed to make the playoffs six times – losing in an appearance in an AFL championship game in 1963 and Super Bowl XX in 1986 by a combined score of 97-20, and four times getting knocked out in the first round.

Still, Patriots fans were loyal – so loyal, in fact, that when the team threatened to leave town and their woeful stadium in 1993, their landlord, a die-hard fan himself, refused the $75 million offered to buy out the remainder of his stadium lease and bought the team instead. At the press conference making the sale of the Patriots official, on February 25, 1994, the new owner, Robert Kraft, made things clear to all Patriots fans – his goal was to bring an NFL championship to New England. In his first 16 years at the helm (1994-2009), the Patriots posted a 183-98 record – the most victories for any NFL team in this time span.

Thanks to Bob Kraft, the sudden turnaround of the Patriots as the 21st century began to unfold was a welcome sight on the New England sports scene. Sell-out home games, no local television blackouts, stable and finacially solvent upper-management, and a quality team on the field made the Patriots' future look rosy. With five Super Bowl appearances and three World Championships, a new state-of-the-art stadium, a natural-born leader as head coach, year-in-year-out knowledgeable assistant coaches, an endless crop of outstanding players, and loyal fans, what more could anyone ask for? How about a franchise quarterback? With Tom Brady, voilà, the New England Patriots have everything going smoothly.

It's easy to look up and find the leading career rusher, receiver, and quarterback in Patriots team history or the final score of all the "big games"; this information is just a book or a click on the computer away. Throughout this book, however, the reader will learn the unique, obscure, fascinating, never-to-forget, "oh-wow" facts, tales, and stories of Patriots history. Keep a supply of post-it-notes by your side to mark the tidbits you want to remember. All the information on these pages was collected by a fan for the enjoyment of all Patriots fans. Let's pass on the legacy of Patriots Pride to future generations of New England Patriots fans. Enjoy.

ONE
THE TEAM

The First Opening Patriots Act

Patriots offensive tackle Tony Discenzo boomed the initial American Football League opening kickoff, on September 9, 1960 at Nickerson Field, into the Denver end zone. Broncos running back Bob McNamara hauled in the kick, sprinted out toward the right side line, but suddenly handed the ball to teammate Al Carmichael on a razzle-dazzle reverse. The AFL was hyping this exciting style of play as a sales pitch; and sure enough, on the first official play of this new league, the 21,597 fans in attendance witnessed such action. Thanks to an alert Tommy Addison, who held his lane on the opposite side of the field, this play was snuffed out at Denver's 17-yard line.

Who Said This Team Wasn't Going To Be Entertaining?

Down three points, 24-21, to the New York Titans (1960/game 2) and kicking off with only 1:50 left in the fourth quarter, the Patriots needed an intervention from the football gods to gain their first American Football League regular-season victory. The Patriots on-sides kick failed and the Titans gained possession of the ball at their own 49-yard line. The game was all but over and to make things even worse, Boston jumped off sides giving the Titans a first and five in Patriots territory. Holding New York to one yard on three plays and utilizing their time outs, Boston forced the Titans to punt. With seconds left in the game, in order to secure a victory, New York just needed to get the punt off and provide good coverage. Titans kicker Rick Sapienza mishandled the snap from center and fumbled the ball. Attempting to recover the loose football, Sapienza bobbled the pigskin and failed to secure the ball. Patriots defensive back Chuck Shonta out-muscled the hapless punter for the loose ball, scooped up the prized possession, and sprinted into the Titans end zone for the game-winning touchdown. With no time remaining on the clock, the Patriots won their first-ever regular season AFL game, 28-24, in miraculous fashion. Originally, the play was listed as a 25-yard fumble return; however, the official scorer later changed the length of the winning touchdown to a 52-yard fumble return. Shonta's score was the first touchdown in franchise history credited to the defense.

The American Football League Cream Of The Crop

Gino Cappelletti, Babe Parilli, and Jim "Earthquake" Hunt are included on the elite list of 17 players who were on a team's roster for each of the ten 14-game seasons of the American Football League (1960-1969). The other 14 individuals are George Blanda, quarterback, Houston/Oakland; Billy Cannon, running back, Houston/Oakland; Larry Grantham, linebacker, New York; Wayne Hawkins, offensive guard, Oakland; Harry Jacobs, linebacker, Boston/Buffalo; Jacky Lee, quarterback, Houston/Denver/KC; Paul Maguire, linebacker/punter, Los Angeles/San Diego/Buffalo; Bill Mathis, running back, New York; Don Maynard, wide receiver, New York; Ron Mix, offensive tackle, Los Angeles/San Diego; Jim Otto, center, Oakland; Johnny Robinson, safety, Dallas/Kansas City; Paul Rochester, defensive tackle, Dallas/Kansas City/New York; and Ernie Wright, offensive tackle, Los Angeles/San Diego/Cincinnati. Three players, Tom Flores, quarterback, Oakland/Buffalo/Kansas City, Jack Kemp, quarterback, Los Angeles/San Diego/Buffalo; and Paul Lowe, running back, Los Angeles/San Diego, missed one season due to injury but were in the league for all 10 years.

Someone Had To Be The First

Running back Billy Lott was the first individual in franchise history to score a touchdown both for and against the Patriots (1960/game 5, 1961/game 5). After playing for the Oakland Raiders in 1960, both Lott and Babe Parilli were traded to Boston for running back Alan Miller and defensive tackle Hal Smith. With both touchdowns coming via the rush, Lott is also the first player in team history to rush for a touchdown both for and against the Patriots.

Defensive lineman Leroy Moore was the first player in team history to score a defensive touchdown both for and against the Patriots (1961/game 11, 1962/game 8). Moore spent the 1960 season playing with the Buffalo Bills, came to Boston and played for the Patriots in 1961 and half of 1962. Halfway through the 1962 season, Moore was let go by Boston and returned to Buffalo. In his first game back in a Bills uniform, Moore scored a touchdown against his former team to complete his "Patriots Daily Double."

Wide receiver/punter Bob Scarpitto was the first individual in franchise history to catch a scoring pass both for and against the Patriots during a game (1963/game 7/against, 1968/game 7/for).

Quarterback Don Trull was the first player in franchise history to both throw a touchdown pass against and for the Patriots (1966/game 9, 1967/game 11). Trull is still the only college quarterback to win multiple Sammy Baugh Trophies (1962 and 1963). This honor, which began in 1959, is presented annually to the nation's top college passer voted by members of the Touchdown Club of Columbus (OH). It is believed that Don Trull, caught in a bidding war between the Houston Oilers and Washington Redskins, was given a three-year, no-cut contract with over $100,000 in bonuses and perks to play for the AFL. His professional career lasted 11 years crisscrossing North American. After four and a half years with the Oilers, Trull spent the balance of 1967 with the Patriots and subsequently returned to the Oilers for the next two years. In 1970, he crossed the northern border and spent two years playing for the Edmonton Eskimos of the CFL. After returning to the USA and taking two years off, Trull played in the World Football League for two more years in 1974 for the Houston Texans and 1975 for the Shreveport Steamers. Trull and Vinny Testaverde, who won the award in 1986, are the only two Sammy Baugh Trophy winners to appear in a game wearing a Patriots uniform.

Veteran AFL quarterback Jack Kemp was the first player to score a touchdown against the Patriots for two different clubs (1960/game 7, 1962/game 11). With this feat, Kemp is also the first player to rush for a touchdown against the Patriots for two different clubs. He is also the first person to toss a touchdown pass against the Patriots for two different teams (1960/game 7, 1963/game 8).

Wide receiver Art Powell is the first player to catch a touchdown pass against the Patriots for two different clubs (1961/game 4, 1963/game 3).

Let's Check Out The Sunday Matinee

The first Sunday afternoon regular-season game in Patriots history was played at Kezar Stadium in San Francisco (1960/game 5). In 1971, Kezar Stadium was the site of several scenes from the Clint Eastwood film *Dirty Harry*.

After losing their first six Sunday afternoon games, five in 1960 and one in 1961, the Patriots won their first Sunday afternoon game in their first-ever Sunday afternoon home game (1961/game 7). The game was played at Nickerson Field in front of 9,398 fans. This crowd still ranks as the second smallest the team would ever draw for a home game (lowest home game attendance was 1960/game 8).

PATRIOTS PASSION

Who Was That Trench Coat Guy?

In their second year of existence, in a game at Nickerson Field (1961/game 9), the Patriots were aided by a 12th player on the field to preserve a 28-21 victory over the Dallas Texans. With 0:02 remaining and the ball resting at the Patriots 2-yard line, the Texans had one last opportunity to score a touchdown and hopefully execute a two-point conversion for a 29-28 victory. Dallas quarterback Cotton Davidson barked out his signals, took the snap from center, and dropped back hoping to toss a touchdown pass. Spotting an open receiver, Davidson zinged a pass in the direction of wide receiver Chris Burford. In the back left side of the end zone, Buford was wide open and awaited the sure touchdown pass. In an utter moment of frenzy, a Patriots fan, wearing a trench coat, standing just behind the back line of the end zone among a crowd of spectators, jumped in front of the startled Texans receiver to knock down the sure touchdown pass. Talk about a Free Safety! The pass was incomplete, the game was over, the fans rushed onto the field and Mr. Trench Coat Defensive Back blended into the crowd. Check it out – a true story; and as any Patriots fans will attest . . . only in Boston to one of our teams can this happen. And usually our team would be on the wrong end of a play such as this.

Guess The Bruins Aren't The Only Ones To Hit The Post?

In the next home game after the 12th-man-on-the-field victory, the Patriots, once again, enjoyed an improbable victory (1961/game 11). Trailing the Oakland Raiders, 17-13, on the second play of the fourth quarter, Gino Cappelletti's 35-yard field goal attempt fell short. Under the rules, any field goal attempt falling short and rolling on the playing field was treated as a punt. The Patriots downed the pigskin at the Raiders 3-yard line. After a 1-yard gain on a running play and two incomplete passes, Boston forced the visitors to punt. Oakland punter Wayne Crow booted a kick to midfield and Patriots return man Ron Burton zigged and zagged his way downfield to the Raiders 12-yard line giving Boston excellent field position. Unfortunately, the Patriots were flagged for off sides and the Raiders accepted the penalty to nullify Burton's 38-yard return. With the ball now at the 9-yard line, Crow was ready to punt again. He had to make sure he didn't step on the back line of the end zone as it would give the Patriots a safety. Crow again handled a smooth snap from center and, once again, got off a sky-high punt. One thing though . . . he was standing a few yards deep in the end zone and his kick ricocheted off the goalpost and rolled free in the end zone. Patriots defensive end Leroy Moore pounced on the loose football good for his first of two career touchdowns (1962/game 8) and yet another strange but true Patriots victory, 20-17. In both games, the Texans and Raiders' improbable plays each occurred in the west end zone (the one closet to the Mass Pike). Until the 1974 season, the goalposts were positioned on the goal line; and at this time, rules did not require the official to place the ball outside the goalpost on the playing field at the hash marks.

See You In September?

The most popular date for the Patriots to open a season is September 9th (a total of seven times – 1960, 1961, 1990, 2001, 2002, 2004, 2007) with a 3-4 record.

After Seeing How Tough This Guy Was, No Wonder We Won The Revolutionary War

During their inaugural season, 1960, on both sides of the Boston Patriots helmet resided a blue Revolutionary War three-cornered hat. During the off-season after their first year in the American Football League, the hat was gone and replaced with a new logo featuring a stern-faced Revolutionary War patriot soldier hiking a football. After owner Billy Sullivan's group was awarded an AFL franchise, "Pat the Patriot" debuted in a 1959 newspaper editorial cartoon created by Boston Globe artist Phil Bissell.

Was The Coach Superstitious?

In the past 50 years, the Patriots played only one regular-season game on a Friday the 13th. In Mike Holovak's head coaching debut, October 13, 1961 (game 6) at Nickerson Field, in front of a crowd of 15,070, Boston played to a 31-31 tie against the Houston Oilers.

The Patriots played four preseason games on a Friday the 13th – each in August. In 1965, they played their second preseason game and lost to the New York Jets, 23-16, in front of 8,000 fans at Allentown High School Stadium in Allentown, PA. In 1999, New England played their first preseason tilt of the year and lost to the Washington Redskins, 20-14, in front of 53,440 fans at Foxboro Stadium; and in 2004, the Patriots, opening their preseason, defeated the Philadelphia Eagles, 24-6, in front of 68,756 fans at Gillette Stadium. To kick off the 2009 preseason New England traveled to Philadelphia and defeated the Eagles, 27-25, in front of 69,144.

These Guys Look Awfully Familiar

The only time in franchise history the Patriots would play the same team (the Dallas Texans) two consecutive weeks was due to a quirk in the 1961 regular-season schedule (games 8 & 9). After beating the Texans 18-17 in the Cotton Bowl on a Gino Cappelletti field goal on the last play of the game, the next week, at Nickerson Field, Boston handed Dallas another loss, 28-21.

In 1997, the New England Patriots played the Miami Dolphins in back-to-back games (1997/games 16 & 17), due to the way playoff seeding turned out. The Patriots traveled to Miami for the regular-season finale then hosted the Dolphins the next week in Foxboro. The Patriots won both games.

Only AFL Game Of Its Kind

The Boston Patriots and Buffalo Bills played in the only non-league championship playoff game in the AFL before the AFL-NFL merger agreement (1963/game 15). They squared off in an East Division playoff game for the right to play the San Diego Chargers in the 1963 American Football League Championship. In 1969, the top two teams of each division qualified for the AFL playoffs; and beginning with the 1970 year, coinciding with the merger, the NFL instituted a wild card playoff spot.

After the 1963 season was completed, between regular season and playoff games, the Boston Patriots became the first professional football team in the post-expansion era to play 16 games in one season. Before the Patriots set this record, the only pro team to play more games than Boston during the season was the Frankford Yellow Jackets, who, in 1926, finished the year with a 14-1-2 record.

Wonder If The Kids Got Caught?

In a light moment during a game at Fenway Park (1966/game 12), the individual tracking play-by-play for the gamebook jotted a unique note on the side of the page. After Jim Nance (elected to the Patriots Hall of Fame in 2009) scored on his 65-yard touchdown run (the longest run of his career) and Gino Cappelletti kicked the extra point, the handwritten note in the typed gamebook said to *"look for kids running away with the ball."*

Friday Night Lights, Boston Style

Facing stiff competition for market share throughout the region from the New York Football Giants Sunday broadcasts on CBS, the Boston Patriots played quite a few of their home games on Friday nights for the first six years. The Patriots played a total of 26 games under the Friday night lights in the City of Boston, posting a

16-8-2, .654 record. The last Patriots Friday night home game was on October 8, 1965, at Fenway Park, against the Oakland Raiders who beat Boston 24-10.

Talk About Seeing Quadruple

In eight different instances, between preseason, regular season, and postseason, the Patriots played the same team four times during one season. In 1960, the Patriots played the Bills twice during the preseason (2-0) and another two times in the regular season (0-2). In 1961, they played the New York Titans twice in both the preseason (1-1) and regular season (0-2) and also played the Bills twice in preseason (2-0) and twice in the regular season (2-0). In 1962, Boston, once again, doubled up in games with the Bills during both the preseason (1-1) and regular season (1-0-1). In 1963, the Patriots played the Bills once in the preseason (0-1), twice during the regular season (1-1), and once again in the East Division playoff game (1-0). They also faced the Chargers once in preseason (0-1), twice in the regular season (0-2) and once in the American Football League Championship game (0-1). In 1964, the Patriots played the Jets twice in both the preseason (0-2) and the regular season (1-1). In 1965, the Patriots, once again, played the Jets twice preseason (0-2) and twice in regular season (1-1). Overall, when playing the same team four times during one season, the Patriots posted a lifetime 13-18-1 record. The team's only four-game sweep occurred in 1961, when the Patriots handed the Bills two losses in both the preseason and the regular season. The only time a Patriots team was beaten four times by a single team during one season was in 1963 when the Chargers defeated them once in preseason, twice during the regular season, and a fourth time for the AFL championship.

Toughest Task Was Keeping Track of the Clipboard

In 1971, Mike Taliaferro was the Patriots back-up quarterback to Jim Plunkett. Plunkett was on the field for every play that required the team to use a quarterback. Taliaferro was the only NFL player to appear on his team's active roster all 14 weeks of the 1971 season who did not participate in a single play during the entire season. In 1977, Tom Owen, serving as the back-up quarterback to Steve Grogan, did not see any action for the entire year. In team history, Grogan was the only Patriots player to take all the snaps from center and the only individual to throw a forward pass for the Patriots for an entire season.

Let's Try To Play All The Games In August And February

The Patriots lifetime regular-season record for the month of August currently stands at 1-0 (1997/game 1) and the team's lifetime record for February stands at 3-1 (2001, 2003, 2004, 2007/all game 19). Overall New England's lifetime combined regular season/postseason record by month breaks down as follows: September, 79-84 (.484), October 105-98-5 (.517); November, 103-99-4 (.510); December, 98-80 (.551); and January, 19-12 (.613).

The earliest date the Patriots opened a regular season is August 31st (1997/game 1). This still remains the franchise's only August regular-season game.

The More Wins, The Less Losses and The Better The Record, The Better The Year

Only eight Patriots teams have concluded the regular season with four or more straight victories (1962, 4; 1976, 6; 1993, 4; 1994, 7; 2001, 6; 2003, 12; 2007, 16; and 2008, 4). On the other end of the spectrum, the Patriots finished six different regular seasons with at least four consecutive losses (1960, 4; 1967, 5; 1975, 6; 1981, 9; 1990, 14; and 1992, 5).

For just the second time in team history, after game 2 in 1962, the Patriots owned a career win-loss record of better than .500, 15-14-1. The club's lifetime record would remain over .500 until 1969 game 2 when the

THE TEAM

Patriots all-time record slumped to 59-60-9. The team's lifetime record did not get back over even until 2006 in game 2 when the Patriots could claim a plus .500 lifetime win-loss record with 357-356-9. After a defeat in game 3 of 2006, the Patriots strung four straight wins together; and as of the close of 2009, the club's all-time regular season/postseason record stands at 408-374-9.

During the 1963, 1968, 1985, 2001 and 2006 seasons, the Patriots were able to post two victories against the same team twice by the end of week six – the earliest time on the schedule – to gain two wins against a single team. In 1963, 1968, 1985, and 2006, the Patriots swept the Buffalo Bills twice; and in 2001, the team owned two victories against the Indianapolis Colts all by the end of week six.

Only once in franchise history (1961), have the Patriots lost twice to the same team by the end of week four. The New York Titans defeated the Patriots (game 1) in Boston, then beat them again (game 4) for a season sweep.

Since becoming part of the National Football League in 1970 through the 2009 season, the Patriots own a 12-9 record in games the week after a bye. During the AFL years, each year through the 1968 season, each team was scheduled a bye week; and during the 1966 and 1967 seasons, each club was assigned two bye weeks. During their AFL reign, the Patriots won their first four post-bye-week games and finished with a 6-4-1 after a bye week. Overall, the Patriots lifetime record after a bye week stands at 18-13-1.

In franchise history, the Patriots have played 96 games in which the club turned in a turnover-free game and forced at least one turnover by their opponent. The team has posted an 84-12 record in these eight-dozen special games. On the other hand, the Patriots played a total of 85 games where they committed at least one turnover while not being able to force the opponent to cough up the ball at all. The Patriots record stands at 12-73 in such a game. The club has played a total of 13 games in which neither team turned over the ball once – a total mistake-free game. The Patriots currently sport a 7-6 record in these games.

The Patriots, 3-7 in AFL season openers, currently stand at 26-24 in their first game of the regular season thanks to a 25-24 victory over Buffalo (2009/game 1). They own a 23-27 lifetime record in the last regular-season game of the year.

The Patriots played the defending Super Bowl champions the following regular season a total of 20 times. Overall, they own a 5-15 record in such a game. New England opened their season twice playing the defending Super Bowl victors (1974/game 1, 1979/game 1). Both games were played at Schaefer Stadium, and the home team beat the Miami Dolphins, 34-24, in 1974 but lost in overtime, 16-13, to the Pittsburgh Steelers in 1979.

The Scoreboard Was Stuck After The Last Game

Between all regular-season and playoff games, the Patriots have taken the field a total of 774 times. During the 1963 season, each AFL team played the remaining seven teams twice during the season. The Patriots traveled to Oakland for an early-season game (game 3) and hosted the Raiders in their first Fenway Park game ever (game 6). The Boston Patriots defeated Oakland twice by a score of 20-14. This remains the only time the Patriots defeated the same team twice by the exact same score during the same season.

After the Patriots suffered a 28-10 loss to Green Bay (1997/game 8), the next time these two teams met during the regular season (2006/game 6), the Packers handed New England another 28-10 defeat. In a similar scenario, when squaring off against the Cincinnati Bengals twice in five years (1979/game and 1984/game 7), New England posted identical 20-14 victories. These remain the only two instances when the Patriots posted back-to-back victories against the same team in separate seasons both by the identical score.

The Patriots reversed the final score against the same opponent in one season only once in club history. They bookend their 2003 regular season with a pair of 31-0 games against the Bills. On opening day, Buffalo shut out the Patriots, 31-0; and then on the last day of the regular season (game 16), New England whitewashed the Bills, 31-0.

By the third game of the 2007 regular season, the Patriots were beginning to sound just like a skipping record on the family's stereo. New England won their two first games of the year by an identical score of 38-14 against the New York Jets and San Diego Chargers. This is the only time in franchise history the Patriots won consecutive games by the exact same score. The club defeated the Buffalo Bills the next week, 38-7; and for the only time in team history, New England posted the same number of points in three straight regular-season games.

New England has posted a unique triple-triple, final-score string (1989/games 1, 2, 3, 1991/games 2, 3, 4, 2006/games 1, 2, 3). It began in the 1989 season with a 1-2 record; and in each game, the Patriots allowed 24 points. In 1991, after their first four games, the club's record stood at 2-2; and in games 2, 3, and 4, New England gave up 20 points in each contest. In 2006, the Patriots started out with a 2-1 record and in each of the first three games surrendered 17 points to their opponent.

Patriots Pro Bowl Tidbits

The Patriots, joining the 1981 San Francisco 49ers and 1999 St. Louis Rams, became just the third team in NFL history to win a Super Bowl Championship after not placing any players on the Pro Bowl squad the previous year.

In 1999, Ty Law became the first, and still only, Patriots player to be voted MVP in the AFC-NFC Pro Bowl. The AFC beat the NFC, 23-10, and Law shared MVP honors with New York Jets wide receiver Keyshawn Johnson. Law intercepted a Randall Cunningham pass, returned it 67 yards for a touchdown, made five tackles, and broke up three passes.

The Patriots placed eight players on the 2006 AFC Pro Bowl roster. Selected to represent New England was center Dan Koppen, linebacker Mike Vrabel, quarterback Tom Brady, offensive tackle Matt Light, cornerback Asante Samuels, offensive guard Logan Mankins, wide receiver Randy Moss and nose tackle Vince Wilfork. For Koppen, Vrabel, Samuels, Mankins and Wilfork, this marked their first appearance in the All-Star game.

For the first time in franchise history, in 1985, New England placed eight players on the year-end AFC Pro Bowl roster. Selected to represent the Patriots were free safety Fred Marion, linebacker Andre Tippett, cornerback Raymond Clayborn, kick returner Irving Fryar, offensive tackle Brian Holloway, running back Craig James, and linebacker Steve Nelson; and making his ninth Pro Bowl appearance was offensive guard John Hannah.

When the 1980 regular season was finished, the Patriots, for the first time, placed seven players on the AFC Pro Bowl roster. Defensive lineman Julius Adams, free safety Tim Fox, offensive lineman John Hannah, cornerback Mike Haynes, wide receiver Stanley Morgan, linebacker Steve Nelson and kicker John Smith were all selected to represent New England at the AFC-NFC- Pro Bowl game.

After a franchise five-year drought of not placing a player on the AFC Pro Bowl team, at the end of the 1976 season, New England sent four players to The Kingdome, in Seattle, WA, for the AFC-NFC Pro Bowl game. This was the second major professional league All-Star game to be played in The Emerald City. On January 15, 1974, the NBA featured the East-West All-Star game at the Seattle Center Coliseum. Four Patriots making their initial appearance in the Pro Bowl were defensive back Mike Haynes, tight end Russ Francis, and offensive lineman Leon Gray and John Hannah.

At the close of the 1971 season, for the first time in club history, no Patriots were selected to play in a postseason All-Star/Pro Bowl game. This dubious distinction was repeated in 1972, 1973, 1974, 1975, 1993, and 2000.

At the end of the 1970 season, Boston center Jon Morris became the first Patriots player to participate in the AFC-NFC Pro Bowl. The NFC won the inaugural pro football All-Star showcase held on January 24, 1971 at the Los Angeles Memorial Coliseum by a score of 27-6.

Eleven Patriots were selected to play in the 1966 AFL All-Star game. Ironically, for unknown reasons, the punting chores for the East squad landed in the lap of Babe Parilli who ended up being named Offensive Most Valuable Player for the game as the East defeated the West, 30-23, at a rain-soaked Oakland-Alameda County Coliseum. Besides Parilli, the other Boston players on the squad were defensive linemen Jim Lee Hunt, Houston Antwine, and Larry Eisenhauer; defensive back Chuck Shonta; linebacker Nick Buoniconti; offensive linemen Jon Morris, Tom Neville, and Lenny St. Jean; running back Jim Nance; and wide receiver/placekicker Gino Cappellitti.

Who's Counting?

The only time in team history that the Patriots played 20 games during the regular season and postseason combined was in 1985. New England became the second NFL team from the expansion era, after the 1980 Oakland Raiders, to play 20 games during a season. As of Super Bowl XLIII, another nine teams have played 20 games in one season (Buffalo Bills, 1992; Denver Broncos, 1997; Tennessee Oilers, 1999; Baltimore Ravens, 2000; Carolina Panthers, 2003; Pittsburgh Steelers, 2005; Indianapolis Colts, 2006; New York Giants, 2007; and Arizona Cardinals, 2008).

At the close of the 2007 regular season, the New England Patriots became the first NFL team to win 16 consecutive games during the regular season. They also became the first NFL team to ever win 18 consecutive games in one season (regular season and playoffs).

A Mirror Image

In 1973/game 1, the Patriots, in Foxboro, dropped their season opener to the Buffalo Bills, 31-13. At Buffalo, in 1980/game 8, New England was defeated by the Bills, again by a score of 31-13. The Patriots won the 2007 AFC championship (2007/game 18) after beating the San Diego Chargers, 21-12. During their 50-year existence, these are the only three Patriots games with a palindrome final score. (Note: On October 4, 2010, the Patriots defeated the Miami Dolphins 41-14, the fourth mirror-image game in franchise history.

With an announced crowd of 60,006 for 1999/game 6, this was the only Patriots home game in franchise history when the attendance read as a palindrome. At Candlestick Park (1980/game 13) against the San Francisco 49ers with a crowd of 45,254, at the Orange Bowl (1991/game 10) playing the Miami Dolphins in front of 56,065 fans, and at Lucas Oil Stadium (2009/game 9) playing the Indianapolis Colts in front of a crowd of 67,476, these three games are the only away games with an announced crowd that read as a palindrome.

Why Didn't This Part Make The Movie?

Eagles wide receiver Vince Papale, who was the inspiration for the 2006 Walt Disney film, *Invincible,* managed to get his name in the gamebook twice during a Patriots-Eagles game (1977/game 11). The storybook portion: in the fourth quarter, after fielding a Spike Jones punt, Mike Haynes was tackled by Papale for a minus 2-yard return. The play he probably would not like to remember, with 0:19 remaining in the second quarter was that he was flagged for running into Patriots kicker Mike Patrick while he was punting.

Monday Night Football Madness

The Patriots debuted on Monday Night football in the fall of 1972 (game 8) hosting the Baltimore Colts at Schaefer Stadium. In front of a sellout crowd of 60,999, New England lost 24-17. The Colts first touchdown, by Sam Havrilak, was off a double reverse play. Baltimore quarterback Marty Domres took the snap and handed the ball off to running back Don Nottingham (nicknamed, "the Human Bowling Ball"). Nottingham ran toward the right behind the line of scrimmage and handed the ball to wide receiver Jim O'Brien (hero of Super Bowl V) who was reversing toward the left side of the field. As he began to gain a full head of steam running to the left, O'Brien tucked the ball into the hands of Havrilak who was reversing toward the right side of the field. The Colts trickery caught the Patriots defense by surprise and Havrilak sprinted 32 yards into the end zone for the first touchdown ever scored during a Foxboro Monday Night Football game.

Although the Patriots own a 18-22 lifetime record while appearing on Monday Night Football (MNF) broadcasts, New England sports a 17-22 lifetime record when playing on Monday nights. The reason for the discrepancy – the Patriots appeared on an ABC special Sunday evening broadcast of MNF and defeated the Oakland Raiders, 21-14 (1978/game 4). With their appearance on ABC's special Sunday night broadcast of Monday Night Football in 1978 (game 4), the Patriots became the only NFL club to appear on a MNF broadcast in two consecutive weeks – the first was a loss to the Baltimore Colts, 34-27, (1978/game 3) and the second was the Patriots appearance on the Sunday evening version of MNF against the Oakland Raiders. To date, even though it was only through a technicality, this is still the only instance when the same NFL team appeared on back-to-back Monday Night Football broadcasts.

In their fourth home-game appearance on MNF (1979/game 1), the evening produced the most memorable moment in Patriots MNF history. With 10:01 left in the second quarter, the crowd of 60,798 set the stage for this emotional moment. Patriots wide receiver Darryl Stingley, after a tragic and life-altering injury, was in attendance at the game watching from the owner's box. When introduced to the crowd, the hometown fans responded with a heartfelt standing ovation and all the Patriots players joined in, as did their opponents, the Pittsburgh Steelers. Many of his teammates, with helmet in hand, raised their arms in the air, giving a salute to their fellow Patriot. After a few minutes of applause, referee Jim Tunney attempted to restart the game; however, the fans remained on their feet clapping for Stingley and play was still on hold. This standing ovation lasted over five minutes and was witnessed by Frank Gifford, Don Meredith, Howard Cosell, and viewers of Monday Night Football around the country.

On December 8, 1980, in the waning seconds of the Patriots-Miami Dolphins MNF broadcast (1980/game 14) and the score tied, 13-13, New England called a time out with 0:03 left in the game. The Patriots had the ball at the Miami 18-yard line and used the stoppage of the clock to get ready for John Smith to kick a 35-yard game-winning field goal. After 10 years of losing to the Dolphins at the Orange Bowl, New England now had the chance to snap this losing streak. How ironic, as Englishman John Smith was trotting on the field to get ready for his field goal attempt, MNF broadcaster Howard Cosell stunned the millions of viewers, saying, *"Yes, we have to say it. Remember this is just a football game, no matter who wins or loses. An unspeakable tragedy confirmed to us by ABC News in New York City: John Lennon, outside of his apartment building on the West Side of New York City, the most famous, perhaps, of all of The Beatles, shot twice in the back, rushed to Roosevelt Hospital, dead on arrival."* Perhaps even more ironic – six years and one day before announcing Lennon's death, December 9, 1974, on a Monday Night Football broadcast (Washington Redskins beat the Los Angeles Rams, 23-17, in LA), Cosell interviewed Lennon live during the halftime break.

THE TEAM

Heisman Trophy, Patriots Style

Each of these winners of the prestigious Heisman Trophy all donned a Patriots uniform for at least one play during a regular season game: running back Joe Bellino, 1960, Navy; quarterback John Huarte, 1964, Notre Dame; quarterback Jim Plunkett, 1970, Stanford; quarterback Doug Flutie, 1984, Boston College; and quarterback Vinny Testaverde, 1986, University of Miami.

In the 1966 season opener at San Diego against the Chargers, with less than six minutes remaining in the game, the Patriots were trailing 24-0. Boston back-up quarterback John Huarte, replacing Babe Parilli at the helm, took his first snap during a regular-season professional football game. With his appearance in this game, Haurte became the first Patriots player to wear a single digit jersey (#7) in a regular-season game.

The pride of Winchester, MA, Patriots running back Joe Bellino, the 1960 Heisman Trophy Winner from the Naval Academy scored only one professional touchdown (1966/game 5). From 1935 to 1969, before the AFL-NFL merger, 27 Heisman Trophy winners played in the AFL or NFL and scored or threw for at least one touchdown during his career. The 1967 Heisman Trophy winner, Gary Beban, of UCLA, played five NFL games, with the Washington Redskins without scoring or passing for a touchdown. With one career touchdown, Bellino ranked last in touchdowns scored by Heisman Trophy winners in pro football who scored at least once.

Late during the 1966 season (game 13), routing the Houston Oilers, midway through the third quarter in one play, the Patriots may very well have created the best trivia fact ever! Leading 31-7, coach Holovak inserted back-up quarterback John Huarte to finish the game. Haurte's first pass attempt was complete, good for a 15-yard gain and a first down. The significance of this play – the player to catch the pass was halfback Joe Bellino. Huarte, the 1964 Heisman Trophy winner from Notre Dame completed a pass to Bellino, the 1960 Heisman Trophy winner from the Naval Academy. For the first time in pro football history, and the only time in AFL history, two Heisman Trophy winners hooked up on a pass completion.

Vinny Testaverde and Doug Flutie are the only two Heisman Trophy winners to toss a touchdown pass both for and against the Patriots during their careers. Facing the Patriots, Testaverde threw 23 touchdown passes while Flutie tossed 8 touchdown passes. Wearing a New England uniform, Flutie passed for 11 touchdowns while Testaverde tossed just 1.

Twice in Patriots history, a Heisman Trophy winner started as quarterback for both teams. Jim Plunkett, 1970 winner from Stanford, started for the Patriots, and Roger Staubach, 1963 winner from the Naval Academy, started for the Cowboys in both contests (1971/game 6 and 1975/game 9).

Another Six Dozen Field Goals Would Be Golden

In team history, the Patriots have beaten the Buffalo Bills 10 times by three points or less while losing 12 games to the Bills within the same margin. No other NFL team has suffered any greater number of losses by three or less points against the Patriots than Buffalo. The Patriots have not lost by this same margin to any other NFL team more than the 12 losses to the Bills. They have won a total of 62 games by three points or less while losing 75 games by the same margin. The Patriots and the Bills share eight season opening games. In a battle of old AFL stalwarts, thanks to a dramatic victory in the first game of their 50th season, the Patriots and Bills now stand deadlocked, 4-4, squaring off to open the regular-season (1965, 1968, 1973, 1984, 1993, 2003, 2006, 2009).

Who Doesn't Love a Happy Ending?

In franchise history, the Patriots captured a victory on the last play of the fourth quarter in four games. Defensive back Chuck Shonta returned a fumble 25 yards for the winning touchdown against the New York Titans (1960/game 2) on the last play of their first regular-season triumph in team history. Gino Cappelletti twice kicked the Patriots to victory as the clock wound down to 0:00 with a 24-yard field goal against the Dallas Texans (1961/game 8) and also a 42-yard field goal while facing the Houston Oilers (1964/game 9). The most recent Patriots contest decided on the last play of the fourth quarter happened in Super Bowl XLIII thanks to Adam Vinatieri's 48-yard winning field goal as the game ended. This game still ranks as the only Super Bowl to end with a game-winning score on the last play of the contest.

One Win Away From One Win To Play In Super Bowl I

Heading into their last game of the 1966 regular season (game 14), the Boston Patriots were about to play the most important game in team history. Beat the opponent, New York Jets, and the Patriots would wait 14 days to play the Kansas City Chiefs on New Year's Day for the American Football League championship and a ticket to play either the Green Bay Packers or the Dallas Cowboys in the inaugural AFL-NFL World Championship Game, aka Super Bowl I – two games – two victories. Boston lost to the Jets, 38-28, to end the season in second place to the Buffalo Bills in the AFL East Division.

After Boston and Kansas City played to a 27-27 tie (1966/game 10), Chiefs head coach Hank Stram offered these words about the Patriots in a post-game interview, *"The people they have playing, they have good football players. It's time people realized Boston has a real good team."*

The First Shall Also Be The Last

In three separate seasons, the Patriots last game of the season was against the same team with whom they opened the preseason. In 1962 (first preseason game, in Providence, RI and game 14), Boston played the Oakland Raiders and lost both games. In 1996 (first preseason game in Green Bay, WI and game 19), New England played the Packers and lost both games. In 2004 (first preseason game at Gillette Stadium and game 19), the Patriots played the Philadelphia Eagles and won both games. The Raiders preseason game in 1962 was the third straight year the Patriots played a preseason game in the capital of Rhode Island. After averaging just over 7,500 fans per game, the Patriots never played another preseason game in the Ocean State.

Two For The Price Of One

In the 10 years of AFL competition, the Patriots offense was able to make 12 out of 21 two-point conversions for a 57 percent success rate; and their defense allowed just 5 two-point conversions in 15 attempts for only a 33 percent success rate. After the AFL and NFL officially combined into one league in 1970, the two-point conversion was eliminated. Beginning in 1994, the NFL adopted the two-point PAT rule. In the first 50 years as a franchise, the Patriots offense has scored 32 two-point conversions in 64 attempts for a 50 percent success rate. On defense, opponents have scored 37 two-point PATs in 67 attempts good for a 55 percent success rate.

Fit To Be Tied

The Boston Patriots played in the most tie games (nine) in the 10-year history of the American Football League. Next closest to the Patriots were the Bills and the Chargers with six tie games each. The only team to not play in any tie games in AFL history is the Denver Broncos.

THE TEAM

The New England Patriots and the Dallas Cowboys are the only two teams of the 26 AFL-NFL merger teams of 1970 who have not played in a tie game since the merger.

Other than the Carolina Panthers, Houston Texans, Jacksonville Jaguars, and Seattle Seahawks (the only NFL teams to never play in a tie game), the Patriots have gone the longest of any of the other 28 NFL teams to not play in a tie game (1967/game 5).

Baby Boomer Trivia

Were you born between April 13, 1941 and April 8, 1959? If so, the following statements are true:

- The first Boston Red Sox World Series Championship during your lifetime was won on October 27, 2004 when the Sox defeated the *St. Louis Cardinals*.

- The first New England Patriots Super Bowl Championship during your lifetime was won on February 3, 2002 when they defeated the *St. Louis Rams*.

- The first Boston Bruins Stanley Cup Championship during your lifetime was won on May 10, 1970 when they defeated the *St. Louis Blues*.

- The first Boston Celtics World Championship during your lifetime was won on April 23, 1957 when they defeated the *St. Louis Hawks*.

Any way you slice it, *"Thank you, St. Louis!"*

TWO
THE COACHES

Six Decades Of Coaching Football

Patriots head coach Lou Saban wrapped up his pro football-playing career with the Cleveland Browns of the All-American Football Conference in 1949. He played for the Browns from 1946-1949 as a star linebacker and was also the team captain. In each of his four seasons, Cleveland won the All-America Football Conference championship. Between professional and college football, Saban's coaching career spanned six decades (1950 to 2000). His first college head-coaching job was at Case Western University in 1950 at the age of 29; and he finished coaching at the college level in 2000 at SUNY Canton. His first pro football head-coaching position was with the Boston Patriots of the AFL in 1960; and his last professional head-coaching gig, in 1994, at the age of 73, was with the Milwaukee Mustangs of the AFL in the Arena Football League. His professional coaching stint began and ended in the AFL.

Maybe We Should Have Kept This Guy

Lou Saban was relieved of his duties as Patriots head coach after just five games into the 1961 season. The club's record was 2-3 and his lifetime record as Boston's head coach was 7-12. The next year, Saban was hired as the head coach of the Buffalo Bills. In 1964 and 1965, he led the Bills to back-to-back AFL championships. After sitting out the 1966 season, Saban returned to the sidelines as head coach of the Denver Broncos and led the show for the next five years. Needing a change of scenery, Saban headed back to Buffalo and took over as head coach for the next four and half years. The first five times the Patriots faced a team coached by Lou Saban after he left town, Boston posted a 4-1-1 record. From there on, it was worse than a nightmare. From 1964 through 1975, the Patriots managed just one victory in a total of 15 meetings when playing a team coached by Saban.

Last Of A Rare Breed

At the time of his death, on March 29, 2009, Lou Saban was the last survivor of the eight head coaches of the original eight American Football League teams. The other seven coaches were Sammy Baugh/New York Titans – died 12/17/2008; Eddie Erdelatz/Oakland Raiders – died 11/10/1966; Frank Filchock/Denver Broncos – died 6/20/1994; Sid Gillman/Los Angeles Chargers – died 1/3/2003; Buster Ramsey/Buffalo Bills – died 9/16/2007; Lou Rymkus/Houston Oilers – died 10/31/1998; and Hank Stram/Dallas Texans – died 7/4/2005.

A Chip Off The Old Block

During the 1960 and 1961 seasons, while serving as the Patriots defensive backfield coach, Joe Collier witnessed the club post two shutouts (1960/game 4, 1961/game 14). Collier's son Joel coached the New England Patriots defensive backs from 2005 through 2007 and saw the defense post two shutouts (2005/game 14, 2006/game 10).

Lucky Preseason Games Didn't Count In The Standings

Mike Holovak owns a 53-47-9, .528, lifetime Patriots coaching record which places him 6th on the all-time winning percentage list of Patriots head coaches for combined regular season and postseason. He ranks 12th out of 13 coaches in the all-time winning percentage for preseason games with a 5-27 record good for a .156 winning percent. Beginning with a 7-6 loss against the Buffalo Bills on September 1, 1962 and ending after a

THE COACHES

19-13 loss to the Bills on August 7, 1966, the Patriots lost a franchise record 17 straight preseason contests all under the direction of Holovak.

A Trailblazer For Many A Good Football Coach

In 1966, former Patriots linebacker Ronnie Loudd joined Mike Holovak's coaching staff as the linebacker coach. This move established Loudd as the first African-American assistant coach in the history of the American Football League.

Before The Alaskan Pipeline, The Patriots Had One Of Their Own

During his seven-plus years in charge of the Patriots sidelines, former Boston College football head coach Mike Holovak maintained an open talent pool between his team's roster and football players from The Heights. Between the years 1961 and 1968, while Holovak controlled all player transactions, 10 individuals who played college football at Alumni Stadium in Chestnut Hill donned a Boston Patriots uniform. Joining coach Holovak via the Boston College football program were Don Allard (quarterback/1962); Jim Colclough (wide receiver/1960-68); Harry Crump (running back/1963); Larry Eisenhauer (defensive end/1961-69); Art Graham (wide receiver/1963-68); Joe Johnson (wide receiver/1960-61); Ross O'Hanley (defensive back 1960-65); Frank Robotti (defensive back-running back/1961); Ed "Butch" Songin (quarterback/1960-61); and Jim Whalen (wide receiver/1965-69).

Did We Cause This?

In three different instances in franchise history, after playing the Patriots in a regular season game, the opposing team fired their head coach. In Mike Holovak's head coaching debut (1961/game 6), the Patriots played to a tough 31-31 tie against the Houston Oilers. Before his team's next game, Oilers owner Bud Adams fired head coach Lou Rymkus, who had led Houston to the AFL championship the year before, and brought Wally Lemm on board to coach the team. Houston would go on to win 10 consecutive games to capture the 1961 AFL Championship trophy. After Boston travelled to Colorado and trounced the Broncos (1964/game 4), 39-10, Denver got rid of head coach Jack Faulkner and replaced him with Max Speedie. Within two years (1966/game 2), after the Patriots, once again, travelled to the Rocky Mountains and beat Denver, 24-10, the Broncos made yet another leadership switch. Speedie was fired and Ray Malavasi was named as the new head coach of the Broncos. In yet another Patriots ironic happenstance, after the 1966 season, Malavasi was out and Denver hired former Patriots/Buffalo Bills head coach Lou Saban to take over the reins of the club.

Talk About A Fresh Start

In 50 years, other than opening day, there were only three games when the Patriots faced a team who was playing under a brand new head coach. During the 1974 season, after suffering a 30-10 loss at the hands of the Philadelphia Eagles the week before and staring with a 0-3 record, Colts general manager Joe Thomas fired head coach Howard Schnellenberger before Baltimore was to square off against New England (game 4). Rather than look outside the organization for a new coach, Thomas appointed himself interim head coach for the remainder of the season. Things didn't start well for Thomas as the Patriots routed the Colts, 42-3.

In 1976, the Detroit Lions started out the year with a 1-3 record and ownership decided to make a change at head coach. After a 24-14 loss to the Green Bay Packers and before hosting the Patriots (1976/game 5), Detroit head coach Rick Forzano was shown the door and the keys to the Lions were handed over to Tommy Hudspeth. The new coach lit a fire under the Lions and they upset New England, 30-10.

PATRIOTS PASSION

Turning to the 1978 season, it was the San Diego Chargers who introduced their new head coach midseason to New England (1978/game 5). The Chargers were soundly beaten by the Green Bay Packers, 24-3, the week before traveling east to meet the Patriots to bring their record to 1-3. San Diego owner Eugene Klein handed head coach Tommy Protho his walking papers and hired Don Coryell to lead the club. New England prevailed, 28-23, thanks to Steve Grogan's 4-yard scoring run that capped off a seven-play/73-yard drive in 1:16. The Chargers reset their focus after this game and finished the year with an 8-3 record. "Air Coryell" was born. Beginning with 1979, San Diego would make the playoffs for the next four years.

What's The Rush?

After the 1968 season, the Patriots bid adieu to Head Coach Mike Holovak and in a bit of a shock, hired Clive Rush to run the team. As the offensive coordinator of the New York Jets, Rush architected the game plan Joe Namath executed to upset the heavily favored (by 22 points) Baltimore Colts, 16-7, in Super Bowl III. Eighteen days after the stunning victory, Sullivan lured Rush to Boston to serve as the third head coach in Patriots history and also as the team's vice president.

A Shocking Development

On February 12, 1969, the Patriots called a press conference for new head coach Clive Rush to introduce the club's new general manager, George Sauer, Jr. After spending seven years as the player personnel director for the New York Jets, Sauer, thanks to some enticement by Rush, along with Patriots owner Billy Sullivan, agreed to come to Boston to call the football shots from the front offices. As Rush grabbed the microphone to begin the press conference, he received a five-second electrical shock that briefly stunned him.

Better Late Than Never

Clive Rush's tenure as the head coach of the Boston Patriots had a tough go of it. After posting a 2-3 record during the preseason, the Patriots struggled to post a victory. After dropping the first seven games of the 1969 season, Boston finally broke into the win column (game 8). The Patriots defeated the Houston Oilers, 24-0. They were one of two AFL teams to hold their opponent scoreless on this day (Denver whitewashed the Chargers, 13-0); and these two games were the last shutouts posted in AFL history. With this victory, his eighth game as Boston's head coach, Clive Rush finally notched his first NFL win. This still remains the longest time period an individual has waited to secure his first regular-season victory as the Patriots head coach.

Still Living In A Giant's Shadow

Long-time football veteran Phil Bengston was brought in to replace John Mazur as the Patriots head coach for the remainder of the 1972 season (game 10). In 1934, at the University of Minnesota, as a tackle, Bengston was voted All-American playing alongside quarterback and future legendary college coach Bud Wilkinson. After serving nine years as an assistant coach with Green Bay, when the Packers won the 1962 NFL, 1965 NFL, 1966 Super Bowl I and 1967 Super Bowl II championships, Bengston was given the indelible task of succeeding Vince Lombardi as head coach of the Packers. In three years, 1968-1970 while Bengston coached the Packers, the team posted a 20-21-1 record.

Sooner Rather Than Later I'll Call You To Come Play For Me Again

During his six years as the Patriots head coach, former Oklahoma Sooners coach Chuck Fairbanks kept a "talent pipeline" from Norman, OK to Foxboro, MA wide open. Between the years 1973 and 1978, during Fairbanks' tenure, 10 different players who donned a University of Oklahoma football uniform would wear a

THE COACHES

New England Patriots game jersey. Joining Coach Fairbanks on the Patriots sidelines were former Sooners Sidney Brown (cornerback/1978); Al Chandler (tight end/1976-79); Ray Hamilton (defensive end/1973-81); Eddie Hinton (wide receiver/1974); Horace Ivory (running back/1977-79); Durwood Keeton (safety/1975); Jack Mildren (safety/1974); Ken Pope (cornerback/1974); Rod Shoate (1975-81); and Steve Zabel (1975-78).

Guess Two Wasn't Better Than One In This Case

After learning that Coach Chuck Fairbanks just signed a contract to become the new head coach at the University of Colorado, New England owner Billy Sullivan suspended his head coach just prior to a Monday Night Football (MNF) game against the Miami Dolphins in the Orange Bowl (1978/game 16). Regardless of the outcome of this game, the Patriots had already clinched the AFC number two seed for the playoffs and were guaranteed a home playoff game on New Year's Eve day. Sullivan just made Fairbanks sit out the season finale on MNF and would reinstate him as head coach for the upcoming playoffs. This was the only game in franchise history the head coach duties of the Patriots were shared by two individuals, Defensive Line coach Hank Bullough and Offensive Backfield coach Ron Erhardt.

Head Of The Class, When It Doesn't Count

Chuck Fairbanks (1973-1978) posted a total 20-13-1, .603-preseason record which currently ranks him at the top of the head coaches' preseason winning percentage list. While serving as head coach, Fairbanks led the Patriots to seven consecutive preseason victories; and under Ron Erhardt, New England won their first preseason game extending the franchise winning streak to a record eight during the preseason. Beginning with the second preseason game in 2002 through the first preseason game in 2004 under Bill Belichick, the Patriots tied their franchise record as New England ripped off another eight preseason-game-winning streak.

How About Some Rust-Oleum To Get Things Working Better?

During the 1990 preseason, the Patriots posted a 0-4 record. Rod Rust, who served just one year at the helm of the New England coaching staff, is the only Patriots head coach to not win any preseason games during his tenure in charge. The Patriots were outscored 132-48 for the four games with an average point differential of just over 21 points per game.

A Mirror Image For Two Coaches

After taking over as New England's head coach in 1993, after a 1-3 preseason, Bill Parcells was not able to garner his first Patriots regular-season win until the fifth game thanks to a 23-21 victory against the Phoenix Cardinals, in Arizona, on October 10. Before the new millennium was one month old, the Patriots named Bill Belichick head coach. During the 2000 preseason, New England played five games due to an appearance in the Hall of Fame game and posted a 3-2 record. Once the games started to count, Belichick collected his first regular-season victory, 28-19, against the Denver Broncos, in Colorado, on October 1. Just like Parcells record in 1993, Belichick wasn't credited with his first Patriots regular-season triumph until in his fifth game of his New England coaching career.

Nothing Better Than Starting Off With A Win

When the Patriots, led by Pete Carroll, beat the San Diego Chargers, 41-7, on August 31, 1997, Carroll became the fourth member of a special group of New England head coaches. Rom Meyer was the first head coach to become a member of this prestigious group thanks to a Patriots victory over the Baltimore Colts, 24-13, on September 12, 1982. Raymond Berry was the second member to enlist in this group after New England beat the New York Jets, 30-20, on October 28, 1984. The third Patriots head coach to enroll in this select group was

Dick MacPherson after the Patriots topped the Indianapolis Colts, 16-7, on September 1, 1991. These four gentlemen are the only individuals to win their head coach debut regular-season games while serving as the Patriots head coach.

Like Father Almost Like Son

Patriots head coach Bill Belichick's father, Steve Belichick, while playing for the Detroit Lions in 1941, returned a punt 77 yards for a touchdown against the Green Bay Packers. This was the only punt return in Belichick's one-year NFL career and is still a Detroit record for the longest punt return by any Lions player who only returned one punt in franchise history. Bill Belichick joins David Shula, head coach of the Cincinnati Bengals from 1992-1996, as one of the only four NFL head coaches in league history to have his father play in the NFL. (His dad, Don Shula, played defensive back in the NFL from 1951-1957 for the Cleveland Browns, Baltimore Colts, and Washington Redskins.) The other two are Mike Nolan, head coach of the San Francisco 49ers from 2005-2008 (His dad, Dick Nolan, played defensive back in the NFL from 1954-1962 for the New York Giants and Dallas Cowboys); and Joe Walton, head coach of the New York Jets from 1983-1989 (His dad, Frank "Tiger" Walton, played offensive guard in the NFL for the Boston Redskins in 1934 and for the Washington Redskins in 1944 and 1945).

THREE
THE OFFENSE

All That Running For Nothing

Running backs Ron Burton (1960/game 6) and Robert Weathers (1983/game 1) share the franchise record for the longest non-touchdown rushing play in team history. Although the Patriots lost both games, each running back exploded for a 77-yard run from the line of scrimmage but didn't find the end zone on the play.

Five In A Row; Isn't That A Straight?

Four different Patriots receivers share the team record for the most consecutive games (five) with at least one touchdown reception. In 1962, Jimmy Colclough caught a scoring pass against the New York Titans (game 12) for the fifth game in a row to establish the franchise record. In 1994, tight end Ben Coates, against the Bengals (game 3) caught a touchdown pass for the fifth game in a row to join Colclough in the Patriots record book. During the 2004 season, Daniel Graham hauled in a scoring strike against the Bills (game 3) for a fifth consecutive game to tie the club record. In his record-breaking 2007 season against Buffalo (game 10), Randy Moss equaled the club record of five consecutive games with a reception for a touchdown thanks to a scoring toss from Tom Brady.

Birth Of A Nickname

During the past half century, Gino Cappelletti has worn many hats for the Patriots. Defensive back, placekicker, wide receiver, team captain, fan, special teams coach, and radio announcer pretty much confirm his status as a "Patriot From Day One." In his playing days (1960-1970), his teammates called him "The Duke" because of his expensive wardrobe including 20 or more pairs of shoes. In the early years of the team, in each Patriots gamebook, every player was always listed by just his last name; but during the Patriots third year in existence (1962/game 3), for the first time in team history, the official statistician keyed in "Cappy" on each PAT kick instead of typing Cappelletti. Maybe he was just taking a shortcut?

Just Stick To Rushing The Ball

In the waning minutes of the third Patriots game ever (1960/game 3), Boston running back Dick Christy attempted a forward pass on a third-and-goal from the Buffalo 11-yard line. This was the first pass in club history not thrown by a quarterback. It was intercepted in the end zone by Buffalo defensive back Billy Atkins. A total of 31 Patriots non-quarterback players completed 35 passes in 80 attempts for 738 yards, 14 touchdowns, and 10 interceptions.

Zero For Patriots Career

Tom Dimitroff attempted just two passes in his Patriots career (1960/game 10) and failed to complete either. Tom Flick was not able to connect with any receivers in his game against the Pittsburgh Steelers (1982/game 8) with his only five pass attempts made while donning New England #10. In 2003, third-string quarterback Damon Haurd threw his only pass as a Patriot late in the season (game 16) with the toss falling incomplete. Dimitroff (0-2), Flick (0-5) and Huard (0-1) are the only three Patriots quarterbacks in club history to attempt at least one forward pass without any completions.

PATRIOTS PASSION

No Zeros On The Scorecard

During the first half-century of Patriots football, in 30 games, both the Patriots and their opponents each registered at least one score in all four quarters. The Patriots sport a 19-11 record in such games.

Starting Off On The Right Arm, Or Maybe Not

Twenty-seven different quarterbacks have started at least one game for the Patriots. An even dozen of the signal-callers won their debut for the good guys. In order of appearance, the following players won their first Patriots start at quarterback: Tom Greene (1960/game 2); Tom Yewcic (1962/game 11); Mike Taliaferro (1968/game 1); Jim Plunkett (1971/game 1); Matt Cavanaugh (1980/game 12); Doug Flutie (1987/game 6); Tom Ramsey (1987/game 11); Marc Wilson (1989/game 13); Hugh Millen (1991/game 4); Scott Zolak (1992/game 10); Tom Brady (2001/game 3); and Matt Cassel (2008/game 2).

Five Patriots quarterbacks haven't posted any wins in at least one start at signal-caller for their team. Jeff Carlson owns a 0-2 record as the Patriots starter with both losses coming in 1992 (games 15 and 16). In 1975, Neil Graff started two games (games 1 and 2), failed to guide New England to any wins, and finished with a 0-2 record. Tom Owen drew a starting assignment for the last game of the 1981 season (game 16) and lost 23-21 for a 0-1 lifetime record. In 1993, Scott Secules started as quarterback in four straight games (1993/games 6/7/8/9), however, was not able to lead the Patriots to victory posting a 0-4 lifetime record. Don Trull was given the keys to the offense late in the 1967 season (games 11/12/13) but couldn't deliver the goods. He posted a 0-3 record as Boston's starting quarterback.

Stick With This Guy, Get Those Guys Off The Field

Jack-of-all-trades Tom Yewcic led Boston to victory in his first three starts at quarterback (1961/games 11/12/13). This is the franchise record for the longest winning streak of a starting quarterback beginning with his first lifetime start for the Patriots.

During the Patriots first year in the NFL, Joe Kapp set a franchise record he'd rather not own. Two decades later, rookie quarterback Tommy Hodson tied the record and both players currently co-share this dubious distinction. Kapp (1970/games 5 through 10) and Hodson (1990/games 11 through 16) both lost their first six starts as quarterback. Kapp finished with a 1-9 lifetime record for the Patriots and Hodson bested this mark ending with a lifetime record of 1-11.

Did He Man The First Down Stakes While His Team Was On Defense?

Ron Burton is the only player in Patriots history to return a kickoff for 90 yards or more, record a pass reception for at least 70 yards, return a punt for 60 yards or more, record a rush from the line of scrimmage for 75 yards or better, and return a missed field goal for a touchdown. He returned a kickoff 91 yards for a touchdown (1961/game 9), scored a touchdown on a 73-yard pass reception (1965/game 6), broke a run for a 77-yard rush (1960/game 6), returned a punt for 62 yards (1961/game 10), and returned a missed field goal 91 yards for a touchdown (1962/game 12). The number 91 stands out in the highlight plays of Ron Burton. Too bad he didn't live to the age of 91 because this gentleman would surely have performed even more kind-hearted deeds than anyone could ever imagine.

THE OFFENSE

A Cloud Of Dust, And A Hearty "Hi-Ho, Silver"

After his 77-yard gallop (1960/game 6) against the Broncos, and a game total for yards rushed of 114, Ron Burton secured a permanent spot in the Patriots record book – the running back carried the ball 16 times for 127 yards. Burton became the first Patriots player to rush for at least 100 yards in a single game.

Hey, Coach, Can I Be A Full-Time Wide Receiver?

Boston center Walt Cudzik was the first Patriots offensive lineman to catch a pass in a regular season. In his case, he reached up, grabbed the ball in mid-air, and rambled up the field clutching the pigskin for an 11-yard gain, a first down; and Butch Songin was credited with a pass completion (1960/game 7). This was Cudzik's only career reception.

Offensive guard Justin Canale caught a deflected Tom Sherman pass and managed to get the ball back to the original line of scrimmage for no gain or loss (1968/game 9).

Center Peter Brock, in the game as an eligible receiver, caught a 6-yard touchdown pass from Steve Grogan (1977/game 11). Offensive lineman Brian Holloway hauled in Steve Grogan's battered pass turning the miscue to a 5-yard gain (1985/game 5).

Offensive guard/tackle Sean Farrell pulled down a Doug Flutie deflected pass and bulldozed up field for a 4-yard gain (1988/game 14).

Offensive guard Joe Andruzzi caught a pass from Tom Brady at the 1-yard line but couldn't get the next yard for a score (2003/game 12) and actually fumbled the ball. However, center Damien Woody saved the day by recovering the loose ball.

Offensive tackle Tom Ashworth, as an eligible receiver, caught a 1-yard pass from Tom Brady for a touchdown (2005/game 14).

Offensive guard Logan Mankins caught an errant Brady pass and was tackled for a 9-yard loss (2007/game 4). The Patriots were flagged for a penalty, an illegal touch of pass on Mankins, but the Bengals declined the infraction and took the 9-yard loss.

Twin Score It/Kick It Games

While visiting the Buffalo Bills (1962/game 8), with the Patriots trailing by 14 points, Gino Cappelletti caught a 6-yard touchdown pass from Babe Parilli and added the extra-point kick to cut their opponent's lead in half. The Bills first touchdown, a 2-yard run, was scored by their big bruising fullback Carlton Chester "Cookie" Gilchrist. He also booted the extra point, his first of four PATs kicked, during the evening. Fast forward to Fenway Park six years later (1968/game 12), Cappelletti's 18-yard touchdown reception from Tom Sherman gave the Patriots an 18-0 lead against the expansion Cincinnati Bengals. As usual, Cappelletti added the extra point to make the score 19-0. Halfway through the final quarter, Bengals wide receiver Rod Sherman hauled in a 27-yard touchdown pass from John Stofa and also added the extra point kick. With Cappelletti's touchdown/extra point kick in each game, Gilchrist's duplicate feat in 1962, combined with Sherman's matching achievement in 1986, they remain the only two Patriots games where a player from each team scored a touchdown and added the extra point kick.

Just Like A Record Skipping – Same Thing Over And Over, Being Less Productive Each Year

On their last possession of a game against the Houston Oilers (1964/game 12), head coach Mike Holovak decided to give Patriots rookie running back J.D. Garrett a chance to run the ball. In seven of the team's last eight plays from the line of scrimmage, Garrett carried the ball for a total of 28 yards. After four straight rushes by the rookie, Ron Burton ran the ball for a 5-yard gain then Garrett carried the football another three times. In his third game as a Patriot (1964/game 4), Garrett rushed for 121 yards and one touchdown on 12 carries. From Grambling State, he spent four years with the Patriots (1964-1967) and his total rushing yardage for the season declined each year from 259 yards in 1964 to 147 yards in 1965, to 21 yards in 1966 and only 7 yards in 1967 before he drifted out of pro football forever.

Same Game, Same Name, Same Fame, Different Teams

Against the Chargers, in San Diego (1967/game 2), wide receiver Art Graham caught a 4-yard pass from Babe Parilli for a Patriots touchdown, and Chargers defensive back Kenny Graham returned an interception thrown by Parilli 68 yards for a San Diego touchdown.

Playing in "Hotlanta" against the Falcons (1989/game 6), Patriots wide receiver Cedric Jones hauled in a 15-yard touchdown thrown by Doug Flutie and later in the game Atlanta running back Keith L. Jones dove over the defensive line for a 1-yard touchdown.

During Super Bowl XXXVIII (2003/game 19), after Carolina wide receiver Steve Smith caught a second quarter 39-yard touchdown pass from Jake Delhomme, New England running back Antowain Smith rushed 2 yards for a score in the fourth quarter.

At Gillette Stadium (2006/game 5), against Miami in the second quarter, Patriots wide receiver Troy Brown caught a 10-yard touchdown pass from Tom Brady, and Dolphins running back Ronnie Brown scored a touchdown on a 2-yard run. These are the only four games in Patriots franchise history when a player from each team with the same surname both scored a touchdown.

End Zone Hat Trick Via The Ground

Running backs Tony Collins (1983/game 3), Sam Cunningham (1974/game 6), Corey Dillon (2006/game 12), Curtis Martin (1996/game 9), and Mosi Tatupu (1983/game 15) share the Patriots club record for most rushing touchdowns in one game each with three. Although Cunningham's three rushing scores netted the most total yards (88), this is the only one of the five games New England lost. Martin's total yardage in three touchdowns was just four yards with a couple of 1-yard runs and a single 2-yard plunge into the end zone.

O.J. Who?

By the end of his rookie year (1969), Patriots running back Carl Garrett, a third-round draft pick from New Mexico Highlands, would leave a lasting memory with the entire AFL. He finished first in the league with 5.0 yards per rush, second in all-purpose yards (1,909) and kickoff return average (28.3 yards), and third in average yards per touchdown (9.3). In a driving monsoon rain at Alumni Stadium against the Miami Dolphins (1969/game 9), Garrett broke away for an 80-yard rush for a touchdown that remained his longest career rush and still the second longest run from the line of scrimmage in Patriots history. *The Sporting News* voted Garrett the 1969 American Football League Rookie of the Year over Buffalo Bills well-publicized rookie running back O.J. Simpson.

THE OFFENSE

Treat The Ball Like Cinderella's Glass Slipper – Don't Lose It

During the 1986 season (games 1 through 6), quarterback Tony Eason set a franchise record for the most consecutive games (six) without throwing any interceptions. During this span, Eason completed 110 passes in 175 attempts (62.8 percent), 1,409 yards passing, and 10 touchdowns and the Patriots were 3-3.

They Knew It Was More Than Just A Hunch, The Brady Bunch

In the 774 regular season/postseason games played in club history, just twice (2007/games 6 and 7) a Patriots quarterback completed a touchdown pass to a receiver with the same last name. Tom Brady tossed a scoring pass to tight end Kyle Brady in both contests.

Tom Brady holds the Patriots team record for consecutive games (regular season and postseason) with a touchdown pass (2006/game 14 to 2007/game 13). The Michigan alumnus tossed at least one touchdown pass in 19 straight games. During this record-setting streak, Brady tossed a total of 54 touchdown passes.

Dallas Cowboys great, Roger Staubach, and Tom Brady share the record for most victories by a quarterback in their first 100 starts during the Super Bowl Era (since 1966). Each signal-caller's team won 76 games of their first 100 professional starts (regular season and postseason). Brady's next defeat came in his 102nd start while Staubach's next loss was not until his 104th contest. Staubach ended his 11-year career with a 96-35 record as starting quarterback while Brady posted 101-27 as the Patriots starting quarterback during his first nine years inclusive of seven full seasons.

Against the Jaguars in Jacksonville (2006/game 15), quarterback Tom Brady set a new franchise record throwing at least one pass completion to 11 different New England players – Troy Brown, Rache Caldwell, Bam Childress, Corey Dillon, Heath Evans, Jabar Gaffney, Daniel Graham, Chad Jackson, Kelvin Kight, Laurence Maroney and David Thomas. To take this one step further, Caldwell, Gaffney, Jackson and Kight all attended the same college, the University of Florida, 55 miles away from the site of this game. Thanks to the receptions by these four individuals, this is the only game in team history that four different players from the same college caught a pass for the Patriots.

Tom Brady is one of eight players to start as the quarterback for at least 20 Patriots regular season games. With a 17-3 record during this time span, Brady ranks number one on this list. Next on the list is Babe Parilli at 13-6-1, Steve Grogan and Tony Eason at 11-9, Jim Plunkett and Drew Bledsoe at 8-12, Mike Taliaferro at 7-13, and Hugh Millen at 5-15.

When Tom Brady connected on 22 of 26 passes (2002/game 8), for a .846 completion rate, he set the Patriots single game completion percentage record. He owns eight of the nine top completion-rate games in team history. "Kentucky Babe" Parilli (1967/game 6), in the Patriots first regular-season game ever against the Miami Dolphins, completed 16 passes in 20 attempts for 281 yards. This .800 completion-rate performance enables Parrilli to own the only non-Tom Brady performance in the team's top nine passing accuracy games.

Hindsight is always 20/20 . . . in the second quarter of his fourth NFL start (2001/game 6), Tom Brady offered a preview of his future success as the Patriots new signal-caller. Faced with a first down and 10 yards to go at the Patriots 9-yard line, Brady completed a pass to wide receiver David Pattern. This completion resulted in a 91-yard touchdown pass and set the franchise record for both the longest pass completion in team history and the longest touchdown reception in team history.

Out of the 128 career starts for Tom Brady, 46 are against pre-merger NFL teams. Brady sports an 87-24 lifetime record as a Patriots starting quarterback; and against the 'old guard' teams of the NFL, his lifetime mark is 38-8. Against the seven other Original Eight AFL teams, he owns a 38-14 record.

PATRIOTS PASSION

Spread The Wealth – I'll Play Catch With Anyone

Wide receiver Irving Fryar is the only player in franchise history to catch at least one touchdown pass from seven different Patriots quarterbacks. The former overall number one draft pick from the University of Nebraska caught 84 lifetime touchdown passes during his 17-year NFL career with 38 scoring receptions in a Patriots uniform. When he played for New England, Fryar hooked up with Steve Grogan (14), Tony Eason (10), Hugh Millen (6), Doug Flutie (3), Tommy Hodson (2), Marc Wilson (2) and Tom Ramsey (1), for a total of 38 touchdown receptions as a Patriot.

During his 129 regular-season games (and counting), Tom Brady tossed 225 touchdown passes spread amongst 38 different teammates. Brady's feat is on top of the franchise's all-time list of total different players to catch a touchdown from a quarterback. Over a 16-year period and 149 regular-season games, Steve Grogan threw 182 touchdown passes to 34 different players. This places Grogan second in franchise history.

Brady – 38

Randy Moss – 36	Bethel Johnson – 4	Charles Johnson – 1
Ben Watson – 17	Antowain Smith – 3	Terry Glenn – 1
Daniel Graham – 17	Chad Jackson – 3	Laurence Maroney – 1
David Patten – 16	Doug Gabriel – 3	Heath Evans – 1
Troy Brown – 15	Donte Stallworth – 3	André Davis – 1
Deion Branch – 14	Jermaine Wiggins – 3	Larry Centers – 1
Christian Fauria – 13	Corey Dillon – 2	Dedric Ward – 1
David Givens – 12	Marc Edwards – 2	Cam Cleeland – 1
Wes Welker – 12	Donald Hayes – 2	Patrick Pass – 1
Kevin Faulk – 10	Tim Dwight – 2	Tom Ashworth – 1
Mike Vrabel – 8	Kyle Brady – 2	David Thomas – 1
Jabar Gaffney – 6	Sam Aiken – 2	Julian Edelman - 1
Reche Caldwell – 4	Chris Baker - 2	

Grogan – 34

Stanley Morgan – 39	Clarence Weathers – 3	Marlin Briscoe – 1
Russ Francis – 22	Al Chandler – 3	Greg Hawthorne – 1
Harold Jackson – 17	Tony Collins – 3	Ike Forte – 1
Irving Fryar – 14	Sam Cunningham – 3	Pete Brock – 1
Don Hasselback – 12	Lin Dawson – 2	Marv Cook – 1
Darryl Stingley – 9	Carlos Pennywell – 2	Ken Toler – 1
Cedric Jones – 8	Horace Ivory – 2	Mark van Eeghan – 1
Derrick Ramsey – 6	Greg Baty – 1	Willie Scott – 1
Andy Johnson – 6	Morris Bradshaw – 1	Sammy Martin – 1
Stephen Starring – 6	Don Calhoun – 1	Craig James – 1
Randy Vataha – 6	Ray Jarvis – 1	Mosi Tatupu – 1
Hart Lee Dykes – 4		

As Easy As Taking Candy From A Baby

Wide receiver/running back, Everett, MA native Bobby Leo (1967/game 13), wide receiver/UMass alumnus Steve Schubert (1974/game 7), wide receiver Al Marshall (1974/game 12), center Pete Brock (1976/game 11) and offensive tackle Tom Ashworth (2005/game 14) share a unique Patriots team record. Each is one of only

THE OFFENSE

five individuals of the 253 players to catch just one pass while wearing a Patriots uniform good for a touchdown. Leo was on the receiving end of a Babe Parilli 25-yard scoring toss; Schubert, with a 21-yard touchdown reception from Jim Plunkett; Brock hauled in a 6-yard pass from Steve Grogan in the end zone; and Ashworth caught a 1-yard pass from Tom Brady.

Gino Cappelletti (1961/game 4) and Adam Vinatieri (2004/game 8) are included on the list of 75 players to throw at least one forward pass for the Patriots during any of the 774 regular-season/postseason games in franchise history. Both were lining up to attempt a field goal when each threw his first and only forward pass as a Patriots player. Cappelletti was readying to boot a field goal, however, the football was snapped directly to him. He spotted Larry Garron running the planned pass route and hit him in stride with a perfect toss good for a 27-yard touchdown pass. Vinatieri, prepared to kick an 11-yard field goal, took the direct snap from center Lonnie Paxton and tossed a pass to a wide-open Troy Brown for a 4-yard touchdown pass. Cappelletti and Vinatieri are the only two Patriots players in team history to record a touchdown on their only career pass attempt – a perfect one for one for six points.

Michael Bishop is the only Patriots quarterback in team history to complete his first regular-season pass attempt for a touchdown (2000/game 6). On the last play of the first half, at Foxboro, against the Colts, head coach Bill Belichick inserted Bishop as quarterback. The rookie, out of the shotgun formation, dropped back and tossed a Hail Mary pass toward the right side of the field. Patriots wide receiver Tony Simmons outjumped the defenders for the ball and came down with the pigskin good for a 44-yard touchdown pass. The Cleveland Indians drafted Bishop as an outfielder in the 28th round of the 1995 MLB Draft just after he graduated from Willis High School (TX), but he declined to sign with the Indians and attended Kansas State University to play football.

Patriots running back Craig James is the only player in franchise history to throw a touchdown on his first two pass attempts of his career (1985/games 3 and 8). In both games, after taking a pitch from the quarterback, the Southern Methodist University grad lofted a pass and connected with fellow running back Tony Collins for a touchdown. The first scoring strike was good for 5 yards and the other touchdown covered 11 yards. Born in Jacksonville, TX on January 2, 1961, his full given name is Jesse Craig James.

Eight different players can boast that they connected with a receiver for a touchdown on their first pass attempt while playing for the Patriots. Tom Yewcic, a back-up quarterback, tossed his first AFL pass lining up as a running back (1961/game 2) to flanker Jim Colclough good for an 18-yard touchdown. Gino Cappelletti hooked up with running back Larry Garron (1961/game 4) on a fake field goal covering 27 yards for a score. Craig James connected with Tony Collins (1985/game 3) with a 5-yard scoring toss and again with Collins (1985/game 8) for an 11-yard touchdown pass. Fan favorite Mosi Tatupu, out of his normal running back position, found Tony Collins open down field and hooked up with his teammate good for a 15-yard touchdown pass (1987/game 7). Rookie running back Jon Vaughn was the first ex-University of Michigan Wolverine to throw a touchdown pass for the Patriots (1991/game 4) connecting with tight end Marv Cook on a 13-yard scoring strike. On a razzle-dazzle play (2001/game 1), wide receiver David Pattern connected with fellow wide receiver Troy Brown for a 60-yard touchdown play on his first NFL forward pass. In team history, Pattern is one of 11 players who own just one pass completion, which still ranks as the longest completion by any Patriots player completing just one lifetime pass. Placekicker Adam Vinatieri (2004/game 8) rounds out this group with a 4-yard touchdown pass to Troy Brown on a fake field goal attempt.

Happy Birthday To Me

Patriots running back Andy Johnson added some spice to his 24th birthday celebration on October 18, 1976 by scoring two touchdowns (game 6). Johnson, thanks to a 4-yard run for a score and a 10-yard touchdown reception from Steve Grogan, became the first Patriots player to score a touchdown while celebrating his birthday.

On September 18, 1977, with a first quarter 34-yard double reverse run, Patriots wide receiver Darryl Stingley garnered the second rushing touchdown of his career (the first coming in 1974/game 4). He added his second touchdown on the day during the second quarter hauling in a 21-yard scoring pass from Steve Grogan. Not a bad way for a person to celebrate his 26th birthday. Stingley became the second of three Patriots players in franchise history to score a touchdown on his birthday.

Irving Fryar's 10-yard touchdown pass from Tony Eason (1986/game 4) against the Denver Broncos, on September 28, 1986, is the last time a Patriots player scored a touchdown while celebrating a birthday on game day (his 24th). In 1997, on the day he turned 35 years old, while playing with the Philadelphia Eagles, Fryar scored his only other birthday touchdown thanks to a 6-yard scoring reception against the Minnesota Vikings. Jim Plunkett, Doug Flutie, and Andy Johnson are the only three Patriots players to toss a touchdown pass on their birthdays. On December 5, 1971, Plunkett, celebrating his 24th birthday, connected with Randy Vataha for touchdowns from 25 yards and 26 yards (game 12). Flutie turned 26 years old on October 23, 1988; and to mark the day, he hooked up with wide receiver Irving Fryar for a 12-yard scoring toss (game 8). Turning 29 years old didn't bother Johnson as he became the first, and still only, Patriots player to both throw and catch a touchdown on his birthday (game 7). On October 18, 1981, Johnson threw a halfback option pass to Stanley Morgan good for 28 yards and a score. Later in the game, he was on the receiving end of a 10-yard touchdown pass from Steve Grogan.

Harlem Globetrotters vs. Washington Generals

Thanks to the Patriots 59-0 lopsided win against the Tennessee Titans (2009/game 6), this game now stands as the team record for the greatest margin of victory (59 points).

Winning A Pick Up Game Against Your Older Adopted Brother

New England's 52-7 win against the Washington Redskins (2007/game 7), by a 45-point swing, remains the greatest margin of victory for the Patriots against a pre-merger NFL franchise.

Where's The End Zone?

Wes Welker holds the club record for most passes caught in a single game without posting a touchdown reception. Against the New York Jets (2009/game 10), Welker hauled in 15 passes good for 192 yards but did not find the end zone.

A Passing Thought

On one Sunday afternoon (1994/game 10), Drew Bledsoe set three Patriots single-game passing records which still stand. Two of the three records also remain the NFL record as well. Against the Minnesota Vikings, Bledsoe tossed 70 passes and connected with a receiver 45 times. His yeoman efforts still sit atop the Patriots record book and also remain the high-water mark in the NFL record book. Bledsoe racked up 426 yards in passing – a total that still stands as the franchise record.

THE OFFENSE

Yo-Yo Football

Steve Grogan (1983/game 10), Tommy Hodson (1992/game 6) and Drew Bledsoe (1995/game 15) are the only three New England players to throw, complete, and catch the football all on the same play. Against Buffalo in 1983, Grogan's pass attempt was deflected back toward the backfield by Bills linebacker Lucius Sanford. Grogan grabbed the loose ball before another Buffalo defender could snag it before hitting the ground. After catching the ball, he was tackled for an 8-yard loss. Hodson, while facing the Dolphins at Joe Robbie Stadium in 1992, after having his pass knocked down, was facing the same predicament as Grogan. Pulling in the loose ball for a reception, Hodson was tackled for a 6-yard loss. Against Pittsburgh in 1995, Steeler's defensive lineman Ray Seals swatted a Bledsoe pass up in the air behind the line of scrimmage. Realizing it was a free football, before hitting the ground, the quick-thinking Bledsoe reached out and pulled the ball in for a reception. He was immediately tackled by a swarm of defenders for a 9-yard loss. Grogan to Grogan, Hodson to Hodson, Bledsoe to Bledsoe were in the record book forever.

In addition to Steve Grogan (1983/game 10), Tommy Hodson (1992/game 6), and Drew Bledsoe (1995/game 15) catching their own passes, Grogan (twice), Matt Cavanaugh, and Tom Brady also caught a forward pass from a teammate during a regular-season game. Running back Andy Johnson passed the ball back to Grogan (1981/game 1) after taking a handoff from the quarterback for a 16-yard gain. This was the first reception in franchise history by a Patriots quarterback after taking the snap and handing the ball off. Head Coach Ron Erhardt liked the play so much he called the same play three weeks later (game 4). This time, with Cavanaugh calling signals, he handed off to Johnson, drifted off to the weak side of the field, and caught the running back's pass for a 9-yard gain. For a third time during the 1981 season, Johnson completed a pass to a quarterback (game 9). Running toward the right side of the field, Johnson stopped dead in his tracks, looked left and fired the ball to Grogan. The tough-as-nail quarterback caught the pass and gained 11 yards good for a first down. In the second-to-last week of the 2001 regular season, Brady began his assault on the Patriots record books with a pass reception. Kevin Faulk, in the last regular-season game ever played in Schaefer/Sullivan/Foxboro Stadium (game 15), threw his first NFL pass connecting with Brady for a 23-yard gain and a first down. Brady now had his name etched in the New England record book for the longest pass reception by a Patriots quarterback.

The Best Running Quarterback In Pro Football History

Steve Grogan was penciled in as the starting quarterback for the Patriots 1976 season, and the front office had enough confidence in the second-year kid to trade away Jim Plunkett after the completion of the 1975 season. Using two first-round draft picks acquired from San Francisco in the trade, after selecting defensive back Mike Haynes with their own first-round pick, New England added center Peter Brock and defensive back Tim Fox to the mix. After a 12-year playoff drought, in 1976, the Patriots posted an 11-3 record and grabbed the AFC wild card playoff berth. During the regular season, Grogan averaged 6.6 yards per rush, posted his only career 100-yard rushing game with 103 yards on just 7 against the New York Jets (game 6) and scored 12 rushing touchdowns for the season. This is still the NFL record for most rushing touchdowns scored in one season by a quarterback.

Exiting The Show In Style

Jim Plunkett completed his last official pass attempt while wearing a Patriots uniform. The play covered 5 yards for a touchdown and the receiver was Darryl Stingley (1975/game 9). Three and a half minutes earlier, Plunkett tossed his second-to-last touchdown pass for New England, good for 34 yards, also to Stingley. With 0:14 left in the third quarter, Plunkett delivered his first of three touchdown passes on the day, good for 37 yards, to tight end Russ Francis.

Taking A Bullet For The Team

After winning their first five games of the 1974 season, New England lost a heartbreaking game at Buffalo, 30-28 (game 6). The next week, heading to the land of 10,000 lakes, the 5-1 Minnesota Vikings would surely be waiting to hand the Patriots a second consecutive loss (game 7). After the Vikings scored a touchdown with 1:29 left in the game, to take a 14-10 lead, things were looking gloomy for Chuck Fairbanks and his over-achieving squad. Minnesota pinned the Patriots deep in their own territory on the kickoff and Jim Plunkett was forced to begin at the New England 14-yard line. Six plays later and 76 yards, with 0:08 left in the game, the Patriots were faced with a second-and-ten just outside the Vikings 10-yard line with no timeouts remaining. Jim Plunkett connected with tight end Bob Windsor at the 3-yard line with 0:05 left in the game, and the big tight end dragged Vikings Jeff Siemon, Paul Krause, and Nate Wright over the goal line for the winning touchdown. Windsor injured his knee on this play and was forced to sit out the remainder of the season. The knee was so badly damaged that he barely played in 1975 before retiring at the age of 33 due to his lack of mobility.

What A Great Starting Five

In the Patriots record book, five players rank in both the club's *Top 25 All-Time Rushing Yards* and *Pass Reception* lists. Sam Cunningham is number 1 in rushing and number 12 in pass receptions. Tony Collins checks in as number 3 and 9, respectively. Kevin Faulk, slowly but surely, climbing on both lists, ranks number 6 in rushing and 4 on the pass-reception honor roll. One of the original Patriots, Larry Garron, claims the number 9 spot in rushing and number 18 spot in receptions. Andy Johnson, aka Mr. Versatility, falls in at number 17 in rushing yards and in pass receptions settles in at number 25. Johnson, with four career touchdown passes, ranks number 1 in franchise history for most scoring tosses by a non-quarterback.

The Genes Must Be In The Family Blood

Credited with 10 fumble recoveries during his illustrious 13-year Hall of Fame career, in the last game of his second year (1974/game 14), John Hannah recovered a Jim Plunkett fumble in the Dolphins end zone for his lone NFL touchdown. John's brother Charley played in the NFL for 12 years (1977-1988) spending 6 years with Tampa Bay and another six years with the Raiders. Another brother, David, played college football at University of Alabama. All three boys played offensive line and each were voted to the SEC All-Conference Team during their college years. Their dad, Herb, played offensive tackle for the New York Giants in 1951 and also played college ball at Alabama. Herb's brother Bill, the boys' uncle, attended Alabama in the late 1950s and also played on the football team as an offensive tackle. Quite appropriately, on April 5, 1951, John Hannah was born in Canton, Georgia and now has a permanent home in Canton, Ohio at the Pro Football Hall of Fame.

Once A Patriot, Always A Patriot

After spending seven years with the Patriots (1965-1971), running back great, Jim Nance, was traded to the Philadelphia Eagles but decided to sit out the next year. In 1973, his AFL/NFL career ended after playing seven games for the New York Jets. In his 101st and final NFL game, Nance rushed the football four times for a total of 20 yards, and the opponent was the New England Patriots (game 9). In 1974, getting an itch for football again, Nance signed on to play in the brand new World Football League (WFL). Playing for the Houston Texans, 11 games into the inaugural season, the club moved to Louisiana and became the Shreveport Steamer. His teammates included ex-Patriots Mike Taliaferro, Don Trull, Darryl Johnson, and former Jets wide receiver and future Hall of Famer Don Maynard. Twelve games into the 1975 season, the WFL ran out of money and closed up shop for good. Nance was voted to the All-WFL Team and finished as the league's second all-time rushing leader with 490 carries for 2,007 yards and a 4.1 average.

THE OFFENSE

Not An Every-Game Happening

After Jim Plunkett's third quarter 5-yard touchdown run against the Bills (1973/game 13), combined with a 6-yard touchdown jaunt by O.J. Simpson before halftime, in the Patriots first game ever at Rich Stadium in Buffalo, wonder how many fans realized New England had just made history? This remains the only game in Patriots history when two former Heisman Trophy winners, one for each team, scored a touchdown during a regular season/postseason game.

Can 100 Yards Get Your Team A Win?

The top 10 Patriots players for total yards rushed have combined for 88 career 100-yard regular-season games. The only running back on the list to not rush for 100 yards in a single game is Kevin Faulk who ranks number 8 on the all-time rushing list. The nine other players to rush for 100 yards in a game at least once rank as follows with the club's record in these games:

1. Sam Cunningham (8-3)
2. Jim Nance (11-4-2)
3. Tony Collins (7-1)
4. Curtis Martin (9-5)
5. John Stephens (5-2)
6. Kevin Faulk (0-0)
7. Don Calhoun (7-2)
8. Larry Garron (3-0)
9. Corey Dillon (11-1)
10. Antowain Smith (6-1)

The Good, The Bad and The Ugly

Russ Francis, Andy Johnson, and Craig James remain the only non-quarterback Patriots players to toss a forward pass during a playoff game. In 1976 (game 15), for the first time in 13 years, the Patriots qualified for the playoffs as a wild card team. Leading the Raiders by a score of 7-3 and deep in Oakland territory, New England hoped to extend their lead to 11, or at least 7. With just over two minutes left in the half, on a double reverse out of the tight end position, Francis tossed a pass toward the goal line and Darryl Stingley. Raiders cornerback Skip Thomas picked the ball off at the 6-yard line returning it to the Oakland 24-yard line. Ken Stabler marched his club 76 yards in six plays for a touchdown, and the Raiders left the field at halftime with a 10-7 lead.

In 1978 (game 17), trailing 24-0 against the Houston Oilers in Foxboro in an AFC divisional playoff game on New Year's Eve day, New England desperately needed to reach into their bag of tricks. Johnson, in shotgun formation, took the snap directly from center and tossed a 24-yard touchdown pass to veteran wide receiver Harold Jackson. This was the highlight of the day as the Patriots lost, 31-14.

In 1986 (game 18), in front of the largest crowd to watch a Patriots regular-season/postseason game (88,936), James hooked up with Tony Collins for an 8-yard reception. On the next play, Tony Eason connected with Lin Dawson for a 13-yard touchdown play.

More Than Just A Scottish Narrow And Secluded Valley

Patriots wide receiver Terry Glenn served as one end of a set of bookends for a unique combination of the careers of quarterbacks Tom Brady and Drew Bledsoe. In his third career start (2001/game 5), Brady tossed his first NFL touchdown, a 21-yard pass, to Glenn. Bledsoe's last regular-season touchdown pass in a New England Patriots uniform (2001/game 16) connected with Glenn for a 16-yard score. During his six-year stay in Foxboro, Glenn caught 22 touchdown passes with the Patriots posting a 14-8 record when he crossed the goal line.

New England picked Terry Glenn, a wide receiver from Ohio State, with the seventh overall selection of the 1996 NFL Draft. A total of five wide receivers were selected in the first round of the 1996 draft. During his 12-year career, Glenn posted 593 receptions, 8,823 yards receiving, and 44 touchdowns. Keyshawn Johnson, out of USC was the overall number one pick, by the New York Jets and retired after 11 years in the NFL with 814 catches, good for 10,871 yards, and 64 touchdowns. The St. Louis Rams selected LSU wide receiver Eddie Kennison with the 18th pick of the first round. He managed to net 548 receptions, 8,345 yards, and 42 touchdowns during his 13-year career. With the very next selection, the Indianapolis Colts tabbed Marvin Harrison hoping the team would land a franchise quarterback in the near future to create a dynamic duo. In 1998 when Peyton Manning joined the Colts, Harrison became the quarterback's favorite target. The Syracuse grad tallied 1,102 receptions, 14,580 yards, and 128 touchdowns during his 13-year stay in the NFL. With the 24th selection of the first round the Buffalo Bills finished the run on wide receivers in round one by choosing Eric Moulds of Mississippi State. In 12 seasons, Moulds hauled in 764 receptions, netting 9,995 yards, and 49 touchdowns. Combined, the "Fantastic Five" wide receivers averaged 12.2 seasons in the league with 746 receptions, 10,523 yards, and 64 touchdowns.

FOUR
THE DEFENSE

More Fun Than A Two-Point Conversion

In their first 791 games that count (756 regular season, 35 playoffs), New England held their opponent to just two points in just two games (1980/game 15, 1993/game 13). At Schaefer Stadium, late in the 1980 season, after a snap from center sailed over Patriots punter Mike Hubach's head, who was standing at his own 25-yard line, he was able to track the loose ball down in the end zone and take an intentional safety. New England went on to a 24-2 victory over the Bills. Also in Foxboro, late in the 1993 season, the Patriots hosted Cincinnati on a cold and windy December afternoon. Leading 7-0 and faced with a fourth and ten from their own 2-yard line with 0:21 left in the game, New England elected to take an intentional safety. With punter Mike Saxon standing in the end zone, the pigskin ended up in the hands of tight end Marv Cook who threw the ball into the stands behind the end zone for a safety. The final score was Patriots 7, Bengals 2.

In just four regular-season games the Patriots held a 2-0 lead thanks to a safety as their first scoring play (1964/game 11, 1965/game 8, 1968/game 12, 1986/game 12), and went on to win all four games. In 1964, at Fenway Park, in a scoreless game, with less than five minutes in the opening quarter, Boston linebacker Jack Rudolph sacked Broncos quarterback Jacky Lee in the end zone for a safety. At Balboa Stadium, 1965, Chargers return specialist Leslie "Speedy" Duncan fielded a Tom Yewcic punt three yards deep in the end zone and attempted to run back. Patriots defensive back Jay Cunningham, down the field quickly on the kick coverage, caught Duncan and brought him down two yards before getting out of the end zone for a safety and Boston led 2-0. In the last Patriots game ever played at Fenway Park, December 1968, Boston squared off against the expansion Cincinnati Bengals. Early in the game with a third and 15 from their own 1-yard line, Bengals rookie running back Paul Robinson (who would go on to win the 1968 AFL Rookie of the Year award) took a handoff from quarterback John Stofa but fumbled the ball back into the end zone. The rookie recovered the loose ball but linebacker Doug Satcher pounced on Robinson and was credited with a safety. On a mild late November afternoon in 1986, New England hosted Buffalo at Sullivan Stadium. On the second play of the game from the line of scrimmage (the Buffalo 24-yard line), Bills quarterback Jim Kelly dropped back to pass. As Patriots linebacker Lawrence McGrew sacked the quarterback for a 12-yard loss, the football was jarred from Kelly and rolled back out through the end zone for a Patriots team safety and a 2-0 lead.

Patriots linebacker Don Blackmon is the owner of a unique team record. During the 1985 season (games 1 and 8), the 6'3" defender sacked Green Bay Packers quarterback Lynn Dickey and later in the year also sacked Tampa Bay Buccaneers quarterback Steve DeBerg both for safeties. This is the only instance when a Patriots player was credited with two safeties in one season. Blackmon is currently the defensive coordinator for the New York Sentinels of the newly formed United Football League (UFL).

During the last half century of Patriots football, the team trailed 2-0 just once (1996/game 16). On the second to last play of the opening quarter, facing a furious New York Giants pass rush, Drew Bledsoe was feeling the pressure from the defense. Standing in his own end zone, the quarterback tried to dump the ball off to avoid a sack but was flagged for intentional grounding, throwing the football from the end zone, and the Giants received credit for a safety. The Patriots won this game, 23-22.

Thank Goodness They Canned This Game, Before Someone Got Hurt

Houston Antwine was named to the Patriots 50th Anniversary Team, Patriots All-1960s Team, and All-Time All-AFL Team as a defensive tackle. In his rookie year, 1961, he started on the offensive line; however, after

PATRIOTS PASSION

Mike Holovak took over the coaching reins during the season, Antwine flipped over to the defensive line. In the 1961 College All-Star Game, Antwine was slightly injured which led to a slow start in training camp.

Someone Had To Be The First One

Dallas Texans running back Abner Haynes became the first player to score four touchdowns in one game against the Patriots (1962/game 1). Haynes scored twice in the second quarter on a 2-yard plunge and a 25-yard gallop. In the third quarter, he ran wide and sprinted 30 yards for a score and completed his grand slam of touchdowns after catching a pass from quarterback Len Dawson good for nine yards and his fourth touchdown of the afternoon.

Bubkes/Nada/Zilch/Goose Eggs/Nothing – Gridiron Style

The only time in a half-century of games that the Patriots were shutout in a regular-season game then posted a regular-season game shutout the next week was in their inaugural 1960 season games 3 and 4. When the Buffalo Bills blanked Boston, 13-0, this was the first regular-season shutout in the history of the new American Football League. A week later, the Patriots blanked the Los Angeles Chargers, 35-0, for the club's first shutout ever (also the only 35-0 game in the 10 years of the AFL). During the last season of the AFL before the 1970 AFL-NFL merger, the Patriots posted their first home-game shutout (1969/game 8). The Patriots 24-0 victory over the Houston Oilers, coupled with the Denver Broncos 13-0 win against the San Diego Chargers on the same day, were the last two shutouts in AFL history. In the 10 years of the AFL, there were 30 shutout regular-season games played. Technically, with the Broncos/Chargers game finishing later in the day than the Patriots/Oilers game, the first and last official AFL shutout games ended with a score of 13-0.

The 24 lifetime shutouts posted by the Patriots defense spans 13 different NFL teams. The Buffalo Bills are the only club to have suffered 4 shutouts at the hands of the New England Patriots (1967/game 5, 1983/game 8, 2003/game 16, 2008/game 16). The 12 other teams the Patriots have blanked are the Arizona Cardinals (1996/game 3), Dallas Cowboys (2003/game 10), Green Bay Packers (2006/game 10), Houston Oilers/Tennessee Titans (1969/game 8, 1973/game 11, 2009/game 6), Indianapolis Colts (1987/game 10, 1993/game 15), Miami Dolphins (1980/game 6, 1982/game 6, 2003/game 13), New Orleans Saints (1983/game 14), New York Jets (1971/game 4, 1974/game 5), Pittsburgh Steelers (1986/game 7), San Diego Chargers (1960/game 4, 1961/game 14), Seattle Seahawks (1977/game 4, 1982/game 7) and Tampa Bay Buccaneers (2005/game 14).

Just two teams have traveled to New England, played the Patriots, and shutout the home team at least twice. The Cleveland Browns managed to blank the Patriots 30-0 (1983/game 12) and 20-0 (1991/game 2). Before Houston relocated to Tennessee and became the Titans, the Oilers shutout the Patriots twice, 16-0 (1968/game 5) and 7-0 (1975/game 1).

The Patriots have been involved in 44 shutout games with an overall record of 24-20 in such contests. The most common score for a Patriots game to end in a shutout is 31-0. They participated in eight regular season games with a 31-0 final score, posting a 4-4 record. The 31-0 victories were at the expense of the Arizona Cardinals (1996/game 3), Buffalo Bills (1983/game 8, 2003/game 16) and Seattle Seahawks (1977/game 4) while the 31-0 whitewashes against the club were at the hands of the Baltimore Colts (1972 game 11), Buffalo Bills (2003/game 1), Kansas City Chiefs (1969/game 2), and St. Louis Cardinals (1970/game 8).

The only time in franchise history that the Patriots posted back-to-back regular-season-shutout games was in the nine-game-strike-shortened 1982 season (games 6 and 7). During the infamous "Snow Plow" game at Schaefer Stadium against Miami, the New England defense, kicker John Smith, and John Deere tractor/snow sweeper driver Mark Henderson, in a blizzard, blanked the Dolphins, 3-0. A week later, the Patriots traveled to Seattle and shutout the Seahawks, 16-0.

The only time in team history the Patriots suffered regular season back-to-back shutouts was during the 1992 season (games 12 and 13). Playing in the Georgia Dome for the first time, New England was whitewashed by the Atlanta Falcons. Back at Foxboro Stadium a week later, the home-field advantage didn't help the Patriots at all, and they were blanked 6-0 by the Indianapolis Colts in a game played with a kickoff temperature of -5°F.

Older Than Dirt

Records are made to be broken; just ask Babe Ruth or Hank Aaron. Many Patriots team records have been set and broken countless times; that's the nature of the game. One team record was set in the Patriots very first season (1960/game 5) and still stands alone at the top of the record book after a half century of games. In the second play of the game from the line of scrimmage, Oakland Raiders running back Jack Larschied took a pitch from quarterback Tom Flores, swept around toward the left side of the field, picked up a few key blocks from his teammates, and didn't stop running until arriving in the end zone with an 87-yard touchdown. This play still ranks as the longest rushing play by an opponent in Patriots history.

Early in the 1962 season (game 3), while hosting the Denver Broncos and leading 34-8, the Patriots defense became a little lax. In the latter part of the fourth quarter, Broncos quarterback George Shaw, out of the University of Oregon, (the overall number one selection of the 1955 NFL draft by the Baltimore Colts) connected with wide receiver Jerry Tarr on a quick post pattern. After catching the ball, Tarr was off to the races and ran the entire length of the field netting a 97-yard touchdown reception. This play still stands as the longest passing play against the Patriots.

Home Grown Talent

Nick Buoniconti was selected by the Patriots in the 13th round of the 1962 AFL Draft. He was born and raised in the Springfield, MA area and came to Boston via University of Notre Dame. Playing with the Fighting Irish as a lineman, most NFL scouts had written Buoniconti off due to his size (5'11" and 220 pounds). The Patriots gambled and drafted the Massachusetts native with plans of converting him to a linebacker. The 13th round selection would prove to be lucky for the Patriots and Buoniconti. It seemed as if this Springfield native already exceeded his limit of bad luck as a youth. Just before the age of 2, little Nick almost went under while swimming off the Connecticut shore. At the age of 3, he fell out of a car; and three years later the lad was hit by a truck. Two years after that, he caught scarlet fever, and within the year broke his arm. Attending Cathedral High School, as a junior he underwent knee surgery. Although not too many people could be aware of Buoniconti's pre-college injury woes, his pro football career is well documented, culminating in his induction into the Pro Football Hall of Fame in 2001.

Where's The Defense?

In the 1962, 1970, 1972, 1981, 1984, 1989, 1990, and 2000 seasons, the Patriots were not able to hold any teams to less than 10 points in any game. On the other end of the spectrum, however, in both 1997 and 2004, they were able to hold six opponents to under 10 points in a game. In 1962, 1964, 1974, 1979, 1987, 2005, 2007, and 2008, the Patriots scored at least 10 points in all games played. Conversely, the Patriots were held to under 10 points in six games in the seasons of 1970, 1991 and 1992. In franchise history, the longest consecutive game streak when the Patriots allowed at least 10 points stands at 33 (from 1988/game 16 to 1990/game 16). The longest consecutive game streak in club history when they scored at least 10 points is 42 games (2006/game 14 through 2009/game 1).

Almost A Double-Double, For The Entire Year

During the 1961, 1984, and 1989 seasons, the scoreboard at every Patriots game was given a good workout. In 1961, both the Patriots and their opponents scored at least 10 points in every game until the last game of the season, when Boston defeated San Diego, 31-0. During the 1984 season, other than a Patriots loss to Miami (game 2), 28-7, New England and the opposing team each reached double figures in points scored in every game. In 1989, the Seattle Seahawks beat the Patriots (game 3) by a score of 24-3. In the Patriots 15 other games that year, both teams posted at least 10 points in each game.

It Worked Last Time; Let's Try It Again

In the first few minutes of a Boston/San Diego game (1963/game 10) which was also the first Sunday afternoon Patriots game to be played at Fenway Park, Chargers quarterback Tobin Rote hooked up with future Hall of Fame wide receiver Lance Alworth on an 18-yard scoring pass to only have the play nullified thanks to an illegal procedure penalty on San Diego. Rote and Alworth liked the play so much the Chargers ran the identical play again. Sure enough, from 23 yards away, San Diego had their touchdown and a 7-0 lead. The Chargers defeated the Patriots, 7-6, and this contest ranks as the lowest scoring non-shutout game in AFL history.

A Dozen For The Defense

Defensive back Prentice McCray is the only player in Patriots history to return two interceptions for touchdowns in one game (1976/game 11). He accomplished this feat in style as both picks came at the expense of "Broadway" Joe Namath, and his two touchdowns covered 63 yards and 53 yards. McCray joins a handful of tandem Patriots defensive players to account for two touchdown returns off interceptions in a single game. The first duo to return interceptions for touchdowns in a single game (1962/game 3) was Fred Bruney, good for 33 yards, and Ron Hall with a 47-yard return. Next was Bob Suci with a length-of-the-field 98-yard return and Jim Lee Hunt for 78 yards (1963/game 9). After McCray turned in his record-setting performance, it was another 16 years before two touchdown thefts in one game would occur. In the only time this task was done under a dome (1992/game 10), David Pool, with a 41-yard jaunt, and Chris Singleton double upped Pool's return with an 82-yard return for a score. Victimizing future Hall of Fame quarterback Dan Marino twice within four minutes in the first quarter (1999/game 6), Andy Katzenmoyer, with a 57-yard return, and Ty Law, scoring on a 27-yard return, became the only duo to accomplish this feat in the same quarter. The last duo to rack up two interceptions for touchdowns in a single game did it twice in the same season (2001/games 3 and 16). Against Colts signal-caller Peyton Manning, Otis Smith returned a theft 78 yards for a score, and Ty Law intercepted a Manning pass and scored from 23 yards out with the pick. In the final game of the regular season, after Law returned an interception 46 yards for a touchdown, Smith raced 76 yards with his pick for the last touchdown of the regular season.

They Made It To The End Zone, But Not Through The Goal Posts

The only time in Patriots history the team allowed their opponents to score at least three touchdowns in the game but did not have any point-after kicks converted against them was against the Broncos (1965/game 13) at Bears Stadium in Denver, CO. The Broncos posted three touchdowns on the scoreboard, however, decided to attempt a two-point conversion after each score. They managed to succeed only once and the Patriots walked away with a 28-20 victory.

Picky, Picky, Picky

Gino Raymond Michael Cappelletti is best known for his kicking and receiving prowess throughout the 10 years the Boston Patriots were charter members of the American Football League. He even played an 11th year

THE DEFENSE

(1970) with the Patriots in their initial season as a member of the National Football League. Cappelletti led the AFL in scoring five times (1961, 1963, 1964, 1965, 1966) and broke the 100-point barrier for six straight years (1961-1966). His 155 points in 1964 were the AFL's all-time season high-point total when the league closed up shop after the 1969 season. When he retired after the 1970 season, the scoring and receiving sections of the Patriots record book resembled a Cappelletti family scrapbook with Gino's name repeatedly appearing.

Before his name was even a passing thought in the scoring and receiving team records, in the fifth game in franchise history (1960/game 5), Cappelletti affixed his name in the Patriots record book where it still remains. Playing defensive back and kicker during his first year in a Patriots uniform, against the Oakland Raiders, at Kezar Stadium in San Francisco, Cappelletti picked off three passes. His three interceptions off Raiders quarterback Tom Flores established a team record for most interceptions in a single Patriots game. Six other Patriots players have intercepted three passes in a single game and join Cappelletti in the team's record book include Ross O'Hanley (1962/game 10); Ron Hall (1964/game 2); Nick Buoniconti (1968/game 6); Mike Haynes (1976/game 11); Roland James (1983/game 8); Asante Samuel (2006/game 11); and Leigh Bodden (2009/game 10).

A Four Pack Of Mighty Powerful Brewskis

During his 13-year career with the Patriots (1996-2008), linebacker Tedy Bruschi intercepted 12 regular-season passes. His first pick was at the expense of Koy Detmer of the Philadelphia Eagles (1999/game 14), and his theft of a Chad Pennington, against the New York Jets (2006/game 6) was the last of his dozen-career interceptions. Add in his two postseason picks against Mark Brunell of the Jacksonville Jaguars (1996/game 18) and Donovan McNabb of the Eagles (2004/game 19) and Bruschi's total interception tally rises to 14. He is also the only player in NFL history to return four straight interceptions for a touchdown. At Oakland (2002/game 10), Bruschi picked off a Rich Gannon and chugged 48 yards for a touchdown. His next interception (2002/game 12) was against the Lions on Thanksgiving Day 2002 on a theft of a Joey Harrington pass, and 27 yards later the linebacker had his second straight interception good for a touchdown. In the second game of the next season (2003/game 2) with the Patriots visiting the City Of Brotherly Love, Bruschi ruined McNabb's hope of a pass completion and intercepted his pass intended for Freddie Mitchell. Number 54 galloped 18 yards with the pick for yet another touchdown. Bruschi's next interception came amid a New England December snowstorm (2003/game 13). With the Dolphins pinned deep in their own territory, quarterback Jay Fielder made an unwise choice and attempted a quick screen pass to the right. Bruschi anticipated the throw, stepped in front of the intended receiver, and intercepted the football with a clear, but somewhat snowy, path to a touchdown. Just before the end zone, Bruschi dropped close to his knees and duck-walked into a slide as he crossed the goal line. The fans loved the unorthodox style Bruschi displayed during his 5-yard interception return as well as the results – six points on the scoreboard. The crowd found a useful need for the freshly fallen snow and tossed Mother Nature's answer to confetti in the air turning Gillette Stadium into a winter wonderland. For anyone who witnessed this event in person, on television, or on a news clip, it is hard to ever forget the moment – from Bruschi's sashay into the end zone to the snow being re-cycled into the dark Foxboro evening.

Was Vince McMahon The Water Boy?

While attending North Dakota State University, Patriots All-Pro linebacker Steve Nelson played on the defensive line alongside Bob Backlund (former World Wide Wrestling Federation champion).

The Name Is Almost The Same

Many a strange gamebook recaps contained a few creative notes while the Boston Patriots were part of the AFL; however, after joining the NFL, they became more cut and dry. In the late 1970s, in one particular game

PATRIOTS PASSION

(1978/game 10), a gamebook had the appearance of a mistake on the final individual statistics page until double-checking the listed information. Early in the second quarter, a Steve Grogan offering was picked off by Buffalo linebacker Shane Nelson. Within five minutes, a pass tossed by Bills signal-caller Joe Ferguson found its way into the arms of Patriots linebacker Steve Nelson. There were two pass interceptions, one by each team and both picks by a linebacker named S. Nelson. This was the only time in franchise history that one player from each team who hauled in an interception had the same last name and the same first initial and both happened in the same quarter.

What A Way To Leave Them With A Lasting Impression

Former Patriots linebacker Jim Cheyunski was a product of Syracuse University, thanks to earning a scholarship after a legendary high school haul at West Bridgewater, MA. In December 1967, Cheyunski played his last college football game, Syracuse vs. UCLA, and the Orangemen defeated the Bruins, 32-14. Gary Beban, the UCLA quarterback and winner of the 1967 Heisman Trophy was sacked for a loss four times at the hands of Cheyunski.

Former Patriots number one draft pick John Charles (1967/defensive back/Purdue) spent three years with the team and scored two career touchdowns both from interceptions (1967/game 8, 1969 game 7).

Maybe Lester Hayes Lent Him Some Stick 'Em

In 87 career games with the Oakland Raiders, future Hall of Fame defensive back Mike Haynes did not fumble the ball once. During the 90 games he wore a New England Patriots uniform, Haynes fumbled the ball 11 times.

FIVE
THE SPECIAL TEAMS

At Least Two Players Had The Day Off

During a half-century of football games, the Patriots played in just four games when the club did not return a kickoff during the contest and ended with no yards in kickoff returns (1969/game 1, 1977/game 4, 1987/game 15, 1993/game 13).

Bring Your "C" Game Or You Can't Kick

During the 10 years of the American Football League, Gino Cappelletti kicked 166 field goals in 319 attempted, booted 334 out of 345 extra-point kicks, made four out of five on two-point conversion attempts, scored 42 touchdowns (all pass receptions), scored 1,130 points and led the AFL in scoring five times (1961, 1963, 1964, 1965, 1966). His total of 155 points in 1964 is the all-time point total in AFL history and tenth in all-time single season scoring in the history of the National Football League. Other than a 48-yard field goal attempt by Walt Cudzik (1960/game 13) and an extra-point attempt by Justin Canale (1967/game 9), Cappelletti was the only Patriots player to attempt a field goal or extra-point kick during Boston's entire 10-year AFL life. According to pro-football-reference.com, Patriots running back Jim Crawford missed his only career field goal attempt (1960/game 3) but in the Patriots archives/gamebook for this game, there is no record of Cowboy Jim giving it a try for a field goal.

Another One Of A Kind

During the 1962 season at Denver (game 9), Broncos placekicker Gene Mingo's 45-yard field goal attempt fell short and Patriots running back Ron Burton returned the kick 91 yards for a touchdown. This is the longest (and only) return of a missed field goal attempt for a touchdown in Patriots history.

Coast To Coast

In 756 regular season games, the Patriots returned 21 kickoffs for a touchdown while their opponents returned a kickoff for six points – a total of 17. Their longest dry spell without scoring a touchdown on a kickoff stands at 156 consecutive games (1962/game through 1973/game 13). Patriots special teams went 256 games straight without letting the other team score any touchdowns on kickoff returns (1978/game 4 through 1994/game 10).

Charlie Warner of the Buffalo Bills is the only opposing player to post a kickoff return of 100 yards or better against the Patriots with his 102-yard touchdown return (1965/game 9). The New York Giants Domenik Hixon returned a Stephen Gostkowski kickoff 74 yards for six points and the shortest touchdown kickoff return allowed by the Patriots in club history (2007/game 16).

The 2007 season for Patriots kickoff returns turned out to be the long and short of it in franchise history. Against the Jets in the season opener (game 1), Ellis Hobbs scooped up the second-half opening kickoff eight yards deep in the right side of the end zone. Never hesitating, he bolted up the field toward the left side, split between two would-be New York tacklers and didn't slow down until arriving in the Jets end zone. This was not just a new Patriots team record but also an NFL record for the longest kickoff return in pro football history (108 yards for a touchdown). Almost halfway into their 16-0 perfect regular season (game 7), back-up defensive back Willie Andrews fielded Jay Feely's kickoff at Miami's 23-yard line and returned the ball 77 yards for the shortest kickoff return for a touchdown in Patriots history.

Let's Do The Hustle

Offensive lineman/placekicker Justin Canale wore a Boston uniform for four years (1965-68) and was a good teammate during his stay. In his last game as a Patriot (1968/game 14), played in the Houston Astrodome, Canale created a few memorable moments for his teammates and for his own scrapbook of the mind. This was their first indoor game ever. Opening the second half, he boomed the kickoff off the crossbar of the Oilers goal post ricocheting out of the back of the end zone without touching the playing field. His next kickoff fielded at the 5-yard line was returned by Larry Carwell. At the Houston 27-yard line, Carwell was tackled and stripped of the ball by a Patriots player who subsequently also recovered the fumble. The player was Justin Canale.

Lifetime Perfection

Offensive lineman Justin Canale (1967/game 9), linebacker Steve Zabel (1976/game 14), placekicker Eric Schubert (1987/game 4) and quarterback Doug Flutie (2005/game 16) remain the only players in franchise history to convert their only Patriots career extra-point attempt kick.

Regular placekicker Gino Cappelletti was thrown out of a 1967 game midway through the fourth quarter after getting into a scuffle with Oilers defensive back W.K. Hicks. When Jim Nance scored on a 5-yard run later in the contest, the Patriots turned to Canale, who handled the kickoff duties, to boot the extra-point. During an August 1965 preseason game against the Jets, in Allentown PA, Canale also booted a 49-yard field goal.

Zabel, according to Patriots lore, finagled his way into getting the opportunity to attempt an extra-point. As Pete Brock recalls, after Steve Grogan scored on a 1-yard run with seconds remaining in a game, Zabel, as a practical joke, replaced kicker John Smith in the huddle for the extra-point attempt. Zabel lined up behind holder Tom Owen and split the uprights for the point-after kick. With 0:04 remaining, Smith handled the kickoff duties on the last play of the game.

Schubert, around for just one game in the 1987 strike-affected season, tacked on the extra point after a Larry Linne 6-yard touchdown reception from Bob Bleier.

Hometown hero Flutie, on his very last NFL/professional football play, lined back in shotgun formation on a Patriots extra point. After Matt Cassel's first NFL touchdown pass, to Tim Dwight from nine yards out, made the score 25-19 (Miami leading the Patriots), Coach Belichick decided to go for two points. Taking the snap, Flutie back-pedaled a few yards then drop kicked the football dead straight through the goal posts for the extra point. On December 21, 1941, Ray "Scooter" McLean of the Chicago Bears executed the last successful NFL drop kick.

Zero For Lifetime

After spending 15 years with the Kansas City Chiefs, three-time Pro Bowl punter Jerrel Wilson joined the Patriots in 1978 to handle the punting duties. During New England's 16-6 victory over the St. Louis Cardinals (game 2), Wilson was called on to perform a task in an NFL game for the first time in his career. Early in the second quarter, Patriots kicker John Smith was shaken up during a kick-off return and unable to continue for the remainder of the game. With less than a minute to the half, Patriots tight end Russ Francis caught a 24-yard touchdown pass, setting the stage for Wilson's first career extra-point kick attempt. The snap was on the mark; holder Tom Owen set the ball down quickly for the extra-point boot but St. Louis safety Roger Wehrli blocked the kick. The Cardinals kept New England off the scoreboard for the entire second half. Wilson remains the only player in team history to not convert his only Patriots point-after kick attempt.

THE SPECIAL TEAMS

Got Tied Up In The Line For The Soda. What Did I Miss?

Allen Carter (1975/game 14), Sammy Martin (1988/game 13) and Bethel Johnson (2004/game 12) are the only Patriots to return a regular-season game-opening kickoff for a touchdown. Each player accomplished this feat while New England played on the road. Against the Colts in Baltimore, Carter settled under the opening kickoff at the 1-yard line and didn't stop until he ran 99 yards for his only career touchdown. According to the stadium clock, only 0:08 seconds ticked off until Carter crossed the goal line. If so, give the man an Olympic Gold Medal. Facing Indianapolis in the Hoosier Dome, Martin returned Dean Biasucci's opening kickoff 95 yards for a touchdown covering the field in 15 seconds. It took 14 seconds for Bethel Johnson to record his 93-yard opening kickoff touchdown return against the Browns.

Not A Good Way To Start Off A Game

Eugene "Mercury" Morris (1970/game 12, 1971/game 12) and Greg Pruitt (1974/game 9) are the only opposing players to return a regular-season game-opening kickoff for a touchdown against the Patriots. Morris' first touchdown romp was at the Orange Bowl while the other two coast-to-coast treks occurred on Schaefer Stadium turf. The first Morris touchdown took 16 seconds to cover 96 yards, and his other return was 365 days later covering 94 yards and 16 ticks off the game clock. Pruitt's kickoff return was good for 88 yards, 16 seconds off the game clock, and the only kickoff return for a touchdown during his 13-year NFL/106 kickoff-returns career.

More Three Pointers Than Larry Bird

If you love three-point plays and football, the two Patriots "field goal fest" games are right up your alley, although the club split the two 12-9 games. Adam Vinatieri and Olindo Mare booted seven field goals in Pro Player Stadium (1998/game 7) for a total of 261 yards and an average length of 37 yards. Vinatieri came up short on a 45-yard attempt in the first half and Mare drilled a 43-yard winning field goal with 10:24 still remaining in overtime. The last game New England played in front of less than 50,000 fans (45,527) was at Ralph Wilson Stadium, and the temperature bordered freezing the entire day. Vinatieri outkicked Buffalo placekicker Shayne Graham to lead the Patriots to victory (2001/game 14). The two kickers booted 227 yards worth of field goals for a 32-yard average. With just over 9:00 left in overtime, the sure kicking Vinatieri nailed a 23-yard field goal to end the game. The two games remain the only contests in club history with the greatest number of successful field goals by both teams (seven) without any other means of scoring points.

This Isn't The First Time I Did It

Tony Franklin is the only placekicker in Patriots history to convert a field goal and an extra-point in games for two different teams (Philadelphia Eagles and Miami Dolphins) on each side of his Patriots kicking career (1981/game 2, 1984/game 3, 1988/game 10).

Can't Tell If They're Coming Or Going

Tony Franklin and Adam Vinatieri are the only placekickers to convert a field goal longer than 50 yards for and against the Patriots. Franklin added his name to Patriots folklore in 1988. While kicking for the Miami Dolphins, he nailed a 51-yard field goal (1988/game 10) after having booted three 50-plus yard field goals during his years as a New England kicker (1985/games 8 and 14, 1987/game 8). Vinatieri booted seven career field goals of greater than 50 yards for the Patriots (1997/game 6, 1998/game 2 and game 14, 1999/game 16, 2000/game 13, 2001/game 13, 2002/game 9) as well as kicking a 52-yard tie-breaking and eventually game-winning field goal wearing an Indianapolis Colts uniform (2008/game 8).

PATRIOTS PASSION

Another Rerun

New England placekicker Greg Davis is the only player to score the game's first points in four consecutive Patriot games (1989/games 3/4/5/6). His first quarter field goals of 35 yards, 35 yards again, 30 yards, and 52 yards respectively are the first points of the game posted on the scoreboard by either team. Davis also scored the first points for New England the week before the streak began (game 2) on a 28-yard field goal but after Miami scored the game's first 24 points. This five-game scoring streak is the only time the same Patriots player was the first individual to post the club's first points of the game.

Someone Moved The Goal Posts After I Kicked The Ball

Walt Cudzik (1960/game 13), Nick Lowery (1978/game 5), Joaquin Zendejas (1983/game 15), and Pat O'Neill (1994/game 7) are the only Patriots players, out of 27, to attempt at least one field goal during a regular-season game and not split the uprights for three points. Cudzik was short on a 48-yard attempt against the Dallas Texans in the Cotton Bowl. Lowery, in Foxboro, missed wide left on an attempted field goal of 45 yards against the San Diego Chargers. Zendejas, also wide left, missed a 41-yard field goal at Anaheim Stadium, and O'Neill was short from 45 yards against the Jets in The Meadowlands.

Piece Of Cake

Tony Franklin (1984/game 12), Greg Davis (1989/game 8) and Adam Vinatieri (1997/game 17) are the only placekickers to celebrate their birthdays by booting field goals for New England. Celebrating his 28th birthday while playing against the Colts, Franklin booted a 28-yard field goal on the last play of the first half and added a 40-yard field goal in the fourth quarter. Davis, after missing a potential game-winning 46-yard field goal on the last play of regulation time, gave himself and the team an extra reason to celebrate the day. Davis gave the Patriots and their fans a gift on his 24th birthday by booting a 51-yard field goal against the Colts in overtime to lead the Patriots to the winner's. Both winning kicks were booted at the Hoosier Dome in Indianapolis. Davis' kick of 51 yards is the longest field goal to end any Patriots overtime game, win or lose. On his 25th birthday, Vinatieri kicked a 22-yard field goal during a 17-3 victory playoff game at Foxboro against Jacksonville.

Tony Franklin (1985/games 8 and 14) and Greg Davis (1989/games 6 and 8) are the only New England players to kick two field goals of at least 50 yards in the same season. Franklin booted a pair of 50-yard field goals during the 1985 season both at Sullivan Stadium against the Los Angeles Raiders and Detroit Lions. Davis converted both kicks on the road – 52 yards in Atlanta against the Falcons and 51 yards against the Colts in Indianapolis.

Success Half The Time Will Get You Last Place

With his late first quarter field goal (1978/game 6), new Patriots placekicker David Posey made good on his first NFL field goal attempt. In franchise history, 13 individuals have attempted at least 20 field goals while donning a Patriots uniform. With 11 successful boots in 22 attempts, good for 50 percent, Posey ranks last in franchise history for field goal accuracy.

Tackling The Big Boys

The Patriots first official NFL regular-season game was played at Harvard Stadium (1970/game 1). How fitting that Gino Cappelletti's kicking foot had the honors of getting the franchise's NFL existence underway. His kickoff was taken at the Miami 9-yard line by Jake Scott and returned the football 25 yards before Bob Gladieux made the tackle. On the first play from the line of scrimmage, Dolphins running back Jim Kiick carried the ball four yards before Boston rookie linebacker Mike "Cat" Ballou made the tackle. The city of Boston now had a National Football League team. Gladieux was released by the team just a few days before this game but decided to attend the game with his buddy despite not having a ticket. Shortly after talking his way into the game through the press gate, the public address announcer called, "Will Bob Gladieux please report to the locker room?" After hearing the message a second time, he headed to the Patriots locker room. Informed he was just activated, Gladieux put on a Patriots jersey #24 and raced onto the field to join the kickoff team. After hearing the announcement, "Tackle by Gladieux," his buddy almost fell off his seat.

Finally, What Took You So Long?

During the American Football League's 10-year tenure, the Boston Patriots was the only team out of the Original Eight – Boston Patriots, Buffalo Bills, Denver Broncos, Houston Oilers, Kansas City Chiefs/Dallas Texans, New York Jets/Titans, Oakland Raiders, and San Diego/Los Angeles Chargers – to not return a punt for a touchdown. It was not until 1976 when the New England/Boston franchise finally returned a punt for a touchdown (1976/game 9). The Patriots were also the last team of the 1970 AFL-NFL Merger clubs (26 teams) to return a punt for a touchdown.

John Smith . . . Yeah Right, What's Your Real Name?

Placekicker John Smith began his American football experience quite successfully. In 1973, he played for the New England Colonials in the Atlantic Coast Football League and led the ACFL in scoring with 93 points (36 PATs, 19 of 21 field goals with a long of 48 yards). The Colonials beat the Bridgeport Jets, 41-17, for the last AFCL championship before the league folded after 11 years. After the 1973 Pro Football Hall of Fame game between the Patriots and the San Francisco 49ers, New England traded John Smith to the Steelers for future compensation. As previously agreed by both the Patriots and the Steelers, Pittsburgh released Smith after a few preseason games. New England convinced the soccer-style kicker to return to the area and kick for the New England Colonials of the AFCL. The next season Smith became the full-time placekicker for the Patriots.

One For The Bad Guys, One For The Good Guys Next Time

Bill Bell is the first placekicker to convert a field goal and point-after touchdown kick for and against New England (1972/game 2, 1973/games 1 and 3). Wearing Atlanta Falcons #37, Bell booted two field goals and two PATs against the Patriots in 1972. With 0:35 left in the game, Bell missed a chip shot 10-yard field goal allowing New England to walk away with a 21-20 victory. The next year, wearing #8 for the Patriots, he kicked a PAT on opening day and a 36-yard field goal in the third game of the season. After the game, Coach Chuck Fairbanks signed Jeff White to handle the placekicking for the team and sent Bell packing. His lifetime statistics for New England were much less than stellar – one for four in field goal attempts and four out of five on PAT attempts.

Who Needs The Sheepskin? Just Let Me Kick The Pigskin

Placekicker Mike "Superfoot" Walker is the only individual to play for the Patriots who never attended college before signing with the team. Walker, recruited by Eddie Andelman, Marc Witkin and Jim McCarthy of Sports Huddle /WHDH-AM 850, was the winner of the Superfoot contest held in the United Kingdom in the spring of 1972. The mission of the contest was to travel to England, get as many soccer players as possible to kick a football through the goal posts consistently, and select the best kicker. Walker inked a contract with New England before the 1972 season and played eight games for the team during the year. He converted 4-11 field goals (21 yards, 38 yards, 36 yards, 36 yards) and was a perfect 15-15 in point-after conversions. After the season, Walker retired and never kicked another football during an NFL game.

TV Dinners, Without Any Blocks

After the completion of the 1967 season, Terry Swanson, in his first of two years as a Patriot, became the first punter in club history with at least 20 attempts to go the entire season without having a kick blocked. During the season, he booted 62 punts and averaged 40.5 yards per kick with a long punt of 62 yards. Swanson signed with Boston as a free agent out of the University of Massachusetts before the season. In the spring of 1967, Swanson won a New England contest for punting sponsored by the Dallas Cowboys.

Before Luciano Pavarotti and Plácido Domingo

Once Babe Parilli arrived in Boston (before the 1961 team) and Gino Cappelletti became comfortable with the quarterback as his holder, field goal and point-after kick attempts flowed much more smoothly. Between Parilli's soft and sure-grip hands and Cappelletti's fluid kicking style, each became a maestro in his respective special team task. The Boston newspaper coined a nickname for the duo – "Grand Opera".

A Few Can't Miss Patriots

Matt Bahr (1993-95), Charlie Gogolak (1970-72), Nick Lowery (1978), Rex Robinson (1982), Scott Sisson (1993), and Mike "Superfoot" Walker (1972) are the only full-time placekickers to not miss any point-after touchdown kick attempts during their Patriots careers. Bahr was perfect converting 73-73 kicks and Gogolak was successful with all his 42 PAT boots. Lowery made 7-7 kicks and Robinson was a perfect 5-5. Both Sisson and Walker, while wearing Patriots uniforms, each split the uprights for extra-point kicks for all 15 attempts.

Almost The Full Length Of A Football Field And Zero Points

Wearing a Patriots uniform for the past 10 years (1999-2008) has fit well for running back Kevin Faulk. He ranks 8th in rushing (3,130 yards), 4th in pass receptions (381 receptions), 8th in pass receiving yards (3,304 yards), 21st in scoring (172 points), 6th in total punt-return yards (901 yards), and first in kickoff return yards (3,954 yards). One unique team record Faulk owns is the longest non-touchdown kickoff return in franchise history. Against the New York Jets (1999/game 9), fielding a John Hall kickoff three yards deep in his own end zone, Faulk covered 95 yards before defensive back Marcus Coleman brought him down at the Jets 8-yard line.

SIX
THE DRAFT

Once Upon A Time... A One-Man Team

Harvey White was one of a group of 33 college players selected by the Boston Patriots in the initial American Football League Draft held on November 22, 1959. On December 2, 1959, the AFL held an additional draft with each club selecting another 20 players. White, a quarterback from Clemson University, was the first player to sign a contract with the Boston Patriots on December 20, 1959. This signal-caller was the first Patriots quarterback to complete a pass, rush the ball for a gain, and be credited with a pass reception all in one season. White played for the Patriots only in the 1960 season and rushed for seven yards on five carries, completed three passes in seven attempts, good for 44 yards, had two receptions netting 24 yards, and never found the end zone.

Not Just The Massachusetts Division I Patriots

The Patriots have participated in the college draft for 50 years and selected a total of 724 players. Sticking with the New England theme, in the past half century the club has chosen a grand total of 48 players from an array of New England colleges – 13 to be specific. Overall, in franchise history, 77 players from 18 different New England higher institutions of learning wore a Patriots uniform for at least one regular-season game.

	Players Dressed for a Patriots Game	*Players Drafted by the Patriots*
American International	2	0
Bates	1	1
Boston College	27	23
Boston University	4	4
Bowdoin	0	1
Brandeis	1	0
Brown	1	2
Central Connecticut	0	1
UConn	3	0
Dartmouth	2	1
Harvard	2	3
Holy Cross	8	4
Maine	2	0
UMass	5	3
Northeastern	5	1
UNH	6	0
Southern Connecticut State	3	2
Tufts	1	0
Williams	1	0
Yale	3	2

PATRIOTS PASSION

Talk About A Tricky Multiple Question

Northwestern running back Ron Burton was the first player selected by the Patriots during the inaugural AFL Draft in November 1959. In the 1959 Heisman Trophy voting, Burton received 10 first-place votes and finished 10th in the balloting. He was also a first-round selection by both the Philadelphia Eagles of the NFL and Ottawa Rough Riders of the Canadian Football League in each league's 1960 draft. Burton signed with the Patriots, and today, although deceased, is still an important member of the local community. Both his parents passed away by the time he became a teenager and was raised by his grandmother. The neighborhood kids teased him relentlessly for being small and living in poverty. These heartless children nicknamed him "Nothing" because he had nothing and they thought Burton would never amount to anything. By his senior year of high school, close to 50 colleges came knocking and offered this talented running back a scholarship. Playing his high school football in Ohio, it was assumed Burton would sign with Ohio State as Buckeyes head coach Woody Hayes was heavily recruiting this All-State/All-American athlete. Burton developed a good rapport with Ara Parseghian, head coach at Northwestern. He decided to head to Evanston, get a good college education, play for the Wildcats, and make a difference in his life and in as many other people's lives as possible. Injuries ended Burton's career after the 1965 season; however, it didn't slow him down from doing good things and leading by example. Burton purchased and donated 305-acres in Hubbardston, MA to form the Ron Burton Training Village (RBTV). Over the past 24 years, the RBTV has served more than 3,000 young men and women in their spiritual, physical, and educational growth. Burton passed away on September 13, 2003 at the age of 67. His legacy will live on forever thanks to the RBTV; and based on its results, Burton is still making a difference in many other lives. No matter how a person measures success, Ron Burton has overachieved in his lifelong goals – he was the only Patriots "territorial draft pick" in team history and continues to have a positive effect on the entire territory. The Ron Burton Training Village has a fantastic everlasting motto: "*Here, we find something great in everybody.*"

Talk About A General Region, Alaska Isn't Much Further Than This Place

In the first AFL Draft in 1960, taking their cue from the National Basketball Association's "territorial rights" scheme, the new football league implemented the same rule. The "territorial rights" player for each club was to be from each team's general region so clubs could sign players familiar to their fans. Each "territorial selection" was not just "picked" by each team, but actually agreed on by consensus with all eight teams. With owner Billy Sullivan and assistant coach Mike Holovak's direct connections with Boston College football, the Patriots expanded their region for this pick. The team's first territorial or "bonus" pick was Gerhardt Schwedes, a running back from Syracuse. Schwedes was on the Patriots for the 1960 season and half of the 1961 schedule. His Boston career was seven games played, 10 rushes for a total of 14 yards, one pass reception for 21 yards and one kick return for no gain.

The only eight "territorial rights" selections in AFL history were assigned to each team on November 22, 1959. The Patriots were given the rights to Gerhardt Schwedes, a running back from Syracuse (also a 4th-round/47th overall selection of the Baltimore Colts); the Buffalo Bills received the rights to Richie Lucas, a quarterback from Penn State (also a 1st-round/4th overall selection of the Washington Redskins); the Dallas Texans left with the rights to SMU quarterback Don Meredith (also a 3rd-round/32nd overall selection of the Chicago Bears); the Denver Broncos ended up with the rights to defensive tackle/kicker Roger LeClerc from Trinity College in Hartford, CT (also a 15th round/177th overall selection of the Chicago Bears in the 1959 NFL Draft); the Houston Oilers netted the prize pick with 1959 Heisman Trophy winner Billy Cannon, a running back from LSU (also a 1st-round/1st overall selection of the Los Angeles Rams); the Los Angeles Chargers were assigned the rights to Notre Dame tight end Monty Stickler (also a 1st-round/11th overall selection of the San Francisco 49ers); the New York Titans tabbed George Izo, a quarterback from Notre Dame (also a 1st-round/2nd overall selection of the St. Louis Cardinals); and the Minneapolis AFL franchise (more on this story in the introduction) reeled in the rights to Wisconsin defensive back Dale Hackbart (also a 5th-round/51st overall selection of the Green Bay Packers). Cannon, LeClerc, Lucas and Schwedes chose the AFL while Hackbart, Izo, Meredith and Stickler opted for the NFL.

You Should Have Seen The One That Got Away

In the 1961 AFL Draft, with the 2nd overall selection, the Patriots tabbed Tulane running back Tommy Mason and in the 5th round chose quarterback Fran Tarkenton from University of Georgia. The Minnesota Vikings, in 1961, were readying for their first season of play in the NFL and with the overall number one pick of the 1961 NFL Draft selected Mason. The Vikings also nabbed Tarkenton with the lead-off pick of the 3rd round. Both players signed with Minnesota, and the prize catch of the 1961 draft for the Patriots turned out to be their 6th-round selection, Boston College defensive tackle Larry Eisenhauer.

In the 1962 AFL draft, in the 1st round with the 6th overall pick, Boston selected Gary Collins, wide receiver/punter from the University of Maryland. Collins, in the 1st round of the 1962 NFL Draft, was the 4th overall selection, by the Cleveland Browns. Looking to shore up the wide receiver position, Cleveland also tabbed John Havlicek of Ohio State with their 7th-round/95th overall selection. Their head coach, Paul Brown, was hoping to flank both sides of his offensive line with Collins and Havlicek as the wide receivers. After competing briefly as a wide receiver in training camp, Havlicek decided to focus his energies on playing basketball for the Boston Celtics. Had he played for the Browns, wonder if he could have stolen the ball from a Philadelphia Eagles player? As for Collins, he signed with the Browns and lasted a decade in the NFL. During his 10-year career, all spent with the Browns, Collins was voted to the Pro Bowl twice and to the NFL 1960s All-Decade Team. By drafting the talented wide receiver out of Maryland, Boston passed on another wide receiver, future Hall of Famer Lance Alworth out of Arkansas.

Dallas Cowboys great, Lee Roy Jordan, was selected to the College Football Hall of Fame in 1983 and his name was added to the Cowboys Ring of Honor in 1989. A five-time All-Pro/Pro Bowl linebacker during his 13-year career with Dallas, Jordan was also a member of the Cowboys Super Bowl VI championship squad. Jordan attended the University of Alabama, played under legendary coach Paul "Bear" Bryant, who once said of his All-American linebacker, *"He was one of the finest football players the world has ever seen. If runners stayed between the sidelines, he tackled them. He never had a bad day; he was 100 percent every day in practice and in the games."* Jordan was selected by the Boston Patriots with their 2nd-round pick/12th overall of the 1963 AFL Draft.

On November 8, 1970, when New Orleans Saints kicker Tom Dempsey kicked a NFL record 63-yard field goal against the Detroit Lions on the last play of the game, to win 19-17, the holder was Joe Scarpati. Lions defensive lineman Alex Karras was on the field when this famous kick split the uprights and was later quoted as saying, *"Dempsey didn't kick the ball, God did. A man couldn't kick it that far."* Scarpati, a native of Brooklyn attended North Carolina State and played defensive back. He was selected by the Patriots in round 13 of the 1964 AFL Draft but ended up playing in the NFL for the Philadelphia Eagles from 1964-1969 and the Saints in 1970.

University of Alabama wide receiver Ray Perkins teamed up with quarterback Joe Namath to lead the Crimson Tide to national championships in 1964 and 1965. After graduating in 1966, Perkins was selected by the Patriots in the 5th round of the AFL draft and 7th round of the NFL draft by the Baltimore Colts. Perkins elected to sign with the Colts and didn't join New England until new Patriots head coach Chuck Fairbanks hired him as receivers' coach in 1974. Since leaving town after the 1977 season, Perkins was later hired as head coach by the New York Giants before the 1979 season. During his four years leading the Giants, Perkins hired assistant coaches Bill Belichick, Bill Parcells, and Romeo Crennel. Parcells returned the favor in 1993 and hired Perkins as the Patriots offensive coordinator. He stayed on board for four years and left after New England lost to Green Bay in Super Bowl XXXI (1996/game 19).

With their last selection in the final AFL Draft (1966) the Patriots picked Paul Soule, a running back, from Bowdoin College. The Dallas Cowboys gave Soule a $1,000 bonus to sign a contract to play defensive back. He didn't make it out of training camp. Ten years later the Cowboys invited Soule's younger brother Jim to preseason camp as a free agent. Jim Soule broke all his brother's rushing records at Bowdoin but suffered the same fate as his brother and was cut by the Cowboys before realizing an NFL career.

Back-To-Back Eagles, Then Double Boilermakers

Just twice in team history, the Patriots used their first round pick in consecutive drafts to select players from the same school. Each happened during their AFL stint. In 1963, Boston selected wide receiver Art Graham in the first round and in 1964 chose quarterback Jack Concannon. Both players hailed from Boston College. After going Big Ten in 1965, drafting defensive tackle Jerry Rush from Michigan State in the first round, in the next two AFL drafts, the Patriots looked to Purdue University for their number one selections. In 1966, defensive tackle Karl Singer was the team's first round pick and in 1967, Boston tabbed defensive back John Charles in the first round.

Do You Want Your Twenty-Five Cents Back?

The Patriots utilized their 1st-round pick four times to select a quarterback. They tabbed signal-caller Jack Concannon out of Boston College with the number one overall selection in the 1964 AFL Draft. Stanford's Heisman Trophy winning quarterback Jim Plunkett was the number one overall selection of the 1971 NFL Draft by the Bay State Patriots (see next story for explanation of the "Bay State"). University of Illinois quarterback Charles Carroll "Tony" Eason, IV, was New England's 1st round/15th overall choice in the 1983 NL Draft. In the 1993 NFL Draft, the Patriots selected Washington State quarterback Drew Bledsoe with the number one overall pick.

The B.S. Patriots

On March 22, 1971, the Boston Patriots officially adopted a new moniker – New England Patriots. During the January 28-29, 1971 NFL Draft, officially all selections by the Patriots were entered into the records credited to the Bay State Patriots.

Someone Fell Asleep At The Switch

The 1963 AFL draft consisted of 29 rounds and going into draft day, the Boston Patriots owned a total of 32 picks. With the entire draft taking place on Saturday, December 2, 1962, officials from each team were going in and out of the room for conference calls. The Patriots didn't make any trades on draft day, made 32 selections and left the draft with 31 new potential players. How can that be, 32 picks, 31 bodies? In the 13th round/100th overall, Boston selected offensive tackle Dave Adams from University of Arkansas. In the 27th round/215th overall, the Patriots drafted offensive tackle Dave Adams from the University of Arkansas – the same Dave Adams the team already picked in the 13th round. There you have – 32 selections, 31 players. To help ease the pain for lifelong Patriots fans about possibly wasting at least one, if not two draft picks, please read on. In the annals of pro football draft history, only one round 13 and one round 27 selection earned a spot in the Pro Football Hall of Fame as a player. In 1962, in round 13 (102nd overall), the Patriots selected linebacker Nick Buoniconti from Notre Dame. In 1953, in round 27 (321st overall), the New York Football Giants took a chance with defensive tackle Rosey Brown from Morgan State College. Both players now reside, via a bust, in Canton, Ohio, at the Pro Football Hall of Fame.

THE DRAFT

The Cream Of The Crop At The Top

Since the first AFL-NFL combined draft that began with the 1967 season, the Patriots made the overall number one selection on the first day a total of four times (1971, 1982, 1984, 1993). To begin the festivities for the 1971 NFL Draft, the Patriots scooped up quarterback Jim Plunkett from Stanford University. Plunkett, the winner of the 1970 Heisman Trophy, is one of 16 winners of this prestigious award to be the overall number one pick in an NFL Draft. New England used its 1982 overall number one selections to pick defensive end Kenneth Sims from University of Texas; selected Irving Fryar, wide receiver from University of Nebraska with the overall 1984 top pick; and in 1993 with the top selection, the team went with quarterback Drew Bledsoe from Washington State.

New England owned the overall number one pick in the 1991 NFL Draft, however, dealt the selection before it was time to make the pick. The Patriots traded the overall number one pick to Dallas, along with their other 1st-round pick/17th overall and a 1991 4th round/110th overall, for two Cowboy 1st-round picks in 1991/11th and 14th overall and their 1991 2nd-round pick/41st overall. When the dust settled, the Cowboys chose Russell Maryland, a defensive tackle from University of Miami (FL) as the overall number one and added wide receiver Alvin Harper from Tennessee and Kevin Harris, a defensive end from Texas Southern with the three picks acquired from New England. With the Cowboys three picks, the Patriots added offensive tackle Pat Harlow from University of Southern California, Arizona State running back Leonard Russell and cornerback Jerome Henderson from Clemson.

Guess This Class Didn't Have A Valedictorian

The 1966 AFL Draft proved to be the least productive in Patriots history. The team's draft class of 1966 is credited with a total of only 143 pro-game appearances – the lowest in team history excluding the classes of 2007, 2008 and 2009. Offensive tackle Karl Singer from Purdue University, the overall number three 1st round pick, played 39 games; 2nd-round pick Jim Boudreaux, defensive end from Louisiana Tech, played 12 games; 5th-round selection John Mangum, defensive tackle from Southern Mississippi, played 28 games; and 9th-round pick linebacker Doug Satcher, also from Southern Mississippi, played 42 games, totaling 121 games in a Patriots uniform for this group. In round 13, Boston finally drafted an offensive-eligible ball carrier, Tom Carr, a fullback from Bates College.

To compare Boston's discrepancies with the NFL in the 1966 draft, Singer was selected by the Cleveland Browns in the 19th round; Boudreaux was also selected by the Browns in the 13th round; while Mangum and Satcher were not selected in the NFL Draft. Overall, the 1966 AFL and NFL Drafts combined produced only one Hall of Fame player – Tom Mack, an offensive guard from Michigan. He was selected number two overall by the Los Angeles Rams in the NFL Draft. In the 10 years of pro football drafts from 1960 through 1969, the 1966 draft class produced only one Hall of Famer. With Mack as the sole 1966 AFL/NFL draftee making it to Canton, the 1966 AFL and NFL Drafts claim the lowest number of players to gain induction into the Pro Football Hall of Fame.

This Guy Spelled His Last Name Wrong And Larry Has It Right

In the 1968 NFL Draft, with the 6th overall pick, the Boston Patriots selected Dennis Byrd, defensive tackle from North Carolina State; and 10 years later, in the 1978 NBA Draft, with the 6th overall pick, the Boston Celtics chose another Bird, this time a Larry Bird, from Indiana State. The 6'4", 260-pound Byrd started as defensive tackle in all 14 games on the Patriots 1968 schedule. After his rookie year, Byrd never played pro football again. Legend speaks of an awkward situation with Byrd's first planned meeting with the Boston press. After selecting the massive defensive player, Coach Mike Holovak invited the media to listen in as a call was placed to the rookie's house. With the entire room listening on speakerphone, when the call was answered,

Holovak inquired, *"May I please speak with Dennis Byrd?"* The person on the other end of the line said that Byrd was not at home. The coach asked how he could reach his new number one draft pick. The unidentified person said, *"He's at the hospital, he just had a knee operation."*

Once A Jumbo Always A Jumbo

Mark Buben, the pride of Auburn, MA, played his college football for the Jumbo of Tufts University and is the only player from Tufts to ever play for the Patriots. Buben played defensive lineman yet still managed to chalk up one career interception in front of the home crowd (1981/game 5). New England linebacker Don Blackmon hit Kansas City quarterback Bill Kenney's arm as he readied to pass and the football popped into the air. Out of midair, Buben snagged the ball and rambled down to the Chiefs 17-yard line. He was credited with a 49-yard interception return and the tackle was credited to Kansas City running back Curtis Bledsoe.

A Good Day At The Office

The only time in team history that New England walked away from the annual college draft with five players selected in the first two rounds was in 1982. With their stockpile of picks, the Patriots kicked off that draft by choosing Kenneth Sims, a defensive end from the University of Texas with the overall number one pick. With an additional 1st round pick, at number 27, they grabbed defensive lineman Lester Williams, out of University of Miami (FL). New England, owning three picks in the 2nd round at numbers 40, 41 and 55 overall, selected running back Robert Weathers from Arizona State, linebacker Andre Tippett of University of Iowa, and offensive tackle Darryl Haley from University of Utah respectively.

SEVEN

THE STADIUMS

Three Victories For The Price Of One Plus A Bonus Win In The Snow

On November 4, 1960 (game 8), by a score of 34-28, for the first time ever, the Patriots won a regular-season home game at Nickerson Field. Their first regular-season victory, 20-14, at Fenway Park, was on October 11, 1963 (game 6). When the team moved south to the suburbs, it won its very first regular-season game played in Foxboro on September 19, 1971, 20-6 (game 1). In the last official NFL game played at Foxboro Stadium, the Patriots won "The Snow Bowl", 16-13 (2001/game 17), in overtime. In each of the four games mentioned, the Patriots' victory was at the expense of the Oakland Raiders.

A Den Of Nightmares For Almost Any Boston Sports Fan

The Patriots managed to post only four wins compared with 15 defeats in 19 Shea Stadium regular-season games (1964-1983). The 19 Shea games are sandwiched between a couple historic Boston sports events. On one side of the Patriots first appearance is an embarrassing Red Sox moment and on the other side, their worst nightmare. On July 7, 1964, in baseball's annual All-Star game at Shea Stadium, Red Sox ace relief pitcher Dick Radatz surrendered a 9th inning three-run walk-off home run to Phillies slugger Johnny Callison. Let's travel forward in time to October 25, 1986 at Shea Stadium, Game 6 of the 1986 World Series. The Red Sox led the Series three games to two, leading 5-3, two outs in the bottom of the 10th inning, no runners on base, Bill Buckner playing first base for the Sox. . . ah, forget the rest, everyone knows the ending. There you have it, two pieces of "Red Sox unpleasant moments", with 15 Patriots losses sandwiched in between. At least the Bruins won the 1972 Stanley Cup on Madison Square Garden ice and a Boston cabbie, in 1979, talked Red Auerbach into not leaving the Celtics to take charge of the New York Knicks. Did anyone say Bucky "Blee-pin'" Dent?

Was Somebody Padding The Attendance?

Only five Patriots regular-season games had an announced crowd of less than 10,000 spectators. The smallest crowd to ever watch a Patriots game was 6,500 when Boston squared off against the Oakland Raiders at Candlestick Park in San Francisco, CA (1961/game 13). The smallest regular-season home crowd was 8,446 when the Patriots hosted Oakland at Nickerson Field winning their first home game in franchise history (1960/game 8). The Patriots' three smallest regular season-crowds were games played against the Raiders (see above and also 1962/game 14).

Homes Away From Home

Thanks to how well the Boston Red Sox 1967 season was unfolding and as the summer progressed, the AFL's president Milt Woodward needed to alter the Boston Patriots schedule to fit in a possible World Series at Fenway Park. To make matters worse, Red Sox owner Tom Yawkey, not wanting the playing surface getting ripped up by football players' cleats, was reluctant to allow the Patriots to play any home games until the entire baseball season was finished. With the 1967 schedule already set, the best the AFL central office was able to do was keep the Patriots on the road for their first four games of the year. Unfortunately, after finishing their west coast swing of week one at Denver, week two at San Diego, week three in Oakland, and then heading to Buffalo in week four, the Patriots were scheduled to face the Chargers again in Boston's home opener at Fenway Park on October 8, 1967 (game 5). With no alternative stadiums in the Boston area available, Patriots owner Billy Sullivan was forced, by the League, to play the Chargers in San Diego again. Therefore, even though technically the Patriots were the home team, this game was played at San Diego Stadium. The game finished tied, 31-31, and this was the last tie game in Patriots history.

To prevent a last-minute location change of their 1968 home-opening game, as the Patriots were forced to do the previous year due to the success of the Red Sox, the executive offices of the AFL suggested Boston's owner Billy Sullivan make alternative plans for his club to host the 1968 home opener against the New York Jets (game 2). Sullivan asked Jets owner Sonny Werblin, who was slated to host the Patriots in late October (game 7) at Shea Stadium, to switch home games with Boston; however, New York's owner refused the offer. Realizing Joe Namath was still a local hero with a lot of Alabama football fans, Sullivan booked Legion Field in Birmingham, AL as the site for the Patriots 1968 "home opener". Two years prior, Boston played the Jets in Selma, AL in a preseason game and the Jets won, 41-3. Only 2,000 fans turned out to cheer for local legend Joe Willie Namath. For their 1968 "home opener", although the official attendance was 29,192, many people swear the stadium was packed and a majority of the crowd cheered for "Broadway Joe" and the Jets. New York won the game, 47-31, and went on to win Super Bowl III in January 1968.

In chronological order, the following stadiums have served the Patriots during their first 49 years as "home" venues: Nickerson Field/Boston, MA; Harvard Stadium/Cambridge, MA; Alumni Stadium/Newton, MA; Fenway Park/Boston, MA; San Diego Stadium/San Diego, CA; Legion Field/Birmingham, AL; Schaffer/Sullivan/Foxboro Stadium, Foxboro, MA; and Gillette Stadium, Foxboro, MA. Originally the new stadium was to be called C.M.G.I. Stadium; however, the name was changed to Gillette Stadium before the first game in 2002. If anyone asks you what C.M.G.I. stands for, that's easy; it is, *Call Me Gillette Instead.*

Can The Patriots Next Super Bowl Appearance Be At One Of These Fields?

After the first 50 years of Patriots football, there are 10 parks/fields/stadiums where the Patriots played at least one regular-season/playoff game yet haven't lost a game at the site. The venues are Nippert Field/Cincinnati, OH (1969/game 10); Tulane Stadium/New Orleans, LA (1972/game 13); Yale Bowl/New Haven, CT (1974/game 2); Metropolitan Stadium/Bloomington, MN (1974/game 7); Memorial Stadium/Champaign, IL (2002/game 9); Ford Field/Detroit, MI (2002/game 12); Lincoln Financial Stadium/Philadelphia, PA (2003/game 2); Reliant Field/Houston, TX (2003/games 11 and 19); M&T Bank Stadium/Baltimore, MD (2007/game 12); and Qwest Field/Seattle, WA (2008/game 13); and Wembley Stadium/London, UK (2090/game 7). The only venues no longer standing are Tulane Stadium and Metropolitan Stadium.

Next Time New England Plays Here, Maybe The Tides Will Change?

Over the same period, there are eight parks where the Patriots played at least one regular-season/playoff game yet do not own any victories at the venue. The sites are Kezar Stadium/San Francisco, CA (1960/game 5); Legion Field/Birmingham, AL (1968/game 2); R.F.K. Stadium/Washington, D.C. (1981/game 8); County Stadium/Milwaukee, WI (1988/game 6); Stanford Stadium/Stanford, CA (1989/game 7); FedEx Field/Landover, MD (2003/game 4); University of Phoenix Stadium/Glendale, AZ (2007/game 19); and Lucas Oil Stadium/Indianapolis, IN (2008/game 8 and 2009/game 9). The only venue no longer standing is County Stadium.

No Kidding, This Is Serious

The Patriots played a regular-season game and the Red Sox played a World Series game in six different stadiums. The first professional venue able to make this claim was Braves Fields – Patriots 1960/Red Sox 1915 followed by the Polo Grounds – Patriots 1960/Red Sox 1912; Fenway Park – Patriots 1963/Red Sox 1912; Riverfront Stadium – Patriots 1970/Red Sox 1975; Busch Stadium – Patriots 1975/Red Sox 1967; and the sixth location to join this elite group was Shea Stadium – Patriots 1964/Red Sox 1986.

THE STADIUMS

Talk About Starting Off On The Wrong Foot

The first point after touchdown attempt at Schaefer Stadium was not successful (1971/game 1). After Oakland Raiders running back Pete Bansazak scored on a 4-yard run, kicker/back-up quarterback George Blanda lined up to boot the extra point. The snap from center slipped through the hands of the holder, Raiders third-string quarterback Ken Stabler, and no kick was attempted.

An Official Making A Call Benefiting The Patriots

In the 1967 gamebook (1967/game 5), a specific post-game comment from Chargers head coach Sid Gillman was rather ironic; and at a later point in Patriots history, one can only wonder, did the referee's make-up call come nine years later (1976/game 15)? In the AFL years, the individual responsible for tracking the Chargers home contests for the gamebook often listed pre-game news and post-game quotes. One interesting point from a certain post-game note – just before Gino Cappelletti booted a third quarter 41-yard field goal to increase the Patriots lead to 31-17, the referee flagged San Diego for a personal foul. Patriots punt returner Jay Cunningham had a tough time fielding a kick, but the official called an interference penalty on the Chargers resulting in an extra 15 yards for Boston. This call allowed the Patriots to kick a field goal after not gaining any yards in three plays from scrimmage. The crowd of 23,620 loudly voiced their displeasure with the call as Gillman was giving the referee more than just an earful. After the game in the locker room, a levelheaded Gillman said, "*I agreed with the fans over that call, it was a bad one, but I was afraid we might get penalized again if the booing continued.*" The official in question was referee Ben Dreith

Even The Locker Room Smells Brand New

In 1971, the Patriots played an inaugural NFL regular-season game in two different stadiums (games 1 and 6) for the only time in franchise history. New England opened the season hosting Oakland at brand new Schaefer Stadium in Foxboro, MA and christened the venue with a 20- 6 victory over the Raiders. In late October 1971, in front of 65,708 Cowboy fans, including former United States President Lyndon Baines Johnson, the Patriots were trampled by Dallas, 44-21, in the first NFL regular-season game to be played at Texas Stadium in Irving.

It's Not Raining, Why Are You Still Playing Indoors?

The Patriots lifetime dome-stadium/indoor game record now stands at 29-24. The franchise's first indoor regular-season game was played in the Astrodome, Houston, TX (1968/game 14). The first indoor regular-season game victory for the Patriots was also at the Astrodome (1973/ game 11). New England did not play an indoor preseason game until 1980 against the Seattle Seahawks at the Kingdome and lost, 30-23. In 1986, in the franchise's second indoor preseason game ever, the Patriots defeated the New Orleans Saints, 38-34, in the Superdome, New Orleans, LA. Overall the Patriots own a 3-4 career record in preseason games played inside.

Between regular-season and playoff games, the Hoosier Dome/RCA Dome, the former home field of the Indianapolis Colts, has served as host in 21 games against the New England Patriots. This stadium, no longer an NFL venue, is currently the site of the most Patriots dome stadium/indoor games with New England holding a 14-7 lifetime record while visiting Indianapolis.

The first time New England played back-to-back games under a dome was in 1987 (games 6 and 7) with consecutive road games against Houston and Indianapolis. The only other times in team history the Patriots played two straight road games indoors (1993/games 7 and 8) were against the Seattle Seahawks and the Colts. New England managed just one win against the Oilers in these four games.

PATRIOTS PASSION

The most dome stadium/indoor games the Patriots played during a regular season/postseason are three in five different seasons. In 1980, New England played in the Kingdome (game 3), Astrodome (game 10) and Superdome (game 16) and posted a 2-1 record. During the 1985 season, the Patriots played in the Kingdome (game 11), Hoosier Dome (game 13) and Superdome (game 20) again finishing with a 2-1 record. In 1988, the Patriots didn't fare too well when playing indoors, losing all three games, at the Hubert H. Humphrey Metrodome, Minneapolis, MN (game 2), Astrodome (game 4) and Hoosier Dome (game 13). The team's fortune turned around the next time they played three indoor games during a single season. During the 1998 season, the club played in the Superdome (game 4), Hoosier Dome (game 8) and Trans World Dome, St. Louis, MO (game 14) posting a 2-1 record. In 2001, New England played in the Hoosier Dome (game 6), Georgia Dome, Atlanta, GA (game 8) and Superdome (game 19) and won all three games.

The Patriots first domed-stadium/indoor victory (1973/game 11) was also their first indoor shutout. New England blanked the Oilers, 32-0. Overall, the Patriots' lifetime record for shutouts in a dome stadium is currently 2-1 (1982/game 7, 1992/game 12).

A 49-Year Regular Season/Post-Season Itinerary By Stadium, By State
*(in chronological order, first game in each new state, **state boldfaced**)*

The Patriots have played a regular-season and/or a post-season game in 72 different stadiums, in 24 states plus Washington, D.C. and two countries. Throw in 49 years of preseason games and Rhode Island, Virginia, Mississippi, Utah and Oklahoma, and that makes 29 states. Toss in Montreal and Toronto as well as Mexico City, now you have four different countries. In addition to the regular AFL/NFL preseason stops, during their 49-year preseason sojourn the Patriots played in an additional 23 stadiums. After New England's visit to London (October 25, 2009 and their 42-14 victory against the Tampa Bay Buccaneers, the club's total stops (preseason/regular season/post-season) will be four different countries, 29 different states, 72 regular-season/postseason stadiums and 95 different venues including preseason locations.

THE STADIUMS

1. Nickerson Field – Boston, **MA**
2. Polo Grounds – New York, **NY**
3. Los Angeles Memorial Coliseum – Los Angeles, **CA**
4. Kezar Stadium – San Francisco, CA
5. Bears/Mile High Stadium – Denver, **CO**
6. War Memorial Stadium – Buffalo, NY
7. Cotton Bowl – Dallas, **TX**
8. Jeppesen Stadium – Houston, TX
9. Candlestick/3-COM Park – San Francisco, CA
10. Balboa Stadium – San Diego, CA
11. Harvard Stadium – Cambridge, MA
12. Frank Youell Field – Oakland, CA
13. Alumni Stadium – Chestnut Hill, MA
14. Fenway Park – Boston, MA
15. Municipal Stadium – Kansas City, **MO**
16. Shea Stadium – Flushing, NY
17. Rice Stadium – Houston, TX
18. Orange Bowl – Miami, **FL**
19. San Diego/Jack Murphy/Qualcomm Stadium – San Diego, CA
20. Oakland-Alameda County/Network Associates Coliseum – Oakland, CA
21. Legion Field – Birmingham, **AL**
22. Astrodome – Houston, TX
23. Nippert Stadium – Cincinnati, **OH**
24. Memorial Stadium – Baltimore, **MD**
25. Busch Stadium – St. Louis, MO
26. Riverfront Stadium – Cincinnati, MO
27. Schaefer/Sullivan/Foxboro Stadium – Foxboro, MA
28. Texas Stadium – Irving, TX
29. Municipal Stadium – Cleveland, OH
30. Three Rivers Stadium – Pittsburgh, **PA**
31. Tulane Stadium – New Orleans, **LA**
32. Soldier Field – Chicago, **IL**
33. Veterans Stadium – Philadelphia, PA
34. Rich/Ralph Wilson Stadium – Orchard Park, NY
35. Yale Bowl – New Haven, **CT**
36. Metropolitan Stadium – Bloomington, **MN**
37. Pontiac Silverdome – Pontiac, **MI**
38. Tampa/Houlihan's Stadium – Tampa, FL
39. Atlanta-Fulton County Stadium – Atlanta, **GA**
40. Lambeau Field – Green Bay, **WI**
41. Kingdome – Seattle, **WA**
42. Superdome – New Orleans, LA
43. R.F.K. Stadium – **Washington, D.C.**
44. Anaheim Stadium – Anaheim, CA
45. Giants Stadium/The Meadowlands – East Rutherford, **NJ**
46. Hoosier/RCA Dome – Indianapolis, **IN**
47. Joe Robbie/Pro Player/Dolphins/Dolphin Stadium – Miami Gardens, FL
48. Hubert H. Humphrey Metrodome – Minneapolis, MN
49. County Stadium – Milwaukee, WI
50. Stanford Stadium – Stanford, CA
51. Sun Devil Stadium – Tempe, **AZ**
52. Georgia Dome – Atlanta, GA
53. Arrowhead Stadium – Kansas City, MO
54. ALLTEL Stadium – Jacksonville, FL
55. Trans World/Edward Jones Dome – St. Louis, MO
56. Cleveland Browns Stadium – Cleveland, OH
57. Paul Brown Stadium – Cincinnati, OH
58. Invesco Field at Mile High – Denver, CO
59. Ericsson/Bank of America Stadium – Charlotte, **NC**
60. Heinz Field – Pittsburgh, PA
61. Gillette Stadium – Foxboro, MA
62. Memorial Stadium – Champaign, IL
63. Ford Field – Detroit, MI
64. The Coliseum/LP Field – Nashville, **TN**
65. Lincoln Financial Field – Philadelphia, PA
66. FedEx Field – Landover, MD
67. Reliant Stadium – Houston, TX
68. M&T Bank Stadium – Baltimore, MD
69. University of Phoenix Stadium Glendale, AZ
70. Lucas Oil Stadium – Indianapolis, IN
71. Qwest Field – Seattle, WA
72. Wembley Stadium – London, **UK**

PATRIOTS PASSION

Shuffle Off To Buffalo

New England has visited Ralph Wilson Stadium nee Rich Stadium, in Buffalo, NY once a year for 35 of the past 36 years. The Patriots own a 20-15 record when squaring off against the Bills at this venue. Other than Schaefer/Sullivan/Foxboro Stadium (237 games), Gillette Stadium (56 games) and Fenway Park (38 games), Ralph Wilson Stadium ranks fourth (35 games) for the most Patriots games played at one specific venue.

Did They Count The Fans Sitting On Top Of The Billboard?

The last time the New England Patriots played in a regular season in front of a crowd of less than 50,000 fans was at Buffalo (2001/game 15). The attendance was 45,527.

Maybe They Should Have Stuck Around In L.A.

When the New England Patriots squared off against the Los Angeles Raiders in an AFC Divisional playoff game (1985/game 18), a crowd of 88,939 showed up to watch the heated rivals at the Los Angeles Memorial Coliseum. Through the end of the 2008 season, this remains the largest crowd to ever attend a Patriots regular-season/postseason game.

Sooner Or Later, The Fans Should Show Up

On August 6, 1976, hoping to capitalize on the potential popularity of the Patriots/former University of Oklahoma head coach Chuck Fairbanks in the Norman, OK area, San Diego Chargers owner Gene Klein booked his club's scheduled preseason home game against New England at Memorial Stadium, the home field for the Oklahoma Sooners. Although the stadium was capable of holding a crowd of 82,112, with Coach Fairbanks no longer on the minds of the football-crazed Sooners fans, a sparse gathering of just 23,800 showed up to watch an NFL preseason game. The Patriots lost the game, 26-17.

Blankety Blank

In franchise history, the Patriots own a 24-20 record when playing in a game ending in a shutout. Their home-field record stands at 14-9; while on the road, their record shakes out at 10-11. By stadium, the Patriots posted a 0-1 at Nickerson Field, 1-1 at Fenway Park, 0-1 at Alumni Stadium, 0-1 at Harvard Stadium, 8-5 at their first haunt at Schaefer/Sullivan/Foxboro Stadium, and 5-0 at the new state-of-the-art Gillette Stadium.

Where There's Fire, There's History

During the first preseason game of 1970 on August 16th at Alumni Stadium at Boston College, a fire broke out underneath the stands. Midway through the second quarter, fans were forced to evacuate onto the playing field while the fire was extinguished. The Washington Redskins were the opponents and Steve Wright, an offensive tackle for the Skins, held a rather distinct record. Wright played in Super Bowl I for the champion Green Bay Packers and also played for the University of Alabama in 1961 when the Crimson Tide won the UPI and AP mythical national championships. Wright is the first individual to play on both a Super Bowl winning team and an NCAA national championship team.

EIGHT
"FIRSTS" ON THE FIELD

First in Franchise History
Touchdown – Jimmy Colclough, 10-yard pass from Butch Songin (1960/game 1)
Rushing touchdown – Walt Livingston, 1-yard rush (1960/game 2)
Interception for a touchdown – Don Webb, 26-yard interception return (1961/game 7)
Fumble recovery for touchdown – Chuck Shonta, 52-yard fumble return (1960/game 2)
Kickoff return for a touchdown – Larry Garron, 89-yard kickoff return (1961/game 6)
Punt return for a touchdown – Mike Haynes, 89-yard punt return (1976/game 9)
Touchdown pass by a non-quarterback – Dick Christy, 10-yard pass to Tom Stephens (1960/game 9)
Field goal – Gino Cappelletti, 35-yard field goal (1960/game 1)
PAT kick – Gino Cappelletti (1960/game 1)
Two-point conversion – Jim Crawford pass from Gino Cappelletti (1960/game 4)
Safety – credited to team (1960/game 7)
Rushing play – Jim Crawford, 5-yard rush (1960/game 1)
Pass completion – Jim Colclough, 1-yard pass from Butch Songin (1960/game 1)
Play for a first down – Walt Livingston, 5-yard rush (1960/game 1)
Interception – Chuck Shonta, 52-yard return (1960/game 1)
Fumble recovery – Gino Cappelletti (1960/game 1)
Quarterback sack – Bob Dee, of Frank Tripucka (1960/game 1)
100-yard-rushing game – Ron Burton, 127 yards (1960/game 6)
200-yard-passing game – Butch Songin, 223 yards (1960/game 6)
100-yard-receiving game – Dick Christy, 124 yards (1960/game 8)
Victory – Patriots 28 New York Titans 24 (1960/game 2)

First at Nickerson Field/Boston University (1960-1962)
Touchdown – Jimmy Colclough, 10-yard pass from Butch Songin (1960/game 1)
Rushing touchdown – Dick Christy, 1-yard rush (1960/game 8)
Interception for a touchdown – Don Webb, 26-yard interception return (1961/game 7)
Fumble recovery for touchdown – Tom Stephens, 17-yard fumble return (1961/game 5)
Kickoff return for a touchdown – Larry Garron, 89-yard kickoff return (1961/game 6)
Punt return for a touchdown – none
Touchdown pass by a non-QB – Dick Christy 10-yard pass to Ted Stephens (1960/game 9)
Field goal – Gino Cappelletti, 35-yard field goal (1960/game 1)
PAT kick – Gino Cappelletti (1960/game 1)
Two-point conversion – Jim Crawford pass from Babe Parilli (1962/game 6)
Safety – credited to team (1960/game 7)
Rushing play – Jim Crawford, 5-yard rush (1960/game 1)
Pass completion – Jim Colclough, 1-yard pass from Butch Songin (1960/game 1)
Play for a first down – Walt Livingston, 5-yard rush (1960/game 1)
Interception – Chuck Shonta, 52-yard return (1960/game 1)
Fumble recovery – Gino Cappelletti (1960/game 1)
Quarterback sack – Bob Dee, of Frank Tripucka (1960/game 1)
100-yard-rushing game – Dick Christy, 105 yards (1960/game 9)
100-yard-passing game – Butch Songin, 264 yards (1960/game 8)
100-yard-receiving game – Dick Christy, 124 yards (1960/game 8)
Victory – Patriots 34 Oakland Raiders 28 (1960/game 8)

PATRIOTS PASSION

First at Harvard Stadium (1962/one game, season 1970)
Touchdown – Larry Garron, 63-yard pass from Babe Parilli (1962/game 2)
Rushing touchdown – Ron Burton, 59-yard rush (1962/game 2)
Interception for a touchdown – none
Fumble recovery for touchdown – none
Kickoff return for a touchdown – none
Punt return for a touchdown – none
Touchdown pass by a non-QB – none
Field goal – Gino Cappelletti 45-yard field goal (1962/game 2)
PAT kick – Gino Cappelletti (1962/game 2)
Two-point conversion – none
Safety – none
Rushing play – Ron Burton 8-yard rush (1962/game 2)
Pass completion – Ron Burton 18-yard pass from Babe Parilli (1962/game 2)
Play for a first down – Ron Burton 18-yard pass from Babe Parilli (1962/game 2)
Interception – Ross O'Hanley 16-yard return (1962/game 2)
Fumble recovery – Jim Lee Hunt (1970/game 1)
Quarterback sack – Tommy Addison, of George Blanda (1962/game 2)
100-yard-rushing game – Ron Burton/118 yards (1962/game 2)
200-yard-passing game – Babe Parilli/207 yards (1962/game 2)
100-yard-receiving game – Ron Sellers/108 yards (1970/game 3)
Victory – Patriots 34 Houston Oilers 21 (1962/game 2)

First at Alumni Stadium/Boston College (one game each 1963, 1964, 1967, season 1969)
Touchdown – Jim Crawford, 4-yard rush (1963/game 1)
Passing touchdown – Art Graham, 33-yard pass from Babe Parilli (1963/game 1)
Interception for a touchdown – none
Fumble recovery for touchdown – Darryl Johnson, 33-yard fumble return (1969/game 8)
Kickoff return for a touchdown – none
Punt return for a touchdown – none
Touchdown pass by a non-QB – none
Field goal – Gino Cappelletti, 31-yard field goal (1963/game 1)
PAT kick – Gino Cappelletti (1963/game 1)
Two-point conversion – none
Safety – none
Rushing play – Larry Garron, 4-yard rush (1963/game 1)
Pass completion – Gino Cappelletti, 25-yard pass from Babe Parilli (1963/game 1)
Play for a first down – Gino Cappelletti, 25-yard pass from Babe Parilli (1963/game 1)
Interception – Dick Felt, 35-yard return (1963/game 1)
Fumble recovery – Ed Philpott (1969/game 6)
Quarterback sack – Nick Buoniconti, of Dick Wood (1963/game 1)
100-yard-rushing game – Jim Nance, 109 yards (1969/game 9)
200-yard-passing game – Babe Parilli, 288 yards (1963/game 2)
100-yard-receiving game – Ron Sellers, 124 yards (1969/game 8)
Victory – Patriots 38 New York Jets 14 (1963/game 1)

"FIRSTS" ON THE FIELD

First at Fenway Park (1963-1968)

Touchdown – Jimmy Colclough, 56-yard pass from Babe Parilli (1963/game 6)
Rushing touchdown – Harry Crump, 1-yard rush (1963/game 7)
Interception for a touchdown – Bob Suci, 98-yard interception return (1963/game 9)
Fumble recovery for touchdown – Jim Lee Hunt, fumble recovered in end zone (1966/game 8)
Kickoff return for a touchdown – none
Punt return for a touchdown – none
Touchdown pass by a non-QB – none
Field goal – Gino Cappelletti, 37-yard field goal (1963/game 6)
PAT kick – Gino Cappelletti (1963/game 6)
Two-point conversion – Jim Colclough pass from Babe Parilli (1964/game 6)
Safety – credited to team (1963/game 11)
Rushing play – Larry Garron, 1-yard rush (1963/game 6)
Pass completion – Jim Colclough, 17-yard pass from Babe Parilli (1963/game 6)
Play for a first down – Jim Colclough, 17-yard pass from Babe Parilli (1963/game 6)
Interception – Ross O'Hanley, 61-yard return (1963/game 6)
Fumble recovery – Nick Buoniconti (1963/game 9)
Quarterback sack – Nick Buoniconti, of Tom Flores (1963/game 6)
100-yard-rushing game – Jim Nance, 108 yards (1966/game 6)
200-yard-passing game – Babe Parilli, 358 yards (1963/game 7)
100-yard-receiving game – Jim Colclough, 110 yards (1963/game 7)
Victory – Patriots 20 Oakland Raiders 14 (1963/game 6)

First at Schaefer/Sullivan/Foxboro Stadium (1971-2001)

Touchdown – Ron Sellers, 33-yard pass from Jim Plunkett (1971/game 1)
Tushing touchdown – Jim Nance, 50-yard rush (1971/game 4)
Interception for a touchdown – Larry Carwell, 53-yard interception return (1971/game 12)
Fumble recovery for touchdown – Randy Vataha, 46-yard fumble return (1973/game 4)
Kickoff return for a touchdown – Mack Herron, 92-yard kickoff return (1973/game 12)
Punt return for a touchdown – Mike Haynes, 89-yard punt return (1976/game 9)
Touchdown pass by a non-QB – Andy Johnson, 24-yard pass to Harold Jackson (1978/game 17)
Field goal – Charley Gogolak, 46-yard field goal (1971/game 1)
PAT kick – Charley Gogolak (1971/game 1)
Two-point conversion – Dave Meggett rush (1995/game 1)
Safety – Richard Bishop (1978/game 8)
Rushing play – Odell Lawson, no gain (1971/game 1)
Pass completion – Roland Moss, 14-yard pass from Jim Plunkett (1971/game 1)
Play for a first down – Carl Garrett, 2-yard rush (1971/game 1)
Interception – Larry Carwell, no return (1971/game 1)
Fumble recovery – Ed Philpott (1971/game 1)
Quarterback sack – Steve Kiner, of George Blanda (1960/game 1)
100-yard-rushing game – Carl Garrett, 111 yards (1970/game 4)
200-yard-passing game – Jim Plunkett, 218 yards (1970/game 9)
100-yard-receiving game – Randy Vataha, 129 yards (1970/game 12)
Victory – Patriots 20 Oakland Raiders 6 (1971/game 1)

PATRIOTS PASSION

First at Gillette Stadium (2002-present)

Touchdown – Christian Fauria, 4-yard pass from Tom Brady (2002/game 1)
Rushing touchdown – Antowain, Smith 42-yard rush (2002/game 3)
Interception for a touchdown – Asante Samuel, 55-yard interception return (2003/game 3)
Fumble recovery for touchdown – Matt Chatham, 38-yard fumble return (2003/game 6)
Kickoff return for a touchdown – Kevin Faulk, 87-yard kickoff return (2002/game 15)
Punt return for a touchdown – none
Touchdown pass by a non-QB – none
Field goal – Adam Vinatieri, 45-yard field goal (2002/game 1)
PAT kick – Adam Vinatieri (2002/game 1)
Two-point conversion – Christian Fauria pass from Tom Brady (2002/game 16)
Safety – Jarvis Green (2003/game 13)
Rushing play – Antowain Smith, 6-yard rush (2002/game 1)
Pass completion – Marc Edwards, 11-yard pass from Tom Brady (2002/game 1)
Play for a first down – Marc Edwards, 11-yard pass from Tom Brady (2002/game 1)
Interception – Mike Vrabel, no return (2002/game 1)
Fumble recovery – Victor Green (2002/game 1)
Quarterback sack – Teddy Bruschi, of Kordell Stewart (2002/game 1)
100-yard-rushing game – Antowain Smith, 100 yards (2003/game 18)
200-yard-passing game – Tom Brady, 294 yards (2002/game 1)
100-yard-receiving game – Troy Brown, 176 yards-David Patten 108 yards (2002/game 3)
Victory – Patriots 30 Pittsburgh Steelers 14 (2002/game 1)

NINE

ODDS & ENDS

My Baby Brother . . . Nothing But a Copycat

Peter Brock (1976-1987) shares a spot in pro football history with his younger brother Stan Brock. Each was selected in the NFL Draft with the 12th overall pick; Pete in 1976 by the New England Patriots; and Stan in 1980 by the New Orleans Saints. Both brothers played their college football at the University of Colorado. Pete started for New England in Super Bowl XX while Stan started for the San Diego Chargers in Super Bowl XXIX. There you have it, the only set of brothers selected in an NFL Draft with the exact overall number pick in different years, both play college ball at the same university and each start a Super Bowl game. Adding to the copycat mode, in 1976, Pete's first pro-football college head coach and in 1979, Stan's last college head coach, in each case was Chuck Fairbanks. Sadly, the brothers played on the losing teams in their only Super Bowl game during their career.

The First Before The Very First Of The First

On July 30, 1960, in the Boston Patriots first preseason game ever, defensive end, Quincy, MA native and future Patriots Hall of Fame member Bob Dee scored the first touchdown in the history of the American Football League. Playing against the Bills in War Memorial Stadium, Buffalo, NY, Dee recovered a fumble in the end zone and Gino Cappelletti added the extra point. The Patriots won the game, 28-7, and finished the preseason with a 4-1 record.

The Defender Wasn't Any Type Of Glad Cling Wrap

In 1957, while playing at North Carolina State, Dick Christy (1960) was named Atlantic Coast Conference (ACC) Player of the Year after leading the Wolfpack to the ACC championship. In his last college game, played on November 23, 1957 against the University of South Carolina, Christy played a game for the ages. To this day, the old-timers from Tobacco Road still reminisce about his performance against the Gamecocks. He led the way to a 29-26 victory scoring all his team's points (four touchdowns, one two-point conversions, one field goal) allowing N.C. State to clinch the Conference title. On the last play of the game, Christy attempted his first career field goal from the 36-yard line. The line drive sailed over the cross bar of the goal posts for a 46-yard game-winning kick. In another side note to Christy's storied college football career, on October 12, 1957, the versatile athlete scored the game's only touchdown and N.C. State defeated Florida State, 7-0. Christy outran a Seminole defensive back down the sideline, and with 0:08 in the half, hauled in a 48-yard scoring pass. During the previous two seasons, the Seminole defensive back in question was recovering from a knee injury and was now attempting to make a comeback. After the 1957 season, he decided to give up football due to his injured knee and move on to a new career. Although his first name was Burton, his teammates called him Buddy; however, once he began anew out in Hollywood, he became known as Burt Reynolds.

Fastest Rendition Of National Anthem On Record

Who is the only person to play for the Red Sox, Celtics, and Bruins? This is the first trivia question all Boston Baby Boomer fans learned during the 1960s. More importantly, who played the organ at Fenway Park during Patriots home games? Was it popular Fenway Park Red Sox and Boston Garden Celtics/Bruins organist John Kiley? Not only did Kiley play for the Sox, Celts, and the Bs, he also performed for the Patriots, or did he?

PATRIOTS PASSION

Clarence Campbell Didn't Suspend The Turk

Jimmy Colclough spent his entire nine-year career (1960-68) with the Patriots, however, spent three months on the New York Jets roster after being traded for quarterback John Huarte. After striking up a friendship with "Broadway Joe" Namath, he was dealt back to Boston before training camp began. In the early 1970s, Colclough partnered with two flamboyant jock superstars to open Bachelors III, a nightclub in New York City. His business partners were former Rookies of the Year in their respective sports – Jets quarterback Joe Namath (1965 AFL) and Bruins center Derek Sanderson (1968 NHL/Calder Trophy). Namath was the beauty, Sanderson was the beast, and Colclough was the brains!

Hey Coach, Remember Me?

Back in the mid 1950s, noticing a "help wanted" ad for college football players placed by the Western Illinois University head coach, future Patriots running back Larry Garron (1960-68), a native of Marks, MI, applied for the "position." The talented athlete honed his football skills while playing for the Fighting Leathernecks coached by Lou Saban, who, in a few years, would become Garron's first pro football head coach with the Patriots in 1960.

Legend To Legend To Legend

In the fall of 1949, at the University of Kentucky, Vito "Babe" Parilli (1961-67) succeeded future NFL Hall of Famer George Blanda as quarterback. Under the tutelage of future member of the College Football Hall of Fame and legendary head coach Paul "Bear" Bryant, Parilli guided the Wildcats to three straight Bowl games earning the nickname "Kentucky Babe." Parilli is the only college football quarterback to lead his school to the Orange Bowl (1950), Sugar Bowl (1951) and Cotton Bowl (1952) in a three-year span. In both the 1957 and 1958 seasons, Parilli served as a mentor for future NFL Hall of Fame quarterback Bart Starr. In 1993, he joined fellow former Patriots defensive end Bob Dee, defensive tackle Jim Lee Hunt, and linebacker Steve Nelson as inductees into the Patriots Hall of Fame.

From Curt Gowdy Country

Running back Jim Crawford (1960-64) was born in Greybull, WY, earning the nickname "Cowboy" from his teammates. As a senior at the University of Wyoming, Crawford accounted for 1,775 total yards of offense and led the nation in rushing with 1,104 yards edging out Syracuse University running back Jimmy Brown who finished the year with 986 yards rushing. The Cowboys finished the season at 10-0, yet they did not appear in any postseason bowls and failed to make either the UPI or AP final Top 20 polls. Crawford wasn't selected until the 14th round of the 1957 NFL Draft by the Pittsburgh Steelers. It took three years, a brand new football league, and the Boston Patriots before he began his professional football career. In four full years and two games in a fifth year (1960-1964), Crawford finished with 1,078 yards rushing and still ranks 24th on the Patriots all-time rushing list.

Move Over Babe

In the opening game of their second year in existence (1961/game 1), the Patriots played the New York Titans at the Polo Grounds; and across the Harlem River, less than a mile away, sits another stadium – Yankee Stadium. At the "House That Ruth Built," 23,154 hearty New Yorkers gathered to witness another New York/Boston contest – the 1961 baseball regular-season finale – Yankees vs. Red Sox. While the Titans and the Patriots combined to post 67 points on the scoreboard, at Yankee Stadium, both teams managed to post a total of only one run. The lone run scored in this game far outweighed the 67 points racked up at the Polo Grounds. The totals on any scoreboard that day, anywhere in the United States, if not in the world, could not hold a candle to the 1-0 score in the Bronx. That one run posted by the Yankees was Roger Maris' fourth inning solo home run off Red Sox hurler Tracy Stallard. This clout was Maris' 61st round-tripper of the year, breaking Babe Ruth's heralded record of 60 home runs in one season.

Two Televisions, Two Games, Two Cites, Two Sports

In the half century of post-expansion Boston sports, the Patriots and Red Sox both played a regular-season and/or postseason game against an opponent from the same city, on the same day, on nine different occasions (1961/game 4, 1968/game 2, 1975/game 4, 1992/game 4, 1997/game 4, 1999/game 1, 2000/game 2, 2006/game 2, 2008/game 2). The Patriots own a 4-5 record in the "Boston gridiron/hardball doubleheaders" while the Red Sox posted a 7-3 record on the same days (in 2006 the Sox played a day/night separate admission doubleheader).

In 1961, while the Patriots dropped a 37-30 tilt to the Titans, the Red Sox lost 1-0 to the Yankees; and both games were played in New York City. In 1968, the Patriots traveled to Birmingham, AL for a home game with the Jets, losing 47-31, and the Red Sox traveled to the Bronx beating the Yankees, 5-1. In 1975, New England, playing the Bengals at Riverfront Stadium, lost 27-10, while the Red Sox lost to the Cincinnati Reds, 3-2, at Fenway Park in Game 2 of the 1975 World Series. In 1992, the Patriots lost to the Jets, 30-21, and the Red Sox closed out their season with an 8-2 victory over the Yankees. In 1997, the Windy City had two teams visiting the Greater Boston area and neither visitor fared well. The Patriots romped over the Chicago Bears, 31-3, and the Red Sox took care of business against the White Sox, 5-2. In 1999, New England squeaked by the Jets, 30-28, and the Sox beat the Yankees and Roger Clemens, 4-1. In 2000, the Patriots lost a heartbreaker, 20-19, to the Jets and the Sox blanked the Yankees, 4-0. In 2006, the home teams won three games against New York. New England beat the Jets, 24-17, and the Sox swept a doubleheader against the Yankees, 6-3 and 4-2. In the 2008 season, the Patriots beat the Jets, 19-10, but the Sox lost to the Yankees, 8-7.

If He Played With The Red Sox, How About Gene Conley As A Roommate

Tom Yewcic (1961-65) served as Patriots full-time punter, third-string quarterback, and a running back in an early "Wildcat" offensive formation. Attending Michigan State, he played quarterback in the fall and catcher in the spring for the Spartans. Yewcic was a member of the Michigan State 1954 Rose Bowl championship team and was also voted the Most Outstanding Player of the 1954 College World Series. After departing Lansing, Yewcic signed a contract with the Detroit Tigers and toiled in the minor leagues for a handful of years. On June 27, 1957, while riding the bench for the Tigers during a brief "cup of coffee" stay in the big leagues, he saw his only action. Inserted into the line-up in the bottom of the sixth inning as catcher, he remained in the line-up for the rest of the game. The contest, at Griffith Stadium, against the Washington Senators ended in a Detroit loss, 7-2. In his only major league at-bat, the two-sport standout struck out against Tex Clevenger. In the bottom of the eighth inning, while catching, Yewcic made his mark on the official scorer's game card. Senators base runner Julio Becquer attempted to steal second base and Yewcic's throw ended up in the outfield. His wild toss allowed the runner to advance to third base (error on the catcher). Becquer decided to try to score and headed toward home plate with a full head of steam. Tigers second baseman Ron Samford retrieved the errant toss and threw the ball to home plate hoping to catch the speedy runner. Yewcic caught the throw and tagged the runner to end the inning. The play was scored, E-2, 2-5-2, giving Tom Yewcic the dubious distinction of receiving credit for an error, an assist, and putout all on the same play. To give this gentleman his due, he tossed an 18-yard touchdown pass to Jim Colclough (1961/game 2) on his very first pro football pass. This feat enabled Yewcic to become the first player to toss a touchdown pass on his first lifetime pass while wearing a Patriots uniform (see *The Offense* section for other seven players to equal this task).

PATRIOTS PASSION

Hi Neighbor, Have a 'Gansett'

As a high school football player in the State of Alabama, Billy Neighbors (1962-65), born in Tuscaloosa, AL, hoped to play for Coach Paul "Bear" Bryant at the University of Alabama; and sure enough, Bryant visited Neighbor's house to recruit the hefty young man to play for the Crimson Tide. The coach promised the teenager if he would stick it out for four years, the team would claim a national championship and each fulfilled his end of this deal. In his senior year (1961), Alabama won the Sugar Bowl, 10-3, over the Arkansas Razorbacks and finished first in both the AP and the Coaches Polls as the consensus number one college football team in the nation. Neighbors was voted consensus All-American as well as All-Conference in the Southeast Conference (SEC). During his entire college career, Billy Neighbors started as offense guard and on the defensive line earning him the top lineman award in the SEC in 1961. In 1973, John Hannah would be the next SEC top lineman award winner to play for the Patriots.

Wonder If Bobby Orr Might Have Been My Teammate?

Patriots quarterback Butch Songin (1960-1961) was a two-sport athlete at Boston College excelling in football and hockey. Although Songin was voted All-East quarterback, he reached the pinnacle of his collegiate athletic career on the "frozen pond." During his junior year, Songin was a vital cog for the Eagles' pucksters as an All-American defenseman on Boston College's 1949 NCAA Hockey Championship team. He repeated as an All-American during the 1949-50 season while serving as team captain.

Tailback University, Linebacker State, Quarterback College

With just four weeks remaining in the 1962 season, Patriots quarterback Babe Parilli was sidelined for the remainder of the year with an injury. Back-up quarterback Tom Yewcic was handed the reins to guide the club, but now the team needed a new second-string signal-caller. Coach Mike Holovak utilized his Boston College pipeline to find a backup and signed former Eagles quarterback Don Allard for the balance of the year. Wearing #12 (wonder if any Patriots quarterback wearing #12 will ever make it big time?), Allard did not see any action; however, he does have a significant claim to fame. In the 1959 NFL draft, the Washington Redskins selected him with the 4th overall pick. He was the highest NFL draft selection from Boston College until quarterback Matt Ryan was selected by the Atlanta Falcons with the 3rd overall pick in the 2008 NFL draft.

It's Now Or Never; Don't Be Cruel; All Shook Up

After graduating from Memphis State in 1963, John "Bull" Bramlett (1969-70) signed with the St. Louis Baseball Cardinals and spent two years in their minor league system as an outfielder. In college, he earned four varsity letters in both football and baseball and was also captain of the baseball team his senior year. He once ran right through an outfield fence pursuing a fly ball so his teammates nicknamed him "Bull." Abandoning a baseball career, Bramlett added about 50 pounds to his 6' 1" frame and tried out for the Denver Broncos. Making the team in 1965, he finished second to quarterback Joe Namath for the AFL's Rookie of the Year award. Bramlett's first of three AFL touchdowns (all while wearing a Broncos uniform) came at the expense of the Patriots (1965/game 3) recovering an Ellis Johnson fumble in the Boston end zone for six points. Growing up in Memphis (aka The River City, The Bluff City, M-Town), Bramlett was a lifelong friend of Elvis Presley.

Ask This Guy For The Mega-Millions Numbers

On the Patriots defensive stats sheets of the early gamebooks, the last four spaces were left blank for, if needed, the names of players not usually on defense or special teams. During a 1964 Friday night game, at Fenway Park, against the Denver Broncos (game 11), the numbers 32 and 56 were handwritten by the keeper of the gamebook on the Patriots side of the defensive sheet. A couple of offensive players from Boston were forced to make a tackle after a Denver interception. The sheet read "Garrett" for running back J.D. Garrett (1964-67) and "Morris" for center Jon Morris (1964-74) respectively. Check out the history of Saturday Live Night, the "Not Ready For Prime Time Players", and you'll get this one.

The Tennis Match Of Ties, Back And Forth, Back And Forth, Again And Again

In addition to ranking as the highest combined total points scored in a single game in Patriots history, the same game is also the highest tie game in the history of the NFL (1964/game 6). On Friday evening, October 16, 1964, at Fenway Park, Boston and the Oakland Raiders combined for 86 points with each club scoring 43 points. For the night, there were 11 touchdowns, nine extra-point kicks, one two-point conversion, and three field goals. The Patriots finished with 500 total yards on offense and 191 yards on kick returns for a grand total of 691 yards gained on the evening. The Raiders totaled 431 yards on offense and 116 yards on kick returns to bring their total yards gained to 547. The teams combined for 1,122 yards gained; and if you throw in the 37 total yards of penalties, the grand total is 1,149 yards covered on the field in 60 minutes of football or over 19 yards per minute.

Does The Job Include Free Gas?

After graduating from the College of Holy Cross in the spring of 1964, Tom Hennessey (1965-66) headed to Iraq to work as a teacher and physical education instructor at the Jesuit College in Baghdad. After one year at this elite secondary school, thanks to the urging of fellow Holy Cross alumnus and all-star defensive end Bob Dee (1960-67), Hennessey decided to take a gamble. He signed with Boston as a free agent, attended training camp in late summer 1965, beat the odds, and made the team as a back-up defensive back.

Two Local Legends Under One Roof In The Same Calendar Year

Wide receiver Jimmy Colclough (1960-68) was born in Medford, MA on March 31, 1936; and five months later, on August 31, 1936, also in Medford, MA, future Red Sox hurler Bill Monboquette was born. Wonder which one was voted Most Athletic during his senior year?

Either Way, No One Wins Or No One Loses

Quarterback Eddie Wilson (1965) played for four years in the AFL (1962-1965) spending his entire career as the backup to Len Dawson of the Kansas City Chiefs and then Babe Parilli of Boston. His lifetime statistics show a total of five career-touchdown passes with the first four scoring tosses posted while wearing a Chiefs uniform. His first three touchdown passes came at the expense of the Patriots, and his final scoring toss was rung up while donning a Boston uniform. Thanks to his ability to punt, he appeared in each of the 56 games in which he suited up. His first career start was at Fenway Park (1963/game 11) for Kansas City against Boston. His other career start (1965/game 6) was also at Fenway Park for the Patriots against the San Diego Chargers. In his 1963 start, the game ended in a 24-24 tie; and his start in 1965 also ended in a tie, 13-13. Wilson's two career starts came in games played at Fenway Park – one for the visiting team, one for the home team – and each game ended in a tie. (The 24-24 game was the first Patriots game the author ever attended, and the 13-13 game is the fifth Patriots game he ever attended.)

This Is The Real Stuff, No Jumping From The Ropes

Attending Syracuse University, Jim Nance (1965-71) captured two NCAA Wrestling Championships (1963 and 1965) and lost only once in his 92 collegiate matches. Seeded number one in the 1964 NCAA Wrestling Unlimited Class championship, Nance lost, 2-1, to Bob Billberg of Morehead State in the quarterfinals.

When Papa Joe Speaks, People Listen, And Good

Quarterback Tom Sherman (1968-69) played three years at Penn State University (1965-67) and started his junior and senior years. In his junior year, Sherman served as the first starting signal-caller in Coach Joe Paterno's illustrious 43-year (and still counting) career as head coach of the Nittany Lions. After their first year together (1966), coach Paterno called Sherman "the most underrated quarterback in the country." In the third to last Patriots game ever played at Fenway Park (1968/game 9), the rookie tossed his fourth and probably most memorable touchdown pass of his life. In a steady rain, Sherman threw a 19-yard scoring strike to Gino Cappelletti. The six points upped Cappelletti's career scoring total to an even 1,000 points. The wide receiver/placekicker was the only player to reach the century mark for points scored in the 10-year history of the American Football League.

Could Hold Practice At The Boston Garden

Joe Kapp (1970) led the University of California, Berkeley, Golden Bears football team to the 1958 Pacific Coast Conference title and a berth in the 1959 Rose Bowl. He was also a member of Cal's 1956-57 and 1957-58 Pacific Coast Conference basketball teams. The basketball team played in the 1958 NCAA tournament, advanced to the West Regions finals, then lost to the University of Seattle Chieftains and Elgin Baylor, 66-62, in overtime. In 1958, Kapp became the last person to play for both the Pacific Coast Conference football and basketball champions in the same year.

Patriots tight end Bob Windsor (1972-75) was the first athlete attending the University of Kentucky to play both varsity football and varsity basketball in the same year (1966). During the season, he appeared in two basketball games for the Wildcats and scored two points. Although not playing in the postseason tournament, Windsor was officially a member of the Kentucky squad that lost to Texas Western University in the historic 1966 NCAA basketball championship game, 72-65.

Patriots defensive tackle Dave Rowe (1971-73) was limited to just three years of high school football due to a curvature of the spine before surgery enabled him to start at Penn State. While playing basketball at Deptford Township High School (NJ), the 6'7" athlete scored 1,231 career points and was recruited by over 40 college basketball programs.

According to team legend, Patriots wide receiver Art Graham (1963-68) wore a pair of lucky rabbits' feet under his uniform socks for the first time in a game (1966/game 10) and caught 11 passes for 134 yards and two touchdowns. Also recognized as the best all-around athlete on the team, he was the leading scorer for the Patriots off-season basketball team. As a regular off-season job, Graham served as a probation officer in the Somerville, MA court system. Either way, in the off-season he was tough on the court.

Always Willing To Help Others

Wide receiver Aaron Marsh (1968-69), a 1968 third-round draft pick out of Eastern Kentucky University, was the first African-American football captain for the Colonels. In 2006, he was inducted into the EKU Athletic Hall of Fame. During his playing days, throughout the Ohio Valley Conference, thanks to his explosive speed, Marsh was known as "Big Play" and voted All-Ohio Valley Conference in both his junior and senior years. Marsh is still coming through in clutch situations. "Big Play" is now also "Big Brother" to at-risk kids.

Still Can't Win A Playoff Game

The Patriots added linebacker Marty Schottenheimer (1969-70) to the 1969 squad to help ease the loss of Nick Buoniconti. Spending two years with the club and wearing #54, Schottenheimer is the only player to don a Patriots uniform then go on to become a head coach in the NFL. Defensive back Fred Bruney closed out his seven-year pro football career with the Patriots (1960-62). In 1985, after Philadelphia fired head coach Marion Campbell with just one game left in the season, Bruney took over on the sidelines as the Eagles had coach. Philadelphia beat the Minnesota Vikings, 37-35, to give Bruney a 1-0 lifetime record as an NFL head coach. The next season, Buddy Ryan was hired to coach in Philadelphia.

Not Exactly Another Jean-Claude Killy

Offensive/defensive lineman Halvor Hagen (1971-72) was born in Oslo, Norway and originally moved to the United States to continue his interest in downhill skiing. After playing defensive end at Shoreline Community Junior College in Seattle, Hagen decided to focus his passion on football and transferred to Weber State. He added over 50 pounds to his agile body and in 1969 was drafted by the Dallas Cowboys in the third round. Early in pre-season 1971, Hagen, defensive back Honor Jackson, and running back Duane Thomas were traded to the Patriots for running back Carl Garrett. Upon arriving at the Patriots training camp, the three new players met New England coach John Mazur in his office. Mazur, a former Marine, was aware that Thomas, after his rookie year in 1970, had called Cowboys head coach Tom Landry "Plastic Man" and criticized the entire Dallas organization. Mazur was not going to put up with any of that guff. Participating in the next Patriots practice, Thomas was called into the huddle to run a pitch play and lined up in the backfield in an upright stance. Mazur requested Thomas get into a three-point stance. Replying, "I don't do three-point stances," Thomas was sent back to Dallas and Garrett returned to the Patriots. The trade was voided but New England kept Jackson and Hagen for the proverbial "future considerations."

Too Bad His Longest Punt Didn't Travel As Far

The Patriots signed Pat Studstill in 1972 to handle the punting chores for the season. This former all-pro wide receiver/punter previously played with the Detroit Lions and Los Angeles Rams. Studstill is one of 10 players to own an unbreakable NFL record. On October 16, 1966 while playing for the Lions, Studstill caught a 99-yard touchdown pass from quarterback Karl Sweetan. With placekickers and punters now a specific isolated task, Studstill, by himself, may hold another record to also never be topped. He led the NFL in punt returns per average (15.8 yards) in 1962, led the league in receiving yards (1,266 yards) in 1966 and led the NFL in punting average (44.5 yards) in 1967. Studstill is the only NFL player to lead the league in punt return average, total receiving yards, and punt average in three different years.

Mike, Joanie, Bernie, Uncle Duke, Zonker, Zeke, Alex, And The Whole Gang

Quarterback Brian Dowling (1972-73) tossed two touchdowns passes (1972/games 12 and 14) and rushed for three scores (1972/games 4/7/12) during his two-year New England career. His five touchdowns were all tallied in games the Patriots lost. Dowling was the captain and starting quarterback for Yale University in 1968 when the Bulldogs squandered a 16-point lead in the last 0:42 of "The Game" allowing Harvard to tie Yale, 29-29. "B.D.", the famous football quarterback in the Doonesbury comic strip, was created by Gary Trudeau in honor of Dowling who was his Yale classmate. His brother, Mike Dowling, is a sports reporter for WCVB-TV's NewsCenter 5.

It Beat A Real Job . . . At Least For One Day

At the end of the 1972 season, offensive lineman Conway Hayman (1972) was elevated from the taxi squad to the active roster for the last game of the year (game 14). Donning #65, he remained on the sidelines all day without playing. This was the closest Hayman ever came to seeing game action in a New England uniform. In 1975, he landed a spot on the Houston Oilers for the next five years. Hayman served as the football head coach at Prairie View A&M University from 1983-1986. His career record of 5-36-0 at this southeast Texas institution is good enough to rank 12th of 26 coaches in lifetime victories for the Panthers.

From Snow White's Dwarf, To Wide Receiver, To Agent, And Good At All Three Jobs

Randy Vataha (1971-76) and Jim Plunkett (1971-75) still share the Stanford University football record for the longest touchdown-pass play in school history. In 1970, the duo hooked up for a 96-yard touchdown pass against Washington State. Before enrolling at Stanford, Vataha attended Golden West Junior College in CA. During the summer, to earn spending money, Vataha worked at Disneyland. His job was to wear a costume and be Bashful, one of Snow White's Seven Dwarfs.

A True Patriot Hero

John Tanner (1973-74) scored his only NFL touchdown, as a linebacker reporting to the referee as an eligible receiver, by catching a 2-yard pass from Jim Plunkett (1974/game 8). After attending Cocoa High School in Orlando, FL, Tanner served three years in the United States Army. He was stationed in Vietnam for two years and served as point man for his patrol in the Central Highlands. After the service, Tanner returned to Florida, attended Brevard Junior College on a basketball scholarship, and teamed up with 7'0" Pembroke Burrows, III, who eventually played for the University of Jacksonville in the 1970 NCAA finals against UCLA. After finishing junior college, Tanner was offered a scholarship to attend Tennessee Tech to play basketball. Once enrolled at Tech, he decided to give up basketball and try out for football. In his senior year, Tanner was a two-way starter (offensive guard and linebacker), captain, and was voted team MVP for the Golden Eagles. The Chargers drafted him in the 9th round of the 1971 NFL Draft and he made the squad. After sitting out the 1972 season, Tanner came to the Patriots preseason camp as a free agent; and liking what he saw, Coach Chuck Fairbanks signed the linebacker to a contract. He was the first Patriots player to serve the United States during the Vietnam conflict and saw front line action. Tanner was a fifth-generation Floridian and, the great-great grandson of W.J. Brack, a steamboat captain and cattle rancher who helped incorporate Orlando and later became the city's first mayor. In 2008, Tanner began a struggle with cancer and on February 5, 2009 lost his battle with this ugly illness at the age of 63.

Just Ahead of His Time

On September 12, 1970, Sam Cunningham (1973-79, 81-82) ran for 135 yards and two touchdowns to lead the Southern California Trojans to a 42-21 road victory in Birmingham, AL over the Crimson Tide of the University of Alabama. It is still often reportedly hinted that Cunningham's play for the day convinced the university's administration and fans to allow legendary Coach Paul "Bear" Bryant to integrate Crimson Tide football. Jerry Claiborne, an assistant coach at Alabama, once said, *"Sam Cunningham did more to integrate Alabama in 60 minutes than Martin Luther King did in 20 years."* Truth be told, Bryant had already integrated his squad. Wilbur Jackson, the first African-American to accept a scholarship by the University of Alabama, was sitting in the stands watching Cunningham's performance. Jackson was a freshman during the 1970-71 season, and the NCAA did not change the "freshmen eligible to play varsity" rule until the 1972-73 season.

ODDS & ENDS

While attending Santa Barbara High School, Sam "Bam" Cunningham won two California Interscholastic Federation (CIF) shot put titles and was timed at 9.80 in the 100-yard dash. Sam "Bam" is the older brother of former NFL All-Pro quarterback (1992) and NFL Comeback-Player-of- the-Year Randall Cunningham.

Better Than A Designated Hitter, And Much Cheaper To Keep Around

Defensive back George Hoey (1972-73) is a cousin of Herb Washington, a world-class NCAA champion sprinter out of Michigan State University. Washington appeared in 105 games with the Oakland A's in 1974-75 without ever batting, playing in the field, or pitching. He served as just a pinch runner. During his career, Washington stole 31 bases in 48 attempts and scored 33 runs. His 1975 Topps baseball card is the only baseball card ever released that uses the "pinch runner" position label. As for Cousin George, his claim to fame was in 1971 while playing for the St. Louis Cardinals. Hoey returned Philadelphia Eagles kicker Tom Dempsey's kickoff 103 yards for his only NFL touchdown.

Coach, Can I Have a 10-Second Break From Practice?

Before enrolling in Kansas State University, running back Mack Herron (1973-75) played football at Hutchinson Junior College (KS). He also competed on the Blue Dragons track team and won the 1967 National Junior College 100-yard dash.

A New Breed Of Football Player

Running back Leon McQuay (1975) is the only NFL player to play three consecutive seasons for three teams from different metropolitan areas with each location beginning with the word "New". McQuay played for the New York Giants in 1974, New England Patriots in 1975, and New Orleans Saints in 1976. He is also the first African-American to earn a scholarship to play football at the University of Tampa (the Spartans fielded a football program from 1933 to 1974).

The Start of Everything, A Real Trendsetter

Closing out his five-year NFL career in a Patriots uniform (1975/game 10), wide receiver Elmo Wright caught four passes for a total of 46 yards with a long reception of 20 yards. Although this game's statistics turned out to be his career numbers for the Patriots and his overall NFL career wasn't too earth shattering (70 receptions, six touchdowns), Wright left a never-ending legacy in the game of football. In 1969, as a junior wide receiver at the University of Houston, Wright became the first player to celebrate his touchdowns with a dance. During the season, he once had to do some high stepping to escape the grasp of a defensive back to stay on his feet. Wright continued to high step after crossing the goal line to the delight of the fans. This high-step touchdown celebration became his signature after each scoring pass he caught. Wright still holds the Cougars record for most touchdown passes caught (34). By the mid-1970s, Wright's touchdown dance became a ritual for many players.

Best Player On The Company's Softball Team

Patriots running back Andy Johnson (1974-76, 1978-81) played shortstop at the University of Georgia and was a 6th round pick of the Baltimore Orioles in the June 1974 Major League Baseball draft. The Orioles also selected Southern Cal running back Anthony Davis, an outfielder on the Trojans 1973 and 1974 NCAA College World Series championship teams as their 15th round choice (Fred Lynn was the MVP of the 1973 USC team). In the 19th round of the 1974 MLB draft, Baltimore selected University of California quarterback Steve Bartkowski who also played first base for the Golden Bears baseball team. The Atlanta Falcons selected Bartkowski with the overall number one pick of the 1975 NFL Draft.

As a senior at Junipero Serra High School (San Mateo, CA), Tom Brady earned two varsity letters in both football and baseball. After graduating, he was drafted in the 18th round of the 1995 MLB draft as a catcher by the Montreal Expos. Junipero Serra High School has its share of famous alumnus in addition to Brady – Barry

Bonds (baseball's all-time home run king), Jim Fregosi (former Angels shortstop, traded to the New York Mets for pitcher Nolan Ryan), John Robinson (former USC head coach, member of the College Football Hall of Fame), Lynn Swan (Super Bowl X MVP) and Michael Shrieve (drummer in the early days for Carlos Santana's band, Santana; at the 1969

Woodstock Festival, after just turning 20 years old, Shrieve was the youngest musician to take the stage at this legendary pop-culture phenomenon).

Let's Make This A National Holiday, At Least With Patriot People

From the 1978 season through the end of the 1981 season, Patriots defensive lineman Julius Adams (1971-85, 1987), linebacker Steve Nelson (1974-87), linebacker Rod Shoate (1975-81) and running back Mosi Tatupu (1978-90) held an unofficial yet uncharted NFL record. The four teammates all share the same birthday, April 26th. (This date also happens to be the birthday of this author.)

Either Way You Slice It, The Results Are The Same

Pro Football and Patriots Hall of Famer offensive guard John Hannah (1973-85) is the only player in franchise history to hold a very unique team record. Hannah is the only New England/Boston Patriots player to have a palindrome last name. Spell his last name forward and you get H-A-N-N-A-H; spell his name backward it is also H-A-N-N-A-H.

Hulk Hogan, The Rock, The Hawaiian Pineapple Crush

On April 26, 1978, during the off-season, New England tight end Russ Francis (1975-80, 1987-88), along with his brother Bill, won the National Wrestling Alliance (NWA) Hawaii Tag Team Championship. After defeating Steve Strong and Chris Markoff, within a month, the Francis boys lost the title to "Big John Studd" and "Playboy Buddy Rose".

Better Than Touchdown Tony On New Year's Day

Matt Cavanaugh (1978-82) was the starting quarterback for the University of Pittsburgh when the Panthers, led by Heisman Trophy winning running back Tony Dorsett, won the 1976 consensus National Championship. Cavanaugh was voted MVP of the 1977 Sugar Bowl, leading Pitt to a 27-3 victory over the Georgia Bulldogs and their national title.

We Finally Did It

Of the 26 teams to be part of the AFL-NFL merger to form the new National Football League in 1970, the Patriots were the last team to score a touchdown on a punt return. Patriots rookie defensive back Michael Haynes (1976-82), at Schaefer Stadium, returned a Buffalo punt 89 yards for the first punt return touchdown (1976/game 9) in franchise history.

Both Attended Clemson, One Wore Number 23, The Other Number 32

Defensive back Rod McSwain spent seven years with New England (1984-90) and for three games during the 1987 season, his brother Chuck, a running back, was a teammate on the Patriots active roster. Not only are the two McSwain brothers Irish twins (Chuck was born February 21, 1961 and Rod was born January 28, 1962), they are also the only set of brothers to play for the Patriots.

PATRIOTS PASSION

An Early Sign Of Great Athletic Ability

As a sophomore at Marshall University, wide receiver Randy Moss finished in fourth place for the 1997 Heisman Trophy Award and received 17 first-place votes. Defensive back Charles Woodson (Michigan) won this prestigious award with quarterbacks Peyton Manning (Tennessee) and Ryan Leaf (Washington State) finishing runner-up and third place respectively. Attending DuPont High School in Rand, WV, Moss was selected to be West Virginia High School Football Player of the Year as a senior. In addition, he was chosen as West Virginia High School Basketball Player of the Year in his junior and senior years, earned three varsity letters in both football and basketball, and also lettered in baseball and track. As a freshman at Florida State, Moss was timed at 4.25 in the 40-yard dash – the second best time for the entire football team just behind Deion Sanders' time of 4.23.

His First NFL Action Was At The Hall Of Fame Where He Will Someday Reside

New England thrice played in the annual NFL Hall of Fame (HOF) preseason game. In 1973, the Patriots lost to the San Francisco 49ers, 20-7; in 1986, the club defeated the St. Louis Cardinals, 21-16; and in 2000, in an HOF rematch, New England shut out the 49ers, 20-0. In the 2000 game, the team's third string quarterback, rookie Tom Brady, saw his first NFL preseason action. Playing behind Drew Bledsoe and Michael Bishop, Brady completed his first pass attempt to Sean Morey good for eight yards and a first down.

Could You Please Switch The Station, Again?

The Patriots last regular-season game in 2007 was against the New York Giants (game 16). New England was looking to wrap up the first 16-0 regular season record in NFL history, and the league was looking to capitalize on the nation's desire to watch this contest. For the first time in televised football history, three separate networks broadcast the same game live (NFL Network, CBS, NBC). This was the first NFL game to be simulcast nationally since January 15, 1967 when Super Bowl I was carried live on CBS and NBC.

Just Like Frank/Brooks Robinson And K.C./Sam Jones, We're Not Related

In two separate games during the 2001 season, Antowain Smith (2001-03) and Otis Smith (1996, 2000-02) each scored a touchdown for the Patriots (games 3 and 16). In the first half of the Colts game in Foxboro, Antowain ran four yards off left guard for a touchdown, and Otis returned a Peyton Manning interception 78 yards for a score. In the last regular-season game of the year, this time Antowain ran off left tackle for a touchdown covering 32 yards. Otis picked off a pass thrown by Chris Weinke, 2000 Heisman Trophy winner, and ran the theft back 76 yards for the last regular season New England touchdown. These are the only two games in franchise history where two Patriots teammates with the same last name both scored a touchdown in the same contest.

Patriots defensive lineman Greg Boyd (1977-78) spent two years playing for New England and his namesake, defensive back Greg Boyd (no relation), who played two games for the Patriots in 1973, remain the only players on the franchise's All-Time roster to share an identical first and last name.

Heads I Win, Tails You Lose

In their first 50 years in business, the Patriots have played 756 regular-season games and 34 playoff games. With 791 official games on the books, they won 396 opening coin tosses while losing 395. Talk about the law of averages!

Through 2009/game 12 at Miami against the Dolphins, the Patriots have played 752 regular-season games and 34 postseason games. With 786 official games on the books, the Patriots won 393 opening coin tosses while losing the exact same number of tosses.

Through 2009/game 12 at Miami against the Dolphins, New England owns a 17-20 lifetime win/loss record in overtime games and a 20-17 record in overtime coin tosses. The Patriots are 9-11 when winning the toss and 8-9 after losing the coin flip. Only once in club history have they lost the overtime toss and received the kickoff (1988/game 15). Deciding to take advantage of 30-mile-per-hour winds, Tampa Bay head coach Ray Perkins, in a 7-7 defensive struggle, elected to take the wind hoping his Buccaneers defense could keep the Patriots offense at bay. After Sammy Martin returned the kickoff 34 yards, Tony Eason marched New England 56 yards in six pass plays down to the Tampa Bay 10-yard line. Jason Staurovsky booted a 27-yard field goal, giving the Patriots their first overtime victory in history after suffering 10 straight overtime losses. This is also the only 10-7 Patriots victory in franchise history.

What's In A Name?

Cornerback Ty Law (1995-2004) and wide receiver P.K. Sam (2004) share the Patriots team record for the least number of letters in their first and last names (five). The individual with the most letters (19) in a first and last name is linebacker Marty Schottenheimer (1969-70).

The most common last name for a Patriots player is Johnson with 15 of them on the team's roster for at least one game in the half-century:

Andy (1974-76 and 1979-81)
Bethel (2003-05)
Billy (1966-69)
Charles (2001)
Damian (1990)
Darryl (1968-71)
Ellis (1965-66)
Garrett (2000)

Joe (1960-61)
Lee (1999-2001)
Mario (1993)
Olrick (2000)
Preston (1968)
Steve (1988)
Ted (1995-2004

Two names – Brown and Williams (12 players each) – finished tied for second place. As for the last name Brown:

Barry (1969-70)
Bill E. (1960)
Chad (2005 and 2007)
Corwin (1993-1995)
Kareem (2007)
Monty (1996)

Preston (1980-82)
Roger (1992)
Sidney (1978)
Troy (1993-2007)
Vincent (1988-95)
Wilbert (2003)

And Williams also with 12:

Brent (1986-93)
Brian (1982)
Brooks (1983)
Derwin (1985-87)
Ed (1984-87 and 1990)
Gemara (2006)

Grant (2000-01)
Jon (1984)
Larry (1992)
Lester (1982-85)
Perry (1987)
Toby (1983-88)

Lightning Strikes Twice Just Once

During a freak December steady downpour in Oakland, CA (2008/game 14), Coach Bill Belichick and the Patriots did something on the field never to be done before in franchise history. Early in the second quarter, New England got burned by Justin Miller of the Raiders as he returned a kickoff 91 yards for a touchdown in 13 seconds. Oakland kicker Sebastian Janikowski booted the ensuing kickoff down to the Patriots 5-yard line to Ellis Hobbs and off he went. Sloshing down the soggy field, Hobbs covered 95 yards giving his team a touchdown all in 13 seconds. This is the only instance in Patriots history when back-to-back kickoffs resulted in consecutive touchdowns.

TEN
SUPER BOWL TIME

In five of their six Super Bowl appearances, New England, between the preseason and regular season, was facing their opponent for the second time during the year. Before Super Bowl XX against the Chicago Bears, during the regular season (1985/game 2), the Patriots faced the Bears and lost, 20-7. In their first preseason game of the 1996 season, New England traveled to Green Bay and dropped a 24-7 decision to the Packers. At the end of the 1996 season, the Patriots were, once again, beaten by the Packers in Super Bowl XXI, 35-21. After dropping a regular-season game to St. Louis, 24-17 (2001/game 10), New England braced for a rematch with the Rams in Super Bowl XXXVI (2001/game 10) and won the big game, 20-17. In 2003, at Super Bowl XXXVIII, New England was meeting the Carolina Panthers for the first time since week three of the 2002 preseason when the Patriots won, 23-3. In 2004, the Patriots would win their opening preseason against the Philadelphia Eagles, 24-6. They would eventually meet the Eagles again in Super Bowl XXXIX and walk off the field with a 24-21 victory. (Please read the following story to learn about the fifth team the Patriots were not facing for the first time in the season at the Super Bowl.)

During the run for the perfect 19-0 season in 2007, for the only time in their six Super Bowl appearances, New England, between the preseason and regular season, was facing their Super Bowl opponent for a third time during the current season. The Patriots defeated the New York Giants, 27-20, at Gillette Stadium to close out their 2007 preseason schedule. Two evenings before New Year's Eve, New England capped off their perfect 16-0 regular season with an exciting nail-biter at Giants Stadium and left the field with a hard-earned 38-35 victory (2007/game 16). As fate would have it, these two territorial rivals would meet again for a third time in about five months in Super Bowl XLII (2007/game 19); however, the game didn't turn out the way the Patriots and all their supporters had hoped.

Super Bowl XX – Sunday, January 26, 1986

@Superdome	1	2	3	4	Final
New England Patriots (15-5)	3	0	0	7	10
Chicago Bears (18-1)	13	10	21	2	46

Attendance: 73,818

National Anthem – Wynton Marsalis
Halftime – Up with People performs "Beat of the Future"
Cost of 30-second commercial – $550,000

MVP – Richard Dent (Chicago)
Favorite – Bears by 10

NEW	Franklin 38 yard field goal
CHI	Butler 28 yard field goal
CHI	Butler 24 yard field goal
CHI	Suhey 11 yard rush (Butler kick)
CHI	McMahon 2 yard rush (Butler kick)
CHI	Butler 24 yard field goal
CHI	McMahon 1 yard rush (Butler kick)
CHI	Phillips 28 yard interception return (Butler kick)
CHI	Perry 1 yard rush (Butler kick)
NWE	Fryar 8 yard pass from Grogan (Franklin kick)
CHI	Safety, Waechter tackled Grogan in end zone

On the last play of the first half, Bears' kicker Kevin Butler split the uprights from 23 yards for his third field goal of the game; however, Butler's kick should not have happened. Chicago had the ball at the Patriots 2-yard line as the last seconds of the first half were winding down. The Bears snapped the ball before the official formally put the ball back into play. Chicago quarterback Jim McMahon stopped the clock with a quick incomplete pass leaving three seconds on the clock. The Bears were then penalized 5 yards for delay of game; and according to NFL rules, 10 seconds should be counted off the clock. If the rules were followed to the letter, the half was to end before Butler was allowed to attempt his kick. Referee Red Cashion and the entire officiating crew ignored this rule and Butler's kick was good. The mistake was reported by NBC broadcasters during halftime and promptly acknowledged by the officials; however, the three points stayed on the scoreboard never to be taken away from the Bears.

The NFL fined Jim McMahon during the play-offs for a violation of the league's dress code for wearing a headband with *Adidas* handwritten on the front. During Super Bowl XX, he wore a headband with *Rozelle* written on the front in reference to NFL czar Pete Rozelle.

Patriots quarterback Steve Grogan attended Ottawa High School (KS) and led his teams to state titles in basketball and track and state runner-up in football. During his senior year at Kansas State, while playing quarterback, he caught a 22-yard touchdown pass.

In 1984, Irving Fryar, from University of Nebraska, was the first wide receiver ever selected with the first overall pick in the NFL Draft by New England. In 1996, Keyshawn Johnson of USC was selected by the New York Jets with the overall first pick of the NFL Draft. Fryar and Johnson are the only two wide receivers selected as the overall number one pick of the NFL Draft.

The Bears recorded the "Super Bowl Shuffle" the day after Chicago lost their first (and only) game of the 1985 season to the Miami Dolphins, 38-24, on Monday Night Football. The recording/video peaked at #41 on the Billboard charts and #75 on the Hot R&B/Hip-Hop Singles. This tune also garnered a Grammy nomination for Best Rhythm & Blues Vocal Performance – Duo or Group.

Before Super Bowl XX, 15 of the 19 previous teams to score first in the Super Bowl turned out to be the winners. In spite of Tony Franklin's 46-yard field goal to open the game's scoring, the odds didn't turn out as usual.

Super Bowl XXXI – Sunday, January 26, 1997

@ Superdome	1	2	3	4	Final
New England Patriots (13-6)	14	0	7	0	21
Green Bay Packers (16-3)	10	17	8	0	35

Attendance: 72,301

<u>National Anthem</u> – Luther Vandross
<u>Halftime</u> – "Blues Brothers Bash" featuring Dan Aykroyd, John Goodman, and Jim Belushi. Performances by ZZ Top and "The Godfather of Soul" James Brown

<u>MVP</u> – Desmond Howard (Green Bay)
<u>Favorite</u> – Packers by 14

GNB	Rison 54 yard pass from Favre (Jacke kick)
GNB	Jacke 37 yard field goal
NWE	Byars 1 yard pass from Bledsoe (Vinatieri kick)
NWE	Coates 4 yard pass from Bledsoe (Vinatieri kick)
GNB	Freeman 81 yard pass from Favre (Jacke kick)
GNB	Jacke 31 yard field goal
GNB	Favre 2 yard rush (Jacke kick)
NWE	Martin 18 yard rush (Vinatieri kick)
GNB	Howard 99 yard kickoff return (Chmura pass from Favre)

Super Bowl XXXI was the first Super Bowl televised by the FOX network with Pat Summerall and John Madden handling the broadcast. This pair also called Super Bowls XXXIII, and XXXVI for FOX. During the waning minutes of Super Bowl XXXVI Madden made it known he thought it best for Tom Brady to take a few knees, allow time for run out and give the Patriots a shot at having a chance to win the game in overtime.

In 1994, Patriots owner James Orthwein (a St. Louis native) offered Robert Kraft, the owner of Foxboro Stadium, $75 million to buy out the remainder of the team's stadium lease. If Kraft agreed, Orthwein would be free to move the New England franchise to St. Louis. Kraft turned down his request and offered $200 million to the owner for his ineptly managed franchise. If the Patriots left town, the Greater Boston area would become the largest metropolitan area in the United States to not have a team in each of the four major league sports (NBA, NFL, NHL, MLB). Orthwein accepted Kraft's offer, which until that time, was the highest price ever paid for a North American professional sports team. As of October 2009, the Los Angeles metro area (which ranks second) is the largest city in the United States without a team from all four major league sports. The largest metropolitan area in the country to not have any major league sports franchises is Austin, TX (ranks 15th in the United States).

Packer kick/punt returner Desmond Howard, named the Super Bowl XXXI MVP, became the first special teams player to win this award. He ran for 154 kickoff-return yards and scored the game-clinching touchdown on a Super Bowl record 99-yard kickoff return. Howard also accounted for a record 90 total yards in punt returns and set the Super Bowl record for total return yards (244) and combined net yards gained (244). Howard became the fourth Heisman Trophy winner to be named Super Bowl MVP (Roger Staubach-VI, Jim Plunkett-XV, Marcus Allen-XVIII).

With their Super Bowl XXXII victory, the Packers extended their league record for the most overall NFL championships to 12 titles.

To honor the recent death of former NFL commissioner Pete Rozelle, who had passed away on December 6, 1996, each player wore a special helmet decal with Rozelle's signature, "Pete," printed across the NFL logo.

Super Bowl XXXVI – Sunday, February 2, 2002

@ Superdome	1	2	3	4	Final
St. Louis Rams (16-3)	3	0	0	14	17
NE Patriots (14-5)	0	14	3	3	20

Attendance: 72,922

<u>National Anthem</u> – Mariah Cary <u>MVP</u> – Tom Brady (New England)
<u>Halftime</u> – U2 <u>Favorite</u> – Rams by 14
<u>Cost of 30-second commercial</u> – $1.9 million

STL	Wilkins 50 yard field goal
NWE	Law 47 yard interception return (Vinatieri kick)
NWE	Patten 8 yard pass from Brady (Vinatieri kick)
NWE	Vinatieri 37 yard field goal
STL	Warner 2 yard rush (Wilkins kick)
STL	Proehl 26 yard pass from Warner (Wilkins kick)
NWE	Vinatieri 48 yard field goal

With the game tied, 17-17, Adam Vinatieri lined up with 0:07 remaining in the game for a 48-yard field goal attempt to win the game. His kick was good and this game remains as the only Super Bowl won on the last play of the contest. After this game, the NFL instituted a new rule that a successful field goal should take no longer than four seconds.

Former President George H.W. Bush became the first United States president, past or present, to take part in the coin toss ceremony in person. He was joined by former Cowboys quarterback Roger Staubach, MVP of Super Bowl VI. President Ronald Reagan participated in the coin toss via satellite hook-up from the White House for Super Bowl XIX, the only Super Bowl to be played on Inauguration Day.

This was the last Super Bowl played on the old AstroTurf playing surface. During the 2003 season, the Superdome installed a new playing field, FieldTurf, a surface that better simulates natural grass. The last two NFL teams to play their home games on AstroTurf were the St. Louis Rams and Indianapolis Colts. Both teams switched to FieldTurf in 2005. Every NFL team now plays on either a natural grass surface or the FieldTurf surface.

The NFL offered New England the option to introduce either their defensive or offensive starting unit during pre-game ceremonies. To display the spirit of **unity and team**, Coach Bill Belichick requested the entire Patriots squad be introduced all at once. The league originally balked at New England's wishes but after the persistence of Belichick and the organization, the Patriots took the field *en masse* for the introduction of the starting line-ups.

In another game for the annals of NFL lore, in a 2002 AFC divisional playoff game, the Patriots defeated the Raiders, 16-13, in overtime, in the last football game ever played at Schafer nee Sullivan nee Foxboro Stadium. This game is best known as "The Tuck Game" although others also consider this contest "The Snow Bowl"; or if you're a Raiders fan, it is probably known as "The Snow Job" (attention Raiders fans, please see 1976/game 15 to understand the meaning of "what goes around, comes around"). Referee Walt Coleman ruled the play was not a fumble, so Tom Brady, out of the University of Michigan, did not fumble, and the hit to cause the fumble, by Charles Woodson, out of the University of Michigan, was inconsequential. As they say, the rest is history!

After his appearance in Super Bowl XLI with the Colts, kicker Adam Vinatieri became the first NFL kicker to play in five Super Bowls and the first to win four Super Bowl rings.

Super Bowl XXXVIII – Sunday, February 1, 2004

@ Reliant Stadium	1	2	3	4	Final
Carolina Panthers (14-6)	0	10	0	19	29
New England Patriots (17-2)	0	14	0	18	32

Attendance: 71,525

National Anthem – Beyoncé
Halftime – Janet Jackson, Justin Timberlake, Outkast, P. Diddy, Kid Rock, and Nelly

Cost of 30-second commercial – $2.2 million
MVP – Tom Brady (New England)
Favorite – Patriots by 7

NWE	Branch 5 yard pass from Brady (Vinatieri kick)
CAR	S. Smith 39 yard pass from Delhomme (Kasay kick)
NWE	Givens 5 yard pass from Brady (Vinatieri kick)
CAR	Kasay 50 yard field goal
NWE	A. Smith 2 yard rush (Vinatieri kick)
CAR	Foster 33 yard rush (pass failed)
CAR	Muhammad 85 yard pass from Delhomme (pass failed)
NWE	Vrabel 1 yard pass from Brady (Faulk pass from Brady)
CAR	Proehl 12 yard pass from Delhomme (Kasay kick)
NWE	Vinatieri 41 yard field goal

The most widely discussed moment of Super Bowl XXXVIII came out of the halftime show. An incident involving Janet Jackson and Justin Timberlake – just as their last song reached the final line, *"I'm gonna have you naked by the end of this song,"* – created a halftime-show controversy centering around a "wardrobe malfunction". Over the next week, after the game, all the major networks kept America abreast, of everyone's reactions.

The NFL, in 1992, released a list of five areas to be considered as potential NFL team locations. The list included Baltimore, St. Louis, Memphis, Jacksonville, and the Carolinas. In 1995, Carolina and Jacksonville entered the NFL and the Rams relocated from Los Angeles to St. Louis; in 1996, the Browns relocated from Cleveland to become the Baltimore Ravens; and in 1997 Memphis had the Tennessee Oilers as tenants at the Liberty Bowl Memorial Stadium before they headed to Nashville as the Titans. So four of the five cities on the NFL's 1992 expansion list gained a team, and the best Memphis did was one year with the Oilers, and now an NFL team 210 miles away.

This was the fourth Super Bowl to be decided on a field goal in the final seconds. Colts kicker Jim O'Brien booted a 32-yard field goal to win Super Bowl V; the New York Giants won Super Bowl XXV when Bills kicker Scott Norwood missed a 47-yard field goal on the last play; New England won Super Bowl XXXVI when Adam Vinatieri split the uprights from 48 yards as the clock expired; and in Super Bowl XXXVIII, Vinatieri nailed a 48-yard field goal with 0:04 left, giving the Patriots their second Super Bowl title in three years.

This was the first Super Bowl to be played in a stadium with a retractable roof (but it was eventually closed during the game). It also marked the first time in four tries that the Patriots played a Super Bowl that was not in New Orleans.

New England placekicker Adam Vinatieri was originally recruited to kick for Army and attended West Point for several weeks in 1991 before deciding to return home to South Dakota. He was a four-year letterman at South Dakota State University as a placekicker and punter. His great-great grandfather was Felix Vinatieri, an Italian immigrant who served as General George Armstrong Custer's bandmaster. According to folklore, General Custer told Felix Vinatieri to head back to camp instead of going ahead with the regiment to Little Big Horn, and this decision saved Vinatieri's life. A collection of Felix Vinatieri's manuscripts and instruments can be found at the National Music Museum located in Vermillion, South Dakota. Adam Vinatieri is also a third cousin to the famous daredevil Evel Knievel.

Super Bowl XXXVIII – Sunday, February 2, 2005

@ ALLTEL Stadium	1	2	3	4	Final
New England Patriots (17-2)	0	7	7	10	24
Phila. Eagles (15-4)	0	7	7	7	21

Attendance: 78,125

National Anthem – Combine choirs of the U.S. Military Academy, the U.S. Naval Academy, the U.S. Air Force the U.S. Coast Guard Academy, and U.S. Army Herald Trumpets

Halftime – Paul McCartney
Cost of 30-second commercial – $2.4 Academy,
MVP – Deion Branch (New England)
Favorite – Patriots by 7

PHI	L.J. Smith 6 yard pass from McNabb (Akers kick)
NWE	Givens 4 yard pass from Brady (Vinatieri kick)
NWE	Vrabel 2 yard pass from Brady (Vinatieri kick)
PHI	Westbrook 10 yard pass from McNabb (Akers kick)
NWE	Dillon 2 yard rush (Vinatieri kick)
NWE	Vinatieri 22 yard field goal
PHI	Lewis 30 yard pass from McNabb (Akers kick)

Deion Branch, Super Bowl XXXIX MVP, caught 11 passes tying the Super Bowl record (Dan Ross, Bengals-XVI, Jerry Rice, 49ers-XXIII) of 133 yards. With 10 receptions in the previous Super Bowl (XXXVIII) against Carolina, Branch set the record for the most combined receptions in consecutive Super Bowls with 21 catches. Branch was the third offensive player to ever win Super Bowl MVP without scoring a touchdown or throwing a touchdown pass, joining NFL Hall of Famers quarterback Joe Namath (New York Jets – III) and wide receiver Fred Biletnikoff (Oakland Raiders – XI).

Due to injuries at the tight end spot, the Eagles were forced to sign Jeff Thomason, a former tight end who was working construction at the time, to a one-game contract for the Super Bowl. Thomason saw time during several plays although never had a ball thrown his way. This was his third Super Bowl, playing in two with the Packers, and winning a ring (XXXI) during Philadelphia head coach Andy Reid's days as a Packer assistant.

Super Bowl XXXIX was broadcast by FOX with Joe Buck handling the play-by-play and color commentators Cris Collinsworth and Troy Aikman. This broadcast team was the first group of announcers since Super Bowl I where none of the individuals in the broadcast booth had ever called a Super Bowl game before.

For the third straight year, each team took the field *en masse*. In prerecorded video segments, Andover native Michael Chiklis introduced the Patriots and Philadelphia-born Will Smith introduced the Eagles.

Each member of the Patriots team received a payment of $68,000 for winning the game. The Eagles each received $36,500. When adjusted for inflation, the Patriots' winnings were actually less than the $15,000 paid to members of the Green Bay Packers for winning Super Bowl I in 1967. That amount of money in 1967 equated approximately $85,000 in 2005.

Paul McCartney performed at halftime as the only act, and his set consisted of the Beatles songs "Drive My Car", "Get Back", "Hey Jude", and from his Wings career, "Live and Let Die."

With the choirs of the U.S. Military Academy, U.S. Naval Academy, U.S. Air Force Academy, U.S. Coast Guard Academy, and the U.S. Army Herald Trumpets joining them for the national anthem, it was the first time in 31 years that all four service academies sang together (the last time was at the second inauguration of President Richard Nixon in 1973).

Super Bowl XLII – Sunday, February 3, 2008

@ University of Phoenix Stadium	1	2	3	4	Final
NY Giants (14-6)	3	0	0	14	17
NE Patriots (18-1)	0	7	0	7	14

Attendance: 71,101

National Anthem – Jordin Sparks
Halftime – Tom Petty and the Heartbreakers
Cost of 30-second commercial – $2.7 million

MVP – Eli Manning (New York)
Favorite – Patriots by 12

NYG	Tynes 32 yard field goal
NWE	Maroney 1 yard rush (Gostkowski kick)
NYG	Tyree 5 yard pass from E. Manning (Tynes kick)
NWE	Moss 6 yard pass from Brady (Gostkowski kick)
NYG	Burress 13 yard pass from E. Manning (Tynes kick)

Broadcast by FOX, Super Bowl XLII ranked as the most-watched Super Bowl of all time until a year later (Super Bowl XLIII). The Patriots/Giants game was viewed by an average of 97.5 million people throughout the United States and 148.3 million total viewers watching some part of the game. This broadcast is the third most-watched TV program of all time in United States Nielsen ratings; the final episode of *M*A*S*H*, "Goodbye, Farewell and Amen", broadcast on February 28, 1983, on CBS, with an average of 105.9 million viewers, still holds the all-time number one slot as the most-watched program. In 2009, Super Bowl XLIII edged this game to capture the second slot averaging 98.7 million viewers for the evening.

This game was a rematch of the final game of this year's NFL season when the Patriots prevailed over the Giants, 38-35, to complete the first 16-0 perfect season in league history. This season finale was the first NFL game ever to be shown on three different networks at the same time (NFL Network, CBS and NBC).
After winning the coin toss (tails) to start the game, New York executed a 16-play, 77-yard march ending with a Lawrence Tynes' 32-yard field goal to take a 3-0 lead. This drive lasted 9:59, featured four third-down conversions (most ever on a Super Bowl opening drive), and now ranks as the longest opening drive in Super Bowl history.

On May 1, 1988, Giants punter Jeff Feagles, out of the University of Miami (FL), signed a free-agent contract with the New England Patriots. As one of the Giants captains, it was Feagles who called tails for the Super Bowl XLII coin toss (see above). In his two-decade long career, he has punted 1,585 times for 65,793 yards with 508 punts inside the 20-yard line (all NFL records), with 12 punts blocked and a 41.6-yards-per-kick average. Feagles, at the age of 41, is the oldest player in NFL history to play in and win a Super Bowl.

Mike Carey, the Super Bowl XLII referee, was the first African-American to be the head official at a Super Bowl. He also officiated the Patriots/Giants 2007 season finale (see above). On October 3, 2005, Carey, with his brother Don, became the first siblings to officiate the same game (Carolina Panthers vs. Green Bay Packers). In December 2005, at the start of overtime between the Detroit Lions and the Packers, Carey was unable to locate a coin for the coin toss. He had given his official NFL coin to a child who served as the Packers honorary captain at the game's opening coin toss. The field judge came to the rescue and provided Carey with a penny for the overtime coin toss.

For the last three Super Bowls, the team to be the second to arrive in the host city has won the game. (The Giants before Super Bowl XLII in the Phoenix area, the Indianapolis Colts before Super Bowl XLI in Miami and the Pittsburgh Steelers before Super Bowl XL in Detroit.)

The Patriots are the only team to play in a Super Bowl game (XXXVI and XLII) in two different seasons after losing their two games of the regular season. The Dallas Cowboys (Super Bowl XXVIII) and New York Giants (Super Bowl XLII) are the only other teams to begin the season with two losses and make it to the The Big Game.

Patriots Firsts and Lasts During a Super Bowl

Babe Parilli (1961-67) is the first ex-Patriots player to appear in a Super Bowl game and win a Super Bowl championship ring. Both achievements happened on January 12, 1969 at Super Bowl III when the New York Jets shocked the entire nation with a 13-3 upset of the 18½-point favorite Baltimore Colts.

Jim Plunkett (1971-75) is the first ex-Patriots player to throw for a touchdown during a Super Bowl game. In Super Bowl XV, Plunkett tossed three scoring passes for the Oakland Raiders during their 27-10 victory over the Philadelphia Eagles. He is also the first ex-Patriot to win the MVP award in a Super Bowl.

Bill Rademacher (1969-70) is the first Patriots player to previously win a Super Bowl championship ring before joining the club. He was a back-up receiver for the Jets Super Bowl III winning team. Rademacher invested his Super Bowl earnings in cucumber and sweet potato plantings in the Caribbean with several former New York teammates.

Gene Thomas (1968) is the first Patriots player to previously participate in a Super Bowl before joining the club. He spent the 1966 and 1967 seasons with Kansas City and saw action on special teams for the Chiefs in Super Bowl I.

Wide receiver Bake Turner (1970) is the first Patriots player to score a touchdown after previously winning a Super Bowl championship ring (Super Bowl III) with the New York Jets. He caught a 12-yard pass from Joe Kapp (1970/game 4). This pass established Kapp as the first Patriots quarterback to throw a touchdown pass after previously playing in a Super Bowl. He played for the Minnesota Vikings in Super Bowl IV, and his team lost to the Kansas City Chiefs, 23-7.

Adam Vinatieri (1996-2005) is the only placekicker in NFL history to boot a field goal and extra point for two different Super Bowl winning teams. He achieved this feat in Super Bowl XXXVI, XXXVIII, and XXXIX for the Patriots and Super Bowl XLI for the Indianapolis Colts.

No player has won a Super Bowl MVP for another team then played for New England. In addition, no players wore a Patriots uniform before joining a different team and then score a touchdown in a Super Bowl.

Super Bowl Firsts and Lasts

Super Bowl I is the only Super Bowl to be broadcast simultaneously by two networks (CBS, NBC). No other NFL game was subsequently broadcast on more than one network until December 2007 when the Patriots/Giants game was carried on CBS, NBC, and the NFL Network (2007/game 16). During Super Bowl I, NBC did not return in time from a commercial break for the second-half kickoff. As the kickoff began to unfold, the officials stopped the game and redid the kickoff once NBC was back on the air. This game is the only Super Bowl to not sellout despite a TV blackout in the Los Angeles area. A few days before the game, local newspapers printed editorials criticizing the exorbitant $12 ticket price and detailing how fans could pirate the TV signal from out-of-town stations.

With both the New York Jets and Indianapolis Colts in the American Football Conference, Super Bowl III is the only Super Bowl that could never take place again as a rematch.

Ed Sabol of NFL Films, on the eve of Super Bowl IV, convinced Chiefs head coach Hank Stram to wear a hidden microphone during the game to record his comments for NFL Films. They agreed to keep this a secret, and this would be the first time a head coach wore a microphone during a Super Bowl.

Super Bowl VI (Dallas Cowboys vs. Miami Dolphins), played at Tulane Stadium, New Orleans, LA, was the last Super Bowl to be blacked out in the TV market where the game was played. (The first six Super Bowls were blacked out.) In 1973, the NFL changed its blackout policy allowing games to be broadcast in the home-team's market if all tickets sold out 72 hours in advance of kickoff.

Super Bowl XII was the first Super Bowl between two teams who met during regular season play. The Cowboys defeated the Broncos, 14-6, on the final Sunday of the regular season.

Super Bowl XIV (Los Angeles Rams vs. Pittsburgh Steelers) was the first Super Bowl where two pre-expansion era teams (pre 1960) met in a Super Bowl. The only other Super Bowl to claim the same is Super Bowl XLI between the Indianapolis Colts and Chicago Bears.

Super Bowl XVI was the first Super Bowl to feature two teams who did not appear in any national prime-time televised football game during the regular season. This was also the first Super Bowl to feature two first-time participants since Super Bowl III. (The only other is Super Bowl XX between New England and Chicago.)

This is also the only Super Bowl between two teams who had losing records the previous season (San Francisco, 6-10 and Cincinnati, 6-10).

New York Giants quarterback Phil Simms, Super Bowl XXI MVP, was the first athlete to appear in the *"I'm Going to Disney World"* television commercial.

Super Bowl XXVIII is the only rematch contest in Super Bowl history. In Super Bowl XXVII the Dallas Cowboys defeated the Buffalo Bills, 52-17. A year later in Super Bowl XXVIII, the Cowboys, once again, prevailed against the Bills – this time by a score of 30-13.

Super Bowl XXXIV is the only Super Bowl played between two teams who were now located in a different city from the city in which each resided when the 1970 AFL-NF merger took place. The St. Louis Rams called Los Angeles home until 1995 when the club headed east to St. Louis. The Tennessee Titans began life as the Houston Oilers, born in 1960, as part of the new upstart AFL. The Oilers won the first two AFL championships (1960 and 1961) and moved to Tennessee before the 1997 season.

Big Game Leftovers

Joe Namath is the only quarterback to win a Super Bowl Most Valuable Player award (III) and not throw a touchdown pass during the game.

Len Dawson was the first quarterback to both win and lose a Super Bowl game as the starting signal-caller. In Super Bowl I, led by Dawson, the Kansas City Chiefs lost to the Green Bay Packers, 35-10. In Super Bowl IV, the Chiefs defeated the Minnesota Vikings, 23-7, and Dawson was voted game MVP.

Tom Flores, Mike Ditka, and Tony Dungay are the only individuals to win a Super Bowl ring as both a player and head coach. Flores earned his jewelry in Super Bowl IV as the back-up quarterback to Len Dawson of the Kansas City Chiefs and in Super Bowls XV and XVIII while serving as head coach of the Raiders. Ditka visited the winner's circle in Super Bowl VI as a tight end with the Dallas Cowboys and in Super Bowl XX as head coach of the Chicago Bears. Dungy won his bling in Super Bowl XIII as a defensive back with the Pittsburgh Steelers and in Super Bowl XLI as the head coach of the Indianapolis Colts.

Tom Flores is the only NFL head coach to win a Super Bowl for two different cities while representing the same franchise. He coached the Oakland Raiders to the Super Bowl XV championship and the Los Angeles Raiders to victory in Super Bowl XVIII. In addition to the Raiders, the Colts are the only other NFL franchise to earn Super Bowl victories representing different cities. While residing in Baltimore, the Colts won Super Bowl V; and after relocating to Indianapolis in 1984, they won Super Bowl XLI.

With his game-tying touchdown reception, Panthers wide receiver Ricky Proehl became the second player to score a touchdown for two different franchises in Super Bowl history (XXXVI with St. Louis Rams, XXXVIII with Carolina Panthers). With his touchdown reception in Super Bowl XXXVII as an Oakland Raider and his seven touchdown receptions while donning a San Francisco 49ers uniform in a Super Bowl (XXIII, XXIV, XXIX), Jerry Rice was the first individual to garner a touchdown for two different franchises in Super Bowl history.

In Super Bowl II, Green Bay cornerback Herb Adderley became the first defensive player to score a Super Bowl touchdown with a 60-yard interception return early in the fourth quarter to seal the Packers victory. Adderley is also the first player to earn a Super Bowl ring with two different teams (Green Bay in Super Bowls I and II and Dallas in Super Bowl VI).

Super Bowl XIII could arguably be called the greatest collection of NFL talent to ever gather for a game. Pittsburgh featured nine future Hall of Famers: Terry Bradshaw, Franco Harris, John Stallworth, Mike Webster, Joe Greene, Jack Lambert, Jack Ham, and Mel Blount. The Cowboys' five future Hall of Famers were Roger Staubach, Tony Dorsett, Randy White, Rayfield Wright, and Jackie Smith. Including Hall of Fame coaches Chuck Noll (Steelers) and Tom Landry (Cowboys), the Orange Bowl gridiron featured 16 future Hall of Famers. Throw in NFL Hall of Famers Ernie Stauter (Cowboys assistant coach), Tex Schramm (Cowboys President/GM), Art Rooney (Steelers owner) and Dan Rooney (Steelers executive) and the total was 20 future Hall of Famers.

Cowboys quarterback Roger Staubach (Super Bowl VI), Raiders quarterback Jim Plunkett (Super Bowl XV), Raiders running back Marcus Allen (Super Bowl XVIII), and kick-returner Desmond Howard (Super Bowl XXXI) are the only Heisman Trophy winners to garner a Super Bowl MVP honor.

The Raiders and the Colts are the only two teams to win separate Super Bowls while representing different cities. The Raiders won Super Bowls XI and XV hailing from Oakland and Super Bowl XVII while residing in Los Angeles. The Colts gained victory in Super Bowl X representing the city of Baltimore and Super Bowl XLI as the Indianapolis Colts.

Super Bowl XXV (Buffalo Bills vs. New York Giants) and Super Bowl XXIX (San Francisco 49ers vs. San Diego Chargers) are the only two Super Bowls where both squads hail from the same state.

Gene Upshaw is the only player to appear in Super Bowls in three decades for the same team. Representing the Raiders, this offensive guard played in Super Bowl II (1968), Super Bowl XI (1976) and Super Bowl XV (1980). Jerry Rice and Bill Romanowski join Upshaw as the only players to appear in Super Bowls in three different decades. Rice played in Super Bowl XXIII (1988), Super Bowl XXIV (1989), Super Bowl XXIX (1994) with San Francisco, and Super Bowl XXXVII (2002) with the Raiders. Romanowski played in Super Bowl XXIII (1988) and Super Bowl XXIV (1989) for the 49ers, Super Bowl XXXII (1997), and Super Bowl XXXIII (1998) with the Broncos, and Super Bowl XXXVII (2002) with Oakland.

Super Bowl Starting Quarterbacks
(Quarterbacks voted Super Bowl MVP in **boldface**)

Super Bowl I
Green Bay Packers 35 Kansas City Chiefs 10
Bart Starr (Alabama) drafted 1956 in the 17th round (200th overall) by Green Bay Packers
Len Dawson (Purdue) drafted 1957 in the 1st round (5th overall) by Pittsburgh Steelers

Super Bowl II
Green Bay Packers 33 Oakland Raiders 14
Bart Starr (Alabama) drafted 1956 in the 17th round (200th overall) by Green Bay Packers
Darryle Lamonica (Notre Dame) drafted 1963 in the 24th round (188th overall) by Buffalo Bills; in the 12th round (168th overall) by Green Bay Packers

Super Bowl III
New York Jets 16 Baltimore Colts 7
Joe Namath (Alabama) drafted 1965 in the 1st round (1st overall) by New York Jets; in the 1st round (12th overall) by St. Louis Cardinals
Earl Morall (Michigan State) drafted 1956 in the 1st round (2nd overall) by San Francisco 49ers

Super Bowl IV
Kansas City Chiefs 23 Minnesota Vikings 7
Len Dawson-Purdue drafted 1957 in the 1st round (5th overall) by Pittsburgh Steelers
Joe Kapp-California drafted 1959 in the 18th round (209th overall) by Washington Redskins

Super Bowl V
Baltimore Colts 16 Dallas Cowboys 13
Earl Morall (Michigan State) drafted 1956 in the 1st round (2nd overall) by San Francisco 49ers
Craig Morton (California) drafted 1965 in the 1st round (5th overall) by Dallas Cowboys; in the 10th round (75th overall) by Oakland Raiders

Super Bowl VI
Dallas Cowboys 24 Miami Dolphins 3
Roger Staubach (Naval Academy) drafted 1964 in the 10th round (129th overall) by Dallas Cowboys; in the 16th round (122nd overall) by Kansas City Chiefs
Bob Griese (Purdue) drafted 1967 in the 1st round (4th overall) by Miami Dolphins

Super Bowl VII
Miami Dolphins 14 Washington Redskins 7
Bob Griese (Purdue) drafted 1967 in the 1st round (4th overall) by Miami Dolphins
Billy Kilmer (UCLA) drafted 1961 in the 1st round (11th overall) by San Francisco 49ers; in the 5th round (39th overall) by Pittsburgh Steelers

Super Bowl VIII
Miami Dolphins 24 Minnesota Vikings 7
Bob Griese (Purdue) drafted 1967 in the 1st round (4th overall) by Miami Dolphins
Fran Tarkenton (Georgia) drafted 1961 in the 3rd round (29th overall) by Minnesota Vikings; in the 5th round (34th overall) by Boston Patriots

Super Bowl IX
Pittsburgh Steelers 16 Minnesota Vikings 6
Terry Bradshaw (Louisiana Tech) drafted 1970 in the 1st round (1st overall) by Pittsburgh Steelers
Fran Tarkenton (Georgia) drafted 1961 in the 3rd round (29th overall) by Minnesota Vikings; in the 5th round (34th overall) by Boston Patriots

Super Bowl X
Pittsburgh Steelers 21 Dallas Cowboys 17
Terry Bradshaw (Louisiana Tech) drafted 1970 in the 1st round (1st overall) by Pittsburgh Steelers
Roger Staubach (Naval Academy) drafted 1964 in the 10th round (129th overall) by Dallas Cowboys; in the 16th round (122nd overall) by Kansas City Chiefs

Super Bowl XI
Oakland Raiders 33 Minnesota Vikings 14
Ken Stabler (Alabama) drafted 1968 in the 2nd round (52nd overall) by Oakland Raiders
Fran Tarkenton (Georgia) drafted 1961 in the 3rd round (29th overall) by Minnesota Vikings; in the 5th round (34th overall) by Boston Patriots

PATRIOTS PASSION

Super Bowl XII
Dallas Cowboys 27 Denver Broncos 10
Roger Staubach (Naval Academy) drafted 1964 in the 10th round (129th overall) by Dallas Cowboys; in the 16th round (122nd overall) by Kansas City Chiefs
Craig Morton (California) drafted 1965 in the 1st round (5th overall) by Dallas Cowboys; in the 10th round (75th overall) by Oakland Raiders

Super Bowl XIII
Pittsburgh Steelers 35 Dallas Cowboys 31
Terry Bradshaw (Louisiana Tech) drafted 1970 in the 1st round (1st overall) by Pittsburgh Steelers
Roger Staubach (Naval Academy) drafted 1964 in the 10th round (129th overall) by Dallas Cowboys; in the 16th round (122nd overall) by Kansas City Chiefs

Super Bowl XIV
Pittsburgh Steelers 31 Los Angeles Rams 19
Terry Bradshaw (Louisiana Tech) drafted 1970 in the 1st round (1st overall) by Pittsburgh Steelers
Vince Ferragamo (Nebraska) drafted 1977 in the 4th round (91st overall) by Los Angeles Rams

Super Bowl XV
Oakland Raiders 27 Philadelphia Eagles 10
Jim Plunkett (Stanford) drafted 1971 in the 1st round (1st overall) by Bay State Patriots
Ron Jaworski (Youngstown State) drafted 1973 in the 2nd round (37th overall) by Los Angeles Rams

Super Bowl XVI
San Francisco 49ers 26 Cincinnati Bengals 21
Joe Montana (Notre Dame) drafted 1979 in the 3rd round (82nd overall) by San Francisco 49ers
Ken Anderson (Augustana [IL]) drafted 1971 in the 3rd round (67th overall) by Cincinnati Bengals

Super Bowl XVII
Washington Redskins 27 Miami Dolphins 17
Joe Theismann (Notre Dame) drafted 1971 in the 4th round (99th overall) by Miami Dolphins
David Woodley (LSU) drafted 1957 in the 8th round (214th overall) by Miami Dolphins

Super Bowl XVIII
Los Angeles Raiders 38 Washington Redskins 9
Jim Plunkett (Stanford) drafted 1971 in the 1st round (1st overall) by Bay State Patriots
Joe Theismann (Notre Dame) drafted 1971 in the 4th round (99th overall) by Miami Dolphins

Super Bowl XIX
San Francisco 49ers 38 Miami Dolphins 16
Joe Montana (Notre Dame) drafted 1979 in the 3rd round (82nd overall) by San Francisco 49ers
Dan Marino (Pittsburgh) drafted 1983 in the 1st round (27th overall) by Miami Dolphins

Super Bowl XX
Chicago Bears 46 New England Patriots 10
Jim McMahon (BYU) drafted 1982 in the 1st round (5th overall) by Chicago Bears
Tony Eason (Illinois) drafted 1983 in the 1st round (15th overall) by New England Patriots

Super Bowl XXI
New York Giants 39 Denver Broncos 20
Phil Simms (Morehead State) drafted 1979 in the 1st round (7th overall) by New York Giants
John Elway (Stanford) drafted 1983 in the 1st round (1st overall) by Baltimore Colts

Super Bowl XXII
Washington Redskins 42 Denver Broncos 10
Doug Williams (Grambling State) drafted 1978 in the 1st round (17th overall) by Tampa Bay Buccaneers
John Elway (Stanford) drafted 1983 in the 1st round (1st overall) by Baltimore Colts

Super Bowl XXIII
San Francisco 49ers 20 Cincinnati Bengals 16
Joe Montana (Notre Dame) drafted 1979 in the 3rd round (82nd overall) by San Francisco 49ers
Boomer Esiason (Maryland) drafted 1984 in the 2nd round (38th overall) by Cincinnati Bengals

Super Bowl XXIV
San Francisco 49ers 55 Denver Broncos 10
Joe Montana (Notre Dame) drafted 1979 in the 3rd round (82nd overall) by San Francisco 49ers
John Elway (Stanford) drafted 1983 in the 1st round (1st overall) by Baltimore Colts

Super Bowl XXV
New York Giants 20 Buffalo Bills 19
Jeff Hostetler (West Virginia) drafted 1984 in the 3rd round (59th overall) by New York Giants
Jim Kelly (Miami [FL]) drafted 1983 in the 1st round (14th overall) by Buffalo Bills

Super Bowl XXVI
Washington Redskins 37 Buffalo Bills 24
Mark Rypien (Washington State) drafted 1986 in the 6th round (146th overall) by Washington Redskins
Jim Kelly (Miami [FL]) drafted 1983 in the 1st round (14th overall) by Buffalo Bills

Super Bowl XXVII
Dallas Cowboys 52 Buffalo Bills 17
Troy Aikman (UCLA) drafted 1989 in the 1st round (1st overall) by Dallas Cowboys
Jim Kelly (Miami [FL]) drafted 1983 in the 1st round (14th overall) by Buffalo Bills

Super Bowl XXVIII
Dallas Cowboys 30 Buffalo Bills 13
Troy Aikman (UCLA) drafted 1989 in the 1st round (1st overall) by Dallas Cowboys
Jim Kelly (Miami [FL]) drafted 1983 in the 1st round (14th overall) by Buffalo Bills

Super Bowl XXIX
San Francisco 49ers 49 San Diego Chargers 26
Steve Young (BYU) drafted 1984/Supplement Draft in the 1st round (1st overall) by Tampa Bay Buccaneers
Stan Humphries (LSU) drafted 1988 in the 6th round (159th overall) by Washington Redskins

Super Bowl XXX
Dallas Cowboys 27 Pittsburgh Steelers 17
Troy Aikman (UCLA) drafted 1989 in the 1st round (1st overall) by Dallas Cowboys
Neil O'Donnell (Maryland) drafted 1990 in the 3rd round (70th overall) by Pittsburgh Steelers

PATRIOTS PASSION

Super Bowl XXXI
Green Bay Packers 35 New England Patriots 21
Brett Farve (Southern Mississippi) drafted 1991 in the 2nd round (33rd overall) by Atlanta Falcons
Drew Bledsoe (Washington State) drafted 1993 in the 1st round (1st overall) by New England Patriots

Super Bowl XXXII
Denver Broncos 31 Green Bay Packers 24
John Elway (Stanford) drafted 1983 in the 1st round (1st overall) by Baltimore Colts
Brett Farve (Southern Mississippi) drafted 1991 in the 2nd round (33rd overall) by Atlanta Falcons

Super Bowl XXXIII
Denver Broncos 34 Atlanta Falcons 19
John Elway (Stanford) drafted 1983 in the 1st round (1st overall) by Baltimore Colts
Chris Chandler (Washington) drafted 1988 in the 3rd round (76th overall) by Indianapolis Colts

Super Bowl XXXIV
St. Louis Rams 23 Tennessee Titans 16
Kurt Warner (Northern Iowa) was not drafted by any NFL teams
Steve McNair (Alcorn State) drafted 1995 in the 1st round (3rd overall) by Houston Oilers

Super Bowl XXXV
Baltimore Ravens 34 New York Giants 7
Trent Dilfer (Fresno State) drafted 1994 in the 1st round (6th overall) by Tampa Bay Buccaneers
Kerry Collins (Penn State) drafted 1995 in the 1st round (5th overall) by Carolina Panthers

Super Bowl XXXVI
New England Patriots 20 St. Louis Rams 17
Tom Brady (Michigan) drafted 2000 in the 6th round (199th overall) by New England Patriots
Kurt Warner (Northern Iowa) was not drafted by any NFL teams

Super Bowl XXXVII
Tampa Bay Buccaneers 48 Oakland Raiders 21
Brad Johnson (Florida State) drafted 1992 in the 9th round (227th overall) by Minnesota Vikings
Rich Gannon (Delaware) drafted 1987 in the 4th round (98th overall) by New England Patriots

Super Bowl XXXVIII
New England Patriots 32 Carolina Panthers 29
Tom Brady (Michigan) drafted 2000 in the 6th round (199th overall) by New England Patriots
Jake Delhomme (Lafayette) was not drafted by any NFL teams

Super Bowl XXXIX
New England Patriots 24 Philadelphia Eagles 21
Tom Brady (Michigan) drafted 2000 in the 6th round (199th overall) by New England Patriots
Donovan McNabb (Syracuse) drafted 1999 in the 1st round (2nd overall) by Philadelphia Eagles

Super Bowl XL
Pittsburgh Steelers 21 Seattle Seahawks 10
Ben Rothlisberger (Miami [OH]) drafted 2004 in the 1st round (11th overall) by Pittsburgh Steelers
Matt Hassellback (Boston College) drafted 1998 in the 6th round (187th overall) by Green Bay Packers

Super Bowl XLI
Indianapolis Colts 29 Chicago Bears 17
Peyton Manning (Tennessee) drafted 1998 in the 1st round (1st overall) by Indianapolis Colts
Rex Grossman (Florida) drafted 2003 in the 1st round (22nd overall) by Chicago Bears

Super Bowl XLII
New York Giants 17 New England Patriots 14
Eli Manning (Mississippi) drafted 2004 in the 1st round (1st overall) by San Diego Chargers
Tom Brady (Michigan) drafted 2000 in the 6th round (199th overall) by New England Patriots

Super Bowl XLIII
Pittsburgh Steelers 27 Arizona Cardinal 23
Ben Rothlisberger (Miami [OH]) drafted 2004 in the 1st round (11th overall) by Pittsburgh Steelers
Kurt Warner (Northern Iowa) was not drafted by any NFL teams

Super Bowl XLIV
New Orleans Saints 31 Indianapolis Colts 17
Drew Brees (Purdue) drafted 2001 in the 2nd round (32nd overall) by San Diego Chargers
Payton Manning (Tennessee) drafted 1998 in the 1st round (1st overall) by Indianapolis Colts

Super Bowl Starting Quarterbacks Ace-In-The-Hole Facts

The Patriots are the NFL team to originally draft the most Super Bowl starting quarterbacks (6). The club drafted Fran Tarkenton/1961/round three/34th overall/Super Bowls VIII, IX, XI; Jim Plunkett/1971/round one/1st overall/Super Bowls XV, XVIII; Tony Eason/1983/round one/15th overall/Super Bowl XX; Rich Gannon/1987/round four/98th overall/Super Bowl XXXVII; Drew Bledsoe/1993/round one/1st overall/Super Bowl XXXI; and Tom Brady/2000/round six/199th overall/Super Bowl XXXVI, XXXVIII, XXIX, XLII.

ELEVEN PATRIOTS ANNIVERSARY TEAMS

50th Anniversary Team

Tackle	Bruce Armstrong
Tackle	Matt Light
Guard	John Hannah
Guard	Logan Mankins
Center	Jon Morris
Tight End	Ben Coates
Wide Receiver	Stanley Morgan
Wide Receiver	Troy Brown
Wide Receiver	Irving Fryar
Quarterback	Tom Brady
Running Back	Jim Nance
Running Back	Sam Cunningham
Defensive End	Julius Adams
Defensive End	Richard Seymour
Defensive Tackle	Houston Antwine
Defensive Tackle	Vince Wilfork
Outside Linebacker	Andre Tippett
Outside Linebacker	Mike Vrabel
Inside Linebacker	Steve Nelson
Inside Linebacker	Nick Buoniconti
Cornerback	Mike Haynes
Cornerback	Ty Law
Safety	Fred Marion
Safety	Rodney Harrison
Kicker	Adam Vinatieri
Punter	Rich Camarillo
Special Teams	Mosi Tatupu
Kickoff/Punt Returner	Kevin Faulk
Offensive Captain	Gino Cappelletti
Defensive Captain	Tedy Bruschi
Head Coach	Bill Belichick

PATRIOTS ANNIVERSARY TEAMS

All-1960s Team

Tackle	Charlie Long
Tackle	Tom Neville
Guard	Billy Neighbors
Guard	Lennie St. Jean
Center	Jon Morris
Tight End	Jim Whalen
Wide Receiver	Jim Colclough
Wide Receiver	Art Graham
Quarterback	Vito "Babe" Parilli
Running Back	Larry Garron
Running Back	Jim Nance
Defensive End	Bob Dee
Defensive End	Larry Eisenhauer
Defensive Tackle	Houston Antwine
Defensive Tackle	Jim Lee Hunt
Outside Linebacker	Tom Addison
Outside Linebacker	Ed Philpott
Middle Linebacker	Nick Buoniconti
Cornerback	Chuck Shonta
Cornerback	Darryl Johnson
Safety	Don Webb
Safety	Ron Hall
Kicker	Gino Cappelletti
Punter	Tom Yewcic
Special Teams	Larry Garron
Kickoff/Punt Returner	Don Webb
Head Coach	Mike Holovak

All-1970s Team

Tackle	Leon Gray
Tackle	Tom Neville
Guard	John Hannah
Guard	Sam Adams
Center	Bill Lenkaitis
Tight End	Russ Francis
Wide Receiver	Stanley Morgan
Wide Receiver	Randy Vataha
Quarterback	Steve Grogan
Running Back	Sam Cunningham
Running Back	Andy Johnson
Defensive End	Julius Adams
Defensive End	Tony McGee
Nose Tackle	Ray Hamilton
Outside Linebacker	Steve Zabel
Outside Linebacker	Steve King
Inside Linebacker	Steve Nelson
Inside Linebacker	Sam Hunt
Cornerback	Raymond Clayborn
Cornerback	Mike Haynes
Safety	Tim Fox
Safety	Prentice McCray
Kicker	John Smith
Punter	Mike Patrick
Special Teams	Mack Herron
Kickoff/Punt Returner	Mosi Tatupu
Head Coach	Chuck Fairbanks

PATRIOTS ANNIVERSARY TEAMS

All-1980s Team

Tackle	Bruce Armstrong
Tackle	Brian Holloway
Guard	John Hannah
Guard	Ron Wooten
Center	Pete Brock
Tight End	Lin Dawson
Wide Receiver	Irving Fryar
Wide Receiver	Stanley Morgan
Quarterback	Steve Grogan
Running Back	Tony Collins
Running Back	Craig James
Defensive End	Julius Adams
Defensive End	Garin Veris
Nose Tackle	Richard Bishop
Outside Linebacker	Andre Tippett
Outside Linebacker	Don Blackmon
Inside Linebacker	Steve Nelson
Inside Linebacker	Johnny Rembert
Cornerback	Raymond Clayborn
Cornerback	Ronnie Lippett
Safety	Roland James
Safety	Fred Marion
Kicker	Tony Franklin
Punter	Rich Camarillo
Special Teams	Irving Fryar
Kickoff/Punt Returner	Mosi Tatupu
Head Coach	Raymond Berry

All-1990s Team

Tackle	Bruce Armstrong
Tackle	Pat Harlow
Guard	Todd Rucci
Guard	Max Lane
Center	Dave Wohlabaugh
Tight End	Ben Coates
Wide Receiver	Terry Glenn
Wide Receiver	Shawn Jefferson
Quarterback	Drew Bledsoe
Running Back	Curtis Martin
Running Back	Leonard Russell
Defensive End	Willie McGinest
Defensive End	Brent Williams
Nose Tackle	Tim Goad
Outside Linebacker	Andre Tippett
Outside Linebacker	Chris Slade
Inside Linebacker	Vincent Brown
Inside Linebacker	Ted Johnson
Cornerback	Maurice Hurst
Cornerback	Ty Law
Safety	Willie Clay
Safety	Lawyer Milloy
Kicker	Adam Vinatieri
Punter	Tom Tupa
Special Teams	Dave Meggett
Kickoff/Punt Returner	Larry Whigham
Head Coach	Bill Parcells

TWELVE
THE OPPONENTS

An Only And Only Game

From 1920 through the end of the 2009 NFL postseason, 13,587 professional football games (regular season and postseason) have been played. From a low of 0-0 recorded a total of 71 times, with the last coming in 1943, to a high of 73-0 recorded only once in 1940, there are 981 different final scores. The most common final score happening 220 times is 20-17; and the Patriots stand at 5-4 in such games with the team's highlight 20-17 victory in Super Bowl XXXVI against the St. Louis Rams. Through six weeks of the 2009 NFL season, 254 different final scores are the only such final scores in professional football history. The Patriots own 14 of them with a 6-7-1 record.

   New England Patriots beat Tennessee Titans 40-23 (2006/game 16)
   New England Patriots beat St. Louis Rams 40-22 New England (2004/game 8)
   New England Patriots beat Cleveland Browns 42-15 (2004/game 12)
   St. Louis Rams beat New England Patriots 32-18 (1998/game 14)
   New England Patriots beat Baltimore Ravens 46-38 (1996/game 5)
   Denver Broncos beat New England Patriots 34-8 (1996/game 1)
   Miami Dolphins beat New England Patriots 39-24 (1979/game 14)
   New York Jets beat Boston Patriots 47-31 (1968/game 2)
   Buffalo Bills beat the Boston Patriots 44-16 (1967/game 13)
   Miami Dolphins beat the Boston Patriots 41-32 (1967/game 14)
   Boston Patriots tied Oakland Raiders 43-43 (1965/game 6)
   Boston Patriots beat Houston Oilers 46-28 (1963/game 13)
   Boston Patriots beat Denver Broncos 33-29 (1962/game 9)
   Los Angeles Chargers beat the Boston Patriots 45-16 (1960/game 7)

Finally A Victory in The Land Of Cheese

When New England traveled to Wisconsin and defeated the Green Bay Packers, 35-0 (2006/game 10), it was the first Patriots regular-season victory at Lambeau Field. This historic and legendary stadium is the last venue of the 26 teams involved in the 1970 AFL-NFL merger where the Patriots were able to secure a victory.

Heisman For The Other Guys

Lions running back Steve Owens became the first Heisman Trophy winner (1969, University of Oklahoma) to catch a touchdown pass in the history of Schaefer Stadium (1971/game 2). Within three minutes, Owens also became the first Heisman Trophy winner to rush for a touchdown on the Patriots new home field.

Johnny Rodgers, the 1972 Heisman Trophy winning running back from the University of Nebraska, to be kind, had at best, a two-year star-crossed NFL career with the San Diego Chargers. Rodgers caught 17 passes and rushed the ball 4 times during his brief stay in the NFL. His last rush attempt in an NFL uniform was at Schaefer Stadium (1978/game 5) and was good for 5 yards.

PATRIOTS PASSION

Better Late Than Never

After the AFL-NFL merger in 1970, the Patriots lost their first 10 games against pre-merger NFL teams before finally garnering a victory against an established NFL club (1971/game 14). New England was unable to achieve a .500 combined record against all the pre-merger NFL teams until the 2006 season. After defeating the Chicago Bears 17-13 at Gillette Stadium (2006/game 11), for the first time in franchise history, the Patriots had more wins than losses (118-117) against the pre-merger NFL franchises. As of the end of the 2008 season, New England owned a 129-121 record against the pre-merger NFL teams.

You're Not The Only One In Our Family Who Can Do It

Thanks to a 33-yard touchdown pass from quarterback Jeff George (1995/game 4), Atlanta Falcons wide receiver Eric Metcalf combined with his dad, former Cardinals wide receiver Terry Metcalf (owner of a 69-yard punt return) for a touchdown (1975/game 7) and became the first father/son tandem to each score a touchdown against the Patriots.

When Peyton Manning connected with Torrance Small for a 3-yard touchdown pass (1998/game 2), coupled with his dad Archie Manning's 26-yard scoring toss to Danny Abramowicz (1972/game 13), the duo earned bragging rights as the first father/son tandem to each toss a scoring pass against the Patriots. The younger Manning son, Eli, after his 7-yard touchdown pass to Brandon Jacobs (2007/game 16), joined his older sibling as the only brothers to throw a touchdown against the Patriots. This play also allowed Eli to team up with his dad, Archie, and brother, Peyton, to become the only father and multiple son combination to each toss a touchdown pass against New England.

The first father/son tandem to both score and toss touchdowns against the Patriots was the Grieses. In the first official NFL regular-season game in Patriots history, the first scoring play was a 5-yard run by Miami quarterback Bob Griese (1970/game 1). In his first start ever against the Patriots (1967/game 14, his first of 15 career 3 or more touchdown-pass games), he tossed his first of 26 career-touchdown passes against New England connecting with wide receiver Jack Clancy for a 3-yards score. His son, Brian, did his half of the job enabling him and his dad to become the first father/son tandem to both throw for and run for a touchdown against the Patriots in one afternoon (1999/game 7). Brian hooked up with wide receiver Rod Smith for a second quarter 28-yard touchdown pass. During the fourth quarter, from a shotgun formation, Brian bolted up the middle and ran 7 yards for a touchdown.

In his first season as a Patriot (2006/game 14), against his ex-team the Houston Texans, Jabar Gaffney became the first player in New England history to catch a touchdown pass, a 6-yard toss from Tom Brady, when his father had already caught a touchdown pass against the Patriots. His dad, Derrick Gaffney, in his second year with the New York Jets (1979/game 15), caught a 13-yard touchdown pass from quarterback Richard Todd.

Buffalo defensive lineman Sam Aaron Adams contributed to giving many a Patriots fan a headache on Opening Day (2003/game 1) thanks to his 37-yard interception return for a touchdown. With this score, he became the first NFL player to score a touchdown against the Patriots whose father previously played for New England. His dad, Sam Edwards Adams was an offensive lineman for New England (1972-1980) starting opposite John Hannah at guard and was voted to the Patriots All-1970s Team.

The New Kids On The Block

Since inception of the 1970 AFL-NFL merger, New England defeated 4 of the 5 expansion teams to join the league in the club's initial regular-season confrontation (1976/game 14 vs. Tampa Bay, 1977/game 4 vs. Seattle, 1995/game 8 vs. Carolina, 1996/game 4 vs. Jacksonville, 1996/game 5 vs. Baltimore, 2003/game 11 vs. Houston) with just the Carolina Panthers owning a victory, 20-17. Including their first meeting ever against the Miami Dolphins (1966/game 11) and Cincinnati Bengals (1968/game 12), the Patriots sport a 7-1 lifetime record when facing an expansion club for the first time.

When the Patriots defeated the Carolina Panthers, 20-10, on December 13, 2009 (game 13), the franchise now owns at least one regular-season victory against every active NFL franchise in a game played in Foxboro.

Holiday Cooking

The Patriots lifetime Turkey Day record currently stands at 1-2 (1984/game 13, 2000/game 12, 2002/game 12). The team owns a 1-3 all-time record for games played on Christmas Eve day (1989/game 16, 1994/game 16, 2000/game 16, 2006/game 15). New England's lifetime record is 0-2 for games played on New Year's Eve day (1978/game 17, 2006/game 16) and 0-2 in games played on New Year's Day (1994/game 17, 2005/game 16). Overall, for these holidays, the Patriots hold a 2-9 lifetime record.

I'm Going To Kansas City To Have Some Fun

Although the Dallas Texans led the AFL in attendance for the 1962 season averaging over 24,000 fans per game, team owner Lamar Hunt went out shopping for a new home for his club. The Dallas Cowboys of the NFL consistently attracted more fans than the Texans. The oil magnate paid visits to Atlanta and Miami in his quest. Catching wind of Hunt's plight, Kansas City, MO, mayor Harold Roe Bartle invited the owner to visit the "Paris of the Plains" (Kansas City has more boulevards than any city except Paris). Bartle, nicknamed "The Chief", due to his involvement as an executive with many local Boy Scout groups, guaranteed Hunt the local fans would purchase three times the season tickets currently on the books of the Texans. The mayor also committed the city to expanding seating capacity of Municipal Stadium. After accepting the offer to relocate the Dallas Texans to Kansas City and taking a liking to Bartle's nickname, Hunt selected the Kansas City Chiefs as the team's new name. In a local "name our new football team" contest, the two most popular choices as team names were "Mules" and "Royals."

Technically, His Last Name Had To Be D.C.; Hello, Houston, We Have Trouble

During the first quarter of a New England/Washington away contest (1981/game 8), Redskins running back Joe Washington caught a 13-yard touchdown from quarterback Joe Theismann. Flash back to the 1968 season with the Patriots playing their first game ever under a dome (Houston Astrodome, game 14). With 2:00 left in the game, Boston third string quarterback Jim "King" Corcoran's pass was intercepted by future Hall of Fame defensive back Ken Houston and returned 22 yards for an Oilers touchdown. Washington and Houston, the individuals not the cities, are the only two players, with the same last name as the home city of the opponent, to score a touchdown against the Patriots. The two games were played in Washington, D.C. and Houston respectively.

Why Can't The Patriots Get Guys Like This?

Irving Fryar, while playing for the Miami Dolphins (1994/game 1), became the only ex-Patriots player to score three touchdowns in a game against his former team. The former Patriots number one overall selection of the 1984 NFL Draft caught three second-half touchdown passes from Dan Marino good for 54 yards, 50 yards, and 35 yards. Fryar ended the day with five catches, 211 yards receiving, and three touchdowns.

Irving Fryar and Curtis Martin are the only two ex-Patriots to score multiple touchdowns in one game against their old mates. In addition to his three-touchdown game in 1994 (see above), Fryar also had a two-touchdown game vs. New England the next year (1995/game 2) with a 67-yard and 31-yard scoring reception. Martin ran for two scores against the Patriots (2000/game 7) and remains the only ex-Patriots player to rush for two or more touchdowns in one game against his former team.

Drew Bledsoe is the only Patriots quarterback in team history to leave the team then turn around and throw a touchdown pass against them. While wearing the blue and red of the Buffalo Bills, Bledsoe tossed five scoring strikes (2002/games 8 and 13, 2003/game1, 2004/game 3).

Babe Parilli is the only quarterback in franchise history to score a touchdown against Patriots after leaving the team. In 1968 (game 7), at Shea Stadium, playing for the New York Jets, after rolling right he sprinted into the end zone for a two-yard score. Jets quarterback Joe Namath had been shaken up on New York's last set of downs from a hit delivered during a Patriots blitz so Parilli finished the day at the helm. This was also his 24th and last touchdown scored in a pro football game.

Running back Carl Garrett, while wearing a New York Jets uniform, became the first ex-Patriots player to score two touchdowns in one season against his former teammates (1975/games 3 and 12).

It's About Time We Beat These Guys

The Dallas Cowboys were the last of the pre-merger NFL teams to lose a game to the Patriots. New England running back Terry Allen broke a 6-6 tie game with a 3-yard touchdown run midway through the fourth quarter, leading his team to a 13-6 victory (1999/game 12). Before this game, the Patriots lost their first seven lifetime regular-season match-ups against the Cowboys (1971/game 6, 1975/game 9, 1978/game 14, 1981/game 3, 1984/game 13, 1987/game 10, 1996/game 15).

International Football

The Patriots played a preseason game outside the borders of the United States for the first time in team history on August 25, 1969. They tackled the Detroit Lions in Montreal, Quebec, Canada and lost, 22-9, in front of a Jarry Park crowd of 8,212. The game was a field goal fest with a total of eight and only one touchdown. Gino Cappelletti booted three-pointers of 37-yards, 41-yards, and 36-yards for the entire Patriots offense. Lions kicker Errol Mann booted five fields and Mel Farr scored the game's only touchdown on a 24-yard run.

On August 9, 1990, the Patriots played their second lifetime preseason game held outside the United States. They traveled north of the border, once again, to Montreal to take on the Pittsburgh Steelers. In front of a crowd of 26,869, in Stade Olympique, the Steelers topped New England, 30-14. This game was originally scheduled to be played on the other side of the Atlantic Ocean in Ireland; however, funding fell through, and the Steelers were forced to play the game in Montreal.

Three years later on August 14, 1993, New England traveled to Canada again, to play the franchise's third international preseason game. After two trips to Montreal, the Patriots headed to Toronto to meet the Cleveland Browns. Playing at the SkyDome, in front of a crowd of 33,201, New England's lifetime international record dropped to 0-3 thanks to a 12-9 loss to the Browns.

On August 27, 1998, after having played just three preseason games outside the United States, all in Canada, New England ventured south of the border to play their last of four lifetime-preseason games outside the United States. The Patriots squared off against the Dallas Cowboys in American Bowl III in Mexico City. In front of 106,424 fans – the largest crowd to ever witness a Patriots game – at the Estadio Azteca (the largest stadium in Central or South America and the fifth largest in the world), New England won, 21-3, to post the franchise's first preseason victory on international soil.

THE OPPONENTS

Still The Same Zip Code

In 1998, with both the New York Giants and New York Jets sharing Giants Stadium for home games, to differentiate this location, the NFL and the Jets front office decided to change the name of the location for each Jets home game and referred to the venue as The Meadowlands.

Same Results As Last Year

Only once has New England played their Super Bowl opponent during the next regular season. After losing to Green Bay, 35-21, in Super Bowl XXI, the Patriots squared off against the Packers the next fall (1997/game 8). The results were the same – New England lost the game, 28-10.

These Are Cy Young Numbers

During his tenure with the Jets, Joe Namath guided New York to a 15-3-1 record and tossed 25 touchdown passes when starting as quarterback against the Patriots.

Next Time, Same Place

For nine consecutive Steelers/Patriots games (1981/game 4 through 1995/game 15), New England traveled to Three Rivers Stadium for a regular-season game against Pittsburgh. Three Rivers Stadium, which opened in July 1970, was located at the confluence of the Allegheny River and Monongahela River, which forms the Ohio River, hence the "three rivers" name. This ranks number one in Patriots history as the most consecutive appearances for the visiting team against one team without playing a game in Foxboro. Over this span, New England posted a 2-7 record against the Steelers.

For six consecutive games (1986/game 3 through 1993/game 3), when meeting Seattle during the regular season, the Patriots hosted the game in Foxboro. This still remains a New England record for most consecutive home games against an opponent without playing in the other team's city. Over this time span, the Patriots posted a 1-5 record against the Seahawks.

Their Coach Got Lucky, The Patriots Had A Bad Day

The first time New England played an AFC playoff game against a pre-merger NFL team (1994/game 17), Cleveland defeated the Patriots, 20-13. Serving as the head coach for the Browns, Bill Belichick earned his first NFL playoff coaching victory.

The Last Name Remains The Same

During a half-century of Patriots games, two different players from the opposing team with the same last name, each scored a touchdown in just three contests. In 1964, at Fenway Park (game 9), Houston Oilers wide receivers Willie Frazier and Charley Frazier (no relation) each caught a touchdown pass from George Blanda. Within a year (1965/game 2), once again, the Frazier tandem both scored touchdowns via a pass from Blanda.

The Jacksonville Jaguars duo of Maurice Jones-Drew and Matt Jones both made the scoring summary when hosting New England (2006/15). Maurice Jones-Drew crossed the goal line twice with touchdown runs of 74 yards and 1 yard. Matt Jones joined his namesake as visitor to the Patriots end zone after being on the receiving end of a David Garrard 33-yard touchdown pass.

Same Last Name, No Relation

Just twice in franchise history, has an opposing player scored a touchdown against the Patriots and the extra point kicked by his teammate with both players sharing the same last name (1965/game 12, 1988/game 2). In 1965, facing the Jets at Shea Stadium, midway through the second quarter, New York wide receiver Bake Turner scored a touchdown on a 50-yard reception from Joe Namath followed by the extra-point boot by Jets placekicker Jim Turner. Playing their first road game of the 1988 regular season in Minneapolis, the Patriots defense allowed Vikings running back Darrin Nelson to scamper eight yards for a touchdown with Minnesota kicker Chuck Nelson splitting the uprights for the extra point.

What Took You So Long To Invite Me Over?

In late October 1988, on a cold and sunny afternoon, the New England Patriots squared off against the Chicago Bears in a rematch of Super Bowl XX (game 9). On the first play of the game from the line of scrimmage, Patriots quarterback Doug Flutie hooked up with Irving Fryar for an 80-yard touchdown pass. Not only is this the only time the Patriots have scored on the first play of the game from the line of scrimmage, but this was also the Bears first regular-season visit ever to Massachusetts to play the Patriots. The Chicago Bears was the last of the other 25 teams involved in the 1970 AFL-NFL merger to be the guest at a New England Patriots regular-season home game.

When New England visited Anaheim to play Los Angeles (1983/game 15), the Rams were generous enough to the Patriots by fumbling and losing the football six times. The only time during his 13-year Patriots career that running back Mosi Tatupu rushed for three touchdowns was in front of many of his University of Southern California friends. Tatupu may have been the only person from the New England squad to recognize any of their surroundings as this was the Patriots very first regular-season visit to California to play the Rams. Los Angeles was the last of the other 25 teams involved in the 1970 AFL-NFL merger to serve as host to the Patriots for a regular-season away game.

Think Of This, Canton Is Just Down The Street From Foxboro

In their first official visit ever to Foxboro (1974/game 13), an array of future Pro Football Hall of Famers roamed along the Pittsburgh Steelers sidelines. Led by head coach Chuck Noll, the Steelers line-up featured defensive back Mel Blount, quarterback Terry Bradshaw, defensive lineman "Mean" Joe Greene, linebackers Jack Hamm and Jack Lambert, running back Franco Harris, wide receivers Lynn Swan and John Stallworth, and center Mike Webster. These 10 individuals would go on to earn a berth in the Professional Football Hall of Fame.

Maybe We Should Trade For This Player?

In 2004, when the Miami Dolphins traveled to Foxboro to meet the Patriots (game 4), Dolphins kicker Olindo Mare was in uniform; however, after warm-ups, a nagging injury forced Mare to sit out the game. Miami punter Matt Turk did not have the experience to fill in as placekicker, thus head coach Dave Wannstedt needed to look elsewhere for a kicker. His search was successful, as a Dolphins versatile back-up wide receiver was able to answer the call for help and fill in rather admirably. This player was called to kickoff three times and his kicks, on average, carried to the New England 17-yard line. He also converted his only extra-point attempt and made good on his only field goal attempt from 29 yards. This individual, during the 2005 and 2006 seasons, playing for the Dolphins, caught 14 passes for 158 yards in three games against the Patriots. New England's front office liked what they saw and acquired him in March 2007 for a second round and seventh round selection in the 2007 NFL draft. The player who served as the emergency kicker for the Dolphins and now wears #83 for the Patriots is wide receiver Wes Welker.

THE OPPONENTS

Once Upon A Time He Was On The Good Guys Team

After catching 28 touchdown passes during his six-year career with New England, Russ Francis played with the San Francisco 49ers for six years and hauled in 12 more touchdown passes all thrown by future Hall of Fame quarterback Joe Montana. In Super Bowl XIX, Francis posted 5 receptions, good for 60 yards, as the 49ers defeated the Miami Dolphins, 38-16 (the only Super Bowl appearance for quarterback Dan Marino). In his first game in Foxboro (1983/game 5) not wearing a Patriots uniform, but still sporting the familiar #81, Francis produced his 32nd career-touchdown reception. This catch would give the 49ers their first lead – a lead they would not relinquish for the balance of the game. The "All-World" tight end rejoined the Patriots late in the 1987 season wearing #49 since wide receiver Stephen Starring donned #81. Francis hung around for the entire 1988 season switching back to #81 before retiring.

He Ruined A Perfectly Nice Saturday Early Evening All Over New England

Referee Ben Dreith is best known in the annals of Boston "Bad Guys" sports history, thanks to his late game "phantom" roughing the passer penalty call against Ray "Sugarbear" Hamilton (1976/game 15). Dreith attended the University of Northern Colorado from 1946 through 1950 and earned 11 varsity letters (four in baseball, four in basketball, three in football). Playing in the Rocky Mountain Athletic Conference, Dreith was a four-year All-Conference selection in baseball and a two-time All-Conference pick in basketball. During his 31 years as a professional football official (1960-1990), Dreith refereed two Super Bowls (VIII – Miami/Minnesota, XV – Oakland/Philadelphia). He also served as referee in eight NCAA regional basketball tournaments. After the 1976 Patriots/Raiders playoff game, during the next 15 years before he retired, Ben Dreith never officiated another New England Patriots game.

Why Did He Always Run So Well Against The Patriots

During his 11-year NFL career, O.J. Simpson managed to score four touchdowns in one game only once and it was against New England (1975/game 10). Simpson's 80-yard touchdown gallop is the longest rush from the line of scrimmage in the history of Schaefer/Sullivan/Foxboro Stadium (1973/game 1). During his stay in the NFL, he amassed six career games of 200 yards or more rushing. The only club to surrender two games to Simpson of 200 plus yards is the Patriots (1973/games 1 and 13). Against New England, he threw five lifetime passes, completing three for a total of 50 yards. Simpson recorded his longest career pass completion, a 34-yard toss, to wide receiver Bob Chandler (1972/game 4). While a senior at the University of Southern California, Chandler, as a sophomore, was Simpson's teammate. Both were voted Most Valuable Players in a Rose Bowl game – Simpson in 1968 and Chandler in 1970.

Perfectly Perfect

During his 21-year/134-game career, veteran quarterback Earl Morrall owns a 67-37-3 lifetime record as a starting quarterback. Against the Patriots, Morrall posted a lifetime 7-0 record – 2-0 while wearing a Baltimore Colts uniform and 5-0 in a Miami Dolphins uniform.

Let Tom Brady Play Right Field And This Guy Play Quarterback. I Don't Think So

Veteran quarterback Roman Gabriel, in his only career start against New England (1973/game 8), led the Philadelphia Eagles to victory. In 159 career starts, the signal-caller posted a respectable 86-64-7 lifetime record. At New Hanover High School in Wilmington, NC, Gabriel broke most of Sonny Jurgensen's high school quarterback records (Jurgensen is a member of the Pro Football Hall of Fame). In 1992, after graduating from the same high school as Gabriel and Jurgensen, former Red Sox outfielder Trot Nixon broke all the passing records at New Hanover High School. In his senior year of high school, Nixon was named the State Player of the Year in North Carolina for both football and baseball.

The Roller Coaster, The Beach, Kelly's Roast Beef And Jimmy DG

Jim Del Gaizo, born in Everett, MA, starred in football at Revere High School, attended Syracuse University and University of Tampa before serving as the third string quarterback for the Miami Dolphins behind Bob Griese and Earl Morrall during their perfect 17-0 season (1972). His pro football debut came against the New England Patriots (1972/game 9) and he tossed two touchdown passes with his career best 145-passing yards. Del Gaizo is the only Massachusetts high school graduate to play football in the Greater Boston League (GBL) and win a Super Bowl ring (Super Bowl VII).

How Many Times Can He Burn Us?

Running back Joe Washington is the only player to return a kick-off, throw a pass, and catch a pass all for a touchdown against the Patriots in a single game (1978/game 3). To make matters worse, this all happened in the fourth quarter, making Washington the only NFL player to score this combination of touchdowns in one quarter. In a steady Monday evening rain, against the Baltimore Colts on the very first play of the final quarter, in front of Frank Gifford, Don Meredith and Howard Cosell, Washington took a pitch from quarterback Bill Troup and tossed a halfback option pass connecting with wide receiver Roger Carr for a 54-yard touchdown pass play. Within four minutes, Washington hauled in a 23-yard touchdown pass from Troup. With 1:22 left in the game, the former Oklahoma Sooner ran 90 yards with a kickoff return, on the soggy field, for the game-winning touchdown.

It Had To Finally Happen One Day, Better Later Rather Than Sooner

The Patriots are the only team of the Original Eight AFL teams to not allow a 50-yard or better field goal during the league's 10 years in business. Super Bowl V hero Jim O'Brien, of the Baltimore Colts, was the first opposing kicker to ever boot a 50-yard field goal against the Patriots (1971/game 3). His kick was also the first 50-yard field goal to be kicked at Schaefer/Sullivan/Foxboro Stadium and the only 50+ yard three pointer in O'Brien's four- year, 60 field-goal career.

In the annals of the American Football League, the Patriots are the only AFL team of the Original Eight to not allow a safety during the league's 10 years in existence. It took the NFL, however, another former AFL team to break this streak (1970/game 9). San Diego Chargers defensive lineman Joe Owens tracked down quarterback Joe Kapp in the south end zone at Harvard Stadium and hauled him down for the first safety scored against the Patriots in franchise history. After racking up 10 safeties during their AFL years to gain a +10 ratio in safeties for/against, as of the end of the 2008 season, including playoff games, New England stands at +1, 26-25, in lifetime safeties recorded/allowed.

Hit The Post, Wide Right, Blocked

Kickers Mark Moseley (512 PATs), Jim Bakken (534 PATs) and Toni Linhart (213 PATs) combined for 1,259 extra-point kicks. This trio also teamed up to help the Patriots set a club record: opponents who failed at least one extra point kick in three consecutive games (1978/games 1, 2, 3). The Washington Redskins Moseley's PAT boot hit the right post, a week later St. Louis Cardinals Bakken was wide right on a PAT attempt, and on Monday Night Football, Baltimore Colts Linhart's low PAT kick was blocked by the backsides of his own offensive line – the only time in franchise history where the Patriots' opponents missed at least one PAT kick in three straight games.

During The Same Year, Touchdown Maker; Years Later, Decision Maker

Future Hall of Fame defensive back Emmitt Thomas accounted for his first of five career touchdowns after intercepting a Babe Parilli pass and returning the theft 57 yards for a score (1967/game 10). Three games later (1967/game 13), Buffalo Bills linebacker Marty Schottenheimer picked off two Don Trull passes. He returned his second interception 45 yards for the only touchdown of his pro football career that ended with two years as a Patriot (1969 and 1970). Thomas and Schottenheimer are the only two individuals to score a touchdown against the Patriots and eventually move on to hold a heading coach position in the NFL. Thomas served as interim head coach for the Atlanta Falcons in 2007 and posted a 1-2 record. Schottenheimer served as head coach for the Cleveland Browns (1984-1988), Kansas City Chiefs (1989-1998), Washington Redskins (2001), and San Diego Chargers (2001-2006). With 200 lifetime regular-season victories as head coach, Schottenheimer holds the dubious distinction of being the NFL coach with the most wins since 1966 to never coach a team in a Super Bowl.

First Few Glimpses Of The Varsity League

The Baltimore Colts were the first pre-merger NFL opponent at a Patriots regular-season home game (1970/game 3) at Harvard Stadium. The highlight of the contest came just before halftime. As he gained 1 yard on a draw play, Boston running back Carl Garrett's facemask was grabbed by Colts linebacker Mike Curtis, resulting in a 15-yard personal foul penalty against Baltimore. On the next play, Mike Taliaferro hooked up with Ron Sellers on a pass good for a 17-yard gain. As both teams retreated to their respective huddles, Garrett and Curtis began a donnybrook. Referee Bernie Ulman, his fellow officials, and players from both teams broke up the fight with both Garrett and Curtis being ejected.

The Patriots first regular-season game ever against an NFC team (1970/game 5) took place at Harvard Stadium and Boston was shutout, 16-0, by the New York Giants. The crowd of 39,091 (re-arrange a few numbers and you get 13,909, the standard Boston Garden sell-out crowd during this same era) was the Patriots largest home crowd of the entire year. This was the eighth consecutive home game in franchise history when attendance increased game by game and still remains the club's record.

The Patriots first regular-season away game ever against a National Football Conference team (1970/game 8) was played at Busch Stadium in St. Louis, MO. Thanks to the Cardinals defeating Boston, 31-0, this was also the first road game shutout against an NFC team in Patriots history.

The Boston Patriots hosted the Baltimore Colts at Harvard Stadium on Sunday, August 13, 1967 in the franchise's first preseason game ever against a National Football League team. The Colts routed Boston, 33-3, with future Hall of Fame quarterback Johnny Unitas completing 9 of 14 passes for 91 yards. For the record, the first NFL quarterback to ever throw a preseason touchdown pass against the Patriots was Terry Southall hooking up with fullback Bob Baldwin for a 71-yard scoring play.

Wonder If Red Auerbach Scouted This Guy?

Oakland Raiders defensive tackle Richard Sligh saw limited action during his team's 48-14 victory over the Patriots (1967/game 7). Although he made his presence known to all the Boston players and fans, Sligh was credited with just one tackle for the afternoon. Sligh, selected by the Raiders, out of North Carolina Central University, in the 10th round of the 1967 AFL Draft, appeared in eight games during his rookie year. He was released after the season and never played another down of professional football. Sligh stood at 7'0" and is the tallest player to ever play in NFL/AFL history.

Boston College Quarterbacks

Denver Broncos quarterback John McCormick played his college football at Boston College and threw his first pro football-touchdown pass against the Boston Patriots (1963/game 4). During his four-year AFL career, John McCormick threw 17 touchdown passes. As of the end of the 2008 season, McCormack is one of 17 Boston College quarterbacks to suit up for an AFL and/or NFL team in the history of pro football. Matt Hasselbeck leads all ex-Eagle signal-callers with 147 career NFL touchdown passes, followed by Doug Flutie with 86 scoring strikes, and then Charlie O'Rourke with 39 tosses for pay dirt (including a total of 25 touchdown passes while playing for the Los Angeles Dons in 1946 and 1947).

Figures The Original Was Against Boston

On September 10, 1978, Oakland Raiders tight end Dave Casper booted forward a fumble into the end zone and recovered the ball for a last-minute winning touchdown against the San Diego Chargers. This play, in NFL lore, was dubbed "The Holy Roller", and after this play, the NFL Rules Committee rewrote the rules the next off-season to make such a play illegal. Just about 10 years earlier (1968/game 4), the Raiders pulled this trick against the Patriots. Oakland quarterback Darryle Lamonica, from the Boston 27-yard line, completed a 14-yard pass to running back Charles Smith. As Smith was being tackled, he fumbled the ball, rolling the pigskin toward the Patriots end zone. Raiders future Hall of Fame wide receiver Fred Biletnikoff picked up the loose football at the 7-yard line and continued on to score a touchdown. Turns out this play was a dress rehearsal for the well-known play during "The Holy Roller" game.

This Fad Will Never Last

With high stakes – the AFL East Division title and a trip to the League Championship game to play the San Diego Chargers – Patriots fans, readying for a quasi-playoff game against Buffalo (1964/ game 14), were treated to a rare site – a unique place kicker with a rather strange style. This guy had an unusual last name, wore a single digit uniform number, and booted the ball with the inside front of his foot. This player was Hungarian-born Pete Gogolak, a graduate of Cornell University, wearing #3 and booting the football soccer-style for the Bills. His first professional football points came via a 13-yard field on September 13, 1964. Guess he wasn't that unlucky. After spending two years with Buffalo, Gogolak signed a contract with the New York Giants, becoming the first player/free agent to leave the AFL for the greener pastures of the NFL.

The Original Family Tree

In head-to-head competition with the seven other charter members of the original American Football League, the Patriots fared best playing the Bills. The Patriots, in 49 years, played Buffalo 98 times, posting a 57-40-1 for a .586 winning percent. On the other end of the rope, in 42 games against the Denver Broncos, the Patriots own a 16-26-0 record for a .381 winning percent. The Broncos remain the only charter AFL member whom Boston/New England has yet to play to a tie. The team to have played the most regular-season/playoff games against the Patriots is the New York Jets/Titans with 99 games (squeezing out the Bills by one game) with the record shaking out at 49-49-1 for .500, lifetime.

A meaningless game in December between the Patriots and Bills is almost not heard about during their long time AFL rivalry. In franchise history, in all the New England/Boston – Buffalo clashes, the two bitter archenemies have met 21 times during the last month of the season. Both teams have entered the December clashes with a losing record in just three games (1960/game 12, 1967/game 13, 1987/game 14). The Patriots hold a 14-7 advantage in such games.

THE OPPONENTS

No Wonder It Was A Rout

The late Will McDonough, columnist for the Boston Globe, had his own theory as to why the San Diego Chargers rolled over the Boston Patriots, 51-10, in the 1963 American Football League Championship game (1963/game 16). As the game unfolded, many Patriots players were amazed at how well tuned San Diego was to all their plays. It seemed as if the Chargers knew exactly what and where the Patriots were going to go and what they would do as each play developed. Story has it that Chargers Head Coach Sid Gillman placed a friendly phone call to Boston Head Coach Mike Holovak offering the Patriots use of a local navy base in the Southern California area for the team's work outs and practices to prep for the title game that was to be played at Balboa Stadium in San Diego. Coach Holovak commanded a PT boat during World War II in the Pacific and sank nine Japanese ships; so, of course, he jumped at Gillman's offer. Rumor has it, Chargers personnel/scouts dressed in navy garb "innocently" observed the Patriots practices, taking notes, and uncovering Boston's entire game plan. Just 10 offensive plays into the Championship Game, 218 total yards of offense and only 7:16 after the opening kickoff, the Chargers led the Patriots, 21-7. From there, it was all downhill for Boston. By halftime, San Diego running back Keith Lincoln touched the ball 11 times (six rushes and five pass receptions) for 242 total yards. Lincoln himself outgained Boston's entire offense by a 2:1 ratio (242 yards vs. 120 yards). Lincoln amassed a total of 349 total yards (206 yards rushing, 123 yards receiving, and 20 yards passing; he was one for one in pass attempts) to outgain Boston's total offense (262 yards) by almost the length of a football field (87 yards). The Chargers' total of 610 yards gained on offense withstood the test of time and remained the record for most total yards gained in a game during the 10 years of the AFL.

Although not being able to pinpoint the exact time during the second half of the Charger's one-sided victory over the Patriots in the 1963 AFL title game, this writer clearly remembers a moment carried live on NBC's broadcast of the game. The network shared a live-camera shot of Chargers players drinking champagne in fancy wine glasses with their viewers while the rout was still in progress. The action-shot was of #99 "Big Cat" Ernie Ladd hollering, smiling, and toasting with his teammates while still in full uniform with his helmet balanced atop his head.

I Know Someone Who Lives There, Maybe You Know Him

From the beginning of recorded pro football (1920), the six New England states contributed 647 individuals to play in the National Football League, American Football League, or All-American Football Conference. By state, the breakdown by birth place of the professional football players is as follows: Connecticut – 167; Maine – 23; Massachusetts – 389; New Hampshire – 21; Rhode Island – 38; and Vermont – 9 (the least of the 50 states). Listed below are some of the individuals:

Connecticut
Floyd Little, born 7/4/1942 in Hartford, CT, played for the Denver Broncos (1967-75). Legend has it that Broncos head coach Lou Saban "fired" Little after fumbling the ball that led to a late-game-leading field goal in 1968 against the Bills. Little refused to leave the game and asked quarterback Marlin Briscoe to "throw the ball as far as you can and I'll catch it." The pair hooked up for a 45-yard pass play enabling Denver to get within a field goal. A few plays later Bobby Howfield kicked a 12-yard winning field goal for Denver.

Maine
Thurlow Cooper, born 3/18/1933 in Augusta, ME, played for the New York Titans (1960-62), caught a 38-yard touchdown pass against the Patriots (1960/game 1), giving the Titans a 24-7 lead. Boston would score 21 unanswered points to chalk up their first regular-season victory ever in franchise history. Thurlow posted eight career touchdown receptions and three were at the expense of the Patriots.

PATRIOTS PASSION

Massachusetts

Rolf Benirschke, born 2/7/1955 in Boston, MA, played for the San Diego Chargers (1977-86), kicked a 29-yard field goal in overtime, and the Chargers beat the Miami Dolphins, 41-38, in an epic AFC 1981 Divisional playoff game.

Joe Bellino, born 3/13/38 in Winchester, MA, played for the Patriots (1965-67) and won the 1960 Heisman Trophy playing running back at the Naval Academy. As a sophomore and junior at Winchester High School he starred on the varsity basketball team as the Sachems won back-to-back Class B state championships.

Angelo Bertelli, born 6/18/1921 in West Springfield, MA, played for the Los Angeles Dons (1946), Chicago Rockets (1947-48), and was awarded the 1943 Heisman Trophy while quarterbacking the Notre Dame Fighting Irish. Known as one of the first true forward passing quarterbacks, his nickname was the "Springfield Rifle."

Ed King, born 5/11/1925 in Chelsea, MA, played for the Buffalo Bisons (1948-49), Baltimore Colts (1950), and was the 66th Governor of the Commonwealth of Massachusetts. King played football at Boston College both on the offensive and defensive lines.

Brian Piccolo, born 10/31/1943 in Pittsfield, MA, played for the Chicago Bears (1966-69) and was the subject of the gut-wrenching 1971 movie "*Brian's Song*." As a senior at Wake Forest, despite leading the nation in scoring and rushing, and named the Atlantic Coast Conference (ACC) Player of the Year, Piccolo was passed over by every AFL and NFL team in the 1965 drafts. ESPN broadcaster Lee Corso speaks of a poignant moment during the life of Brian Piccolo. In his junior year, Wake Forest hosted Maryland (Corso was an assistant coach for Maryland) and during warm-ups, Piccolo demonstrated courage that would surface again in 1969 when he began his eight-month battle with cancer. Maryland's roster included Darryl Hill, the first and only African-American player in the ACC, and the Wake Forest fans were being rude and unkind, yelling and sneering relentlessly at Hill. Piccolo walked over to the Maryland bench and walked stride-in-stride with Hill to the area in front of the student section of the stands. Brian Piccolo put his arm around Hill's shoulder, silencing the crowd.

New Hampshire

Adolph Kissell, born 9/11/1920 in Nashua, NH, played for the Chicago Bears (1942).
Ed Kissell, born 9/29/1929 in Nashua, NH, played for the Pittsburgh Steelers (1952, 54).
John Kissell, born 5/14/1923 in Nashua, NH, played for the Buffalo Bisons (1948-49) and Cleveland Browns (1950-52, 54-56).

Vito Kissell, born 6/13/27 in Nashua, NH, played for the Buffalo Bisons (1949) and Baltimore Colts (1950). Four brothers played pro football: Adolph attended Boston College, played halfback; Ed attended Wake Forest, played defensive back; John attended Boston College, played offensive and defensive line; and Vito attended Holy Cross, played linebacker and fullback.

Rhode Island

Bill Osmanski, born 12/29/1915 in Providence, RI, played for the Chicago Bears (1939-47).
Joe Osmanski, born 12/26/1917 in Providence, RI, played for the Chicago Bears (1946-49) and New York Bulldogs (1949). Both brothers attended Holy Cross and played fullback. Bill was one of six former Crusaders (including former Celtics great, Bob Cousy) inducted into the Holy Cross Athletic Hall of Fame when established in 1956. In 1939, he was voted the MVP in the College All-Star game against New York Giants (NY won, 9-0). Joe, who starred in both football and baseball, was elected to the Crusaders Hall of Fame in 1980.

THE OPPONENTS

Hank Soar, born 8/17/1914 in Alton, RI, played for the New York Giants (1939-44, 46) and scored 10 NFL career touchdowns (six rushing/two receiving/two interception returns). Out of the halfback option play, Soar threw three career-touchdown passes all against the Brooklyn Tigers. He also caught the game-winning touchdown pass, good for 23 yards, in the 1938 NFL Championship game (Giants 23, Green Bay Packers 17). Soar coached the Providence Steamrollers of the Basketball Association of America (now the NBA) in 1947. After guiding the team to a 2-17 record, he was let go mid-season. Soar turned to baseball and in 1950 became an American League umpire. Before retiring after the 1971 season, he was involved first-hand in quite a few memorable baseball moments. Soar was the first base umpire during Don Larsen's perfect game in the 1956 World Series (Yankees vs. Brooklyn Dodgers). He also served as the crew chief in the 1969 World Series (Baltimore Orioles vs. "The Amazin' Mets").

Vermont

Steve Wisniewski, born 4/7/1967 in Rutland, VT, played for the Oakland/Los Angeles Raiders (1989-2001). In a 1997 poll of over 150 NFL players by *Sports Illustrated*, Wisniewski was voted the "dirtiest player in the NFL." Playing offensive guard he was voted to the NFL 1990s All-Decade Team. "Wiz" also played on the Penn State Nittany Lions 1986 National Championship team.

PATRIOTS PASSION

Patriots running back "Cowboy" Jim Crawford (*left*, #30 - note original tri-corner hat logo) breaks through the Oakland Raiders (sans helmet decals) defense during a preseason game played on August 28, 1960. Boston doubled up Oakland, 28-14, in front of 4,000 spectators (note crowd in background). The game was played in Amherst, MA, the only time the Patriots would ever play in this town. According to the Patriots Media Guide, Walt Cudzik (*left*, #54) is the only player other than Gino Cappelletti to attempt a field goal for Boston during their 10-year AFL history (one missed FG attempt in 1960). According to pro-football reference.com, Cudzik and Crawford are the only players other than Cappelletti to attempt a field goal during the Patriots AFL years (one for each player). I'll go with the Media Guide information. (Photo courtesy of the New England Patriots)

Ron Burton (*right*) was the first player drafted by the Patriots, in the first AFL draft ever, on November 22, 1959. His life was cut down at the age of 67, but his dream will live on forever. Here's this author's only challenge: if you enjoy this book (who wouldn't), please make a donation to the Ron Burton Training Village in honor of #22 and mail it to The Ron Burton Training Village, P.O. Box 2, Hubbardston, MA 01452. It's for an excellent cause - investing in our youth. Thank you very much. (Photo courtesy of the New England Patriots)

Jimmy Colclough (*left*) was the Patriots first "go-to" receiver in team history. He played in every Patriots game for the franchise's first nine years. Colclough attended Quincy High School (MA) and lived across from this author's house in the Hough's Neck section of Quincy. Barely remembering the moment, in the spring of 1960, this author caught his first football pass ever thrown by Jimmy Colclough. His return toss to Colclough was intercepted by his dad, Timmy King, and the author's football career was over. After meeting Joe Namath of the Jets in the mid-1960s, Colclough remained friends with "Broadway Joe" until his passing on May 16, 2004. Jimmy Colclough, was my first favorite pro football player"ever. (Photo courtesy of the New England Patriots)

PATRIOTS PASSION

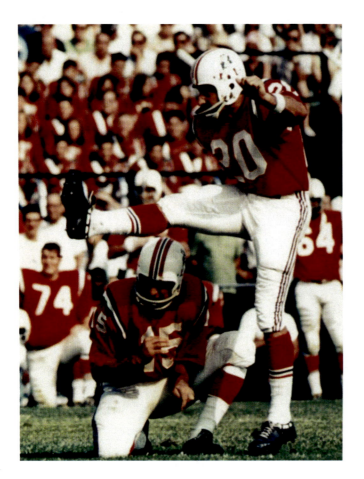

Babe Parilli (#15) and Gino Cappelletti (#20) (*both left*) were nicknamed the "Grand Opera." Cappelletti is the only placekicker to boot a field goal for Boston during the 10 years of the AFL and the Patriots, the only team in AFL history to have just one player account for every field goal during their 10-year stint in the AFL. Cappelletti (1964) and Jim Nance (1966) are the only teammates to win separate AFL Most Valuable Player awards without sharing the honor with other players. After graduating from the University of Minnesota in 1955, Cappelletti played quarterback for Sarnia, in the Ontario Rugby Football Union (ORFU/an amateur Canadian football league). In 1955, he played for the Sarnia Imperial, spent 1956 in the U.S. Army, in 1957 led the Sarnia Golden Bears (same team, new nickname) to the league championship. In 1960 while playing for the Patriots, Cappelletti became the first (and still only) AFL/NFL player to run for a two-point conversion, throw a pass for a two-point conversion, catch a pass, intercept a pass, return a punt and a kickoff in the same season. Born in Rochester, PA, a suburb of Pittsburgh, Parilli is one of many NFL quarterbacks born in Western Pennsylvania, giving the area the nickname "Cradle of Quarterbacks (Dan Marino, Joe Montana, Joe Namath, Jim Kelly, George Blanda, Marc Bulger, Jeff Hostetler, Johnny Unitas, Gus Frerotte).(Photo courtesy of the New England Patriots)

Opening Night, Schaefer Stad., August 15, 1971. (*right*) New England beat the New York Giants, 20-14, in front of 60,423 fans. Gino Cappelletti registered the first points scored in the stadium with a 1st quarter 36-yard field goal. After the field goal, Rocky Thompson (born in Paget, Bermuda and college roommate with future one-day Patriots running back Duane Thomas) returned Cappelletti's kick-off 90 yards for the first touchdown in Schaefer Stadium history. On the ensuing kick-off, New England's Carl Garrett returned the ball 53 yards to the Giants 44-yard line. On the next play, Garrett took a hand-off from quarterback Mike Taliaferro, broke two tackles and scampered 44 yards for the Patriots first touchdown ever in Foxboro. Note the traffic jam in the parking lot and on Route 1 South. The author attended this game with Brian Buckley and ran into Kevin O'Neill during the game. (Photo courtesy of the New England Patriots)

PATRTIOTS PASSION

Steve Nelson (*left*) played his college football at North Dakota State University. One of his teammates in college continued on to win a few championships in professional wrestling. Within the pages of this book the answer to this mystery is answered! Nellie missed just three games during his 14-year Patriots career. Steve Nelson, John Forbes (father of Michael Forbes, who played for Nellie at Curry College), Mosi Tatupu, Rod Shoate, Julius Adams and this author all share the same birthday, April 26th. It should be a national holiday. (Photo courtesy of the New England Patriots)

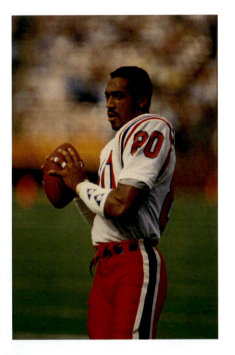

Irving Fryar (*right*), from the University of Nebraska, was chosen by New England with the number one overall draft pick in 1984. Fryar joins Jim Plunkett - Stanford University - 1971; Kenneth Sims - University of Texas - 1982; and Drew Bledsoe - Washington State - 1993, as the only four players selected by the Patriots with a number one overall pick in an NFL draft. Fryar and Keyshawn Johnson (New York Jets - 1996) are the only two wide receivers selected with the number one overall pick in NFL draft history. Fryar also holds the Patriots records for catching at least one touchdown pass from the most different quarterbacks (seven - Tony Eason; Steve Grogan; Tom Ramsey; Doug Flutie; Marc Wilson; Tom Hodson; Hugh Millen). He has caught an NFL touchdown pass from 19 different players. (Courtesy of the New England Patriots)

Mr. Robert Kraft (*left*), a fan's fan, an owner's owner, a fan's owner and an owner's fan...any way you slice it, Mr. Kraft is the best thing to ever happen to the Patriots. Here is Coach Bill Belichick shaking hands with Mr. Kraft after the Patriots defeated the Giants (2007/game 16), to post the first 16-0 regular-season record in NFL history. Had Mr. Kraft not rescued the Patriots from a sure departure to St. Louis in 1994, New England NFL football fans may still have the blues. When the Boston Lobsters entered the World TeamTennis in 1974, Mr. Kraft was the owner. He met his wife, the former Myra Hiatt, on February 2, 1962, at Ken's, a deli in the Copley Square area. Sitting at tables next to each other, as Myra was leaving, both exchanged a quick wink. Within 24 hours, Mr. Kraft tracked Myra down at the Brandeis library, and just like the story of Mr. Robert Kraft purchasing the Patriots to prevent a get-away to St. Louis, the rest is history, two happy stories. (Photo courtesy of the New England Patriots/Photo by David Silverman)

PATRIOTS PASSION

Kevin Faulk (*left*) ended his collegiate career at LSU ranked fifth in NCAA history in both all-purpose yards (6,833 yards) and total touchdowns (53 - 46 rushing, four receiving, two punt return, one kickoff return). He is also the only LSU Tiger to rush for over 1,000 yards in three separate seasons. Faulk's first NFL pass was completed to Tom Brady, good for 23 yards (2001/game 15). Despite coming up short for a first down against the Colts (2009/game 9), Faulk is Mr. Reliable for the Patriots on 3rd and short situations. So far, Faulk has rushed for 3,550 yards (a 4.2 yard average); however, has yet to record a 100-yard rushing game. With 3,550 yards, this ranks him as the all-time NFL rushing leader of all non 100-yard rushing game players in league history. (Photo courtesy of the New England Patriots/Photo by David Silverman)

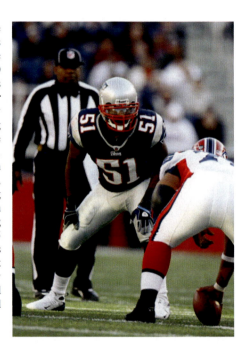

Jerod Mayo (*right*) won the 2008 Associated Press Defensive Rookie of the Year, receiving 49 of the 50 votes (the other vote was cast for Bengals linebacker Keith Rivers). The only other Patriots player winning this award was defensive back Mike Haynes, in 1976. While attending Kecoughtan High School, in Hampton, VA, in addition to excelling at linebacker, as a senior, in seven games as a running back, Mayo rushed for 1,245 yards, scored 13 touchdowns and added five two-point conversions. (Photo courtesy of the New England Patriots/Photo by David Silverman)

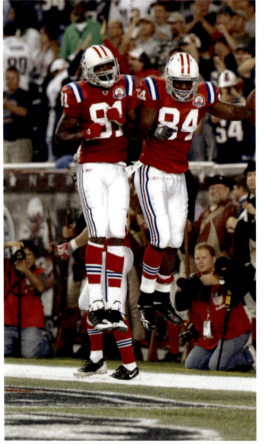

Randy Moss (#81) and Ben Watson (#84) (*both left*) celebrate after Watson scored the go-ahead touchdown/winning touchdown on Opening Night, 2009, at Gillette Stadium, against the Buffalo Bills, on Monday Night Football. As of October 16, 2010, the Patriots own an 19-22 record when playing on a Monday Night Football broadcast, yet own a 18-22 record in games played on Monday. There is an explanation and the answer lies within the pages of this book. Moss and Los Angeles Lakers Hall of Famer Jerry West share the honor of both having their name on the same trophy. In 1956 West, while attending East Bank High School (WV), was named West Virginia Player of the Year in basketball. As a student at DuPont High School (WV), in 1993 and 1994, Moss was named West Virginia Player of the Year in basketball. As a junior in high school, Watson helped lead Northwestern (Rock Hill, SC) High School to the state championship. He was also a member of the National Honor Society and Fellowship of Christian Athletes. (Photo courtesy of the New England Patriots/Photo by David Silverman)

PATRIOTS PASSION

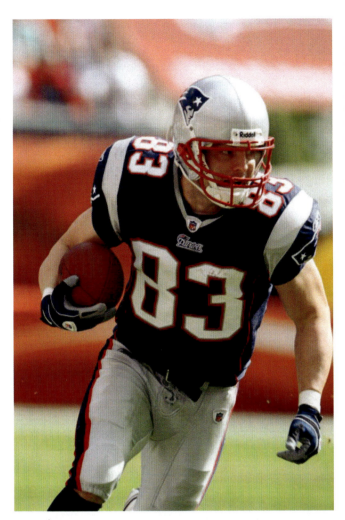

Wes Welker (*left*) was acquired by the Patriots on March 5, 2007 from the Dolphins, for a 2nd-round and 7th-round pick in the 2007 NFL Draft. The two players Miami ended with were Samson Satele, center, University of Hawaii, now with the Oakland Raiders; and Abraham Wright, linebacker, University of Colorado, no longer in the NFL. During the 2004 season, against the Patriots (game 4) while playing for the Dolphins, Welker became the first player in NFL history to kick a field goal (29 yards); kick an extra-point (one); kick-off (three kick-offs, averaging 53 yards per kick); return a kick-off (five returns/101 yards/20.0 yard average); and return a punt (five returns/41 yards/8.1 yard average) in the same game. In the rematch (2004/game 14) Welker returned a punt 71 yards before Patriots special team player Je'Rod Cherry brought him down at the two-yard line. (Photo courtesy of the New England Patriots/Photo by David Silverman)

Julian Edelman (*right*) was not invited to the 2009 NFL Combine, however did workout at the Pro Day held at Kent State University. His 20-yard short shuttle time of 3.92 seconds was faster than any of the times at the NFL Combine. His first action in a Patriots game was on August 13, 2009 in a pre-season game in Philadelphia vs. the Eagles. After fair-catching a first quarter punt early in the second quarter, Edelman returned a punt 75 yards for a touchdown. With two touchdown receptions against the Baltimore Ravens in the 2009 NFL playoffs, Julian became the first rookie to catch two touchdown passes in a NFL playoff since 1995 (David Sloan, Detroit Lions). After wheeling and dealing draft picks in 2008 and 2009 involving multiple teams, each of the teams ended up with: Jacksonville/Derek Cox, Austen Lane; Oakland/Lamarr Houston, Travis Goethel; Chicago/Gaines Adams (passed away of heart disease 1/17/2010); Tampa Bay/Arrelious Benn; and New England Patriots/Ron Gronkowski and Julian Edelman. Wonder which team made out the best? At 5'10" and 195 pounds, it is no wonder Edelman's favorite movie is *Rudy*. (Photo courtesy of the New England Patriots/Photo by David Silverman)

PATRIOTS PASSION

Tom Brady (*left*), heading into the BYE week of the 2010 season, holds the Patriots record for throwing at least one touchdown pass to 40 different receivers (see The Offense chapter for list). Brady increased this number from 38 to 40 in the 2010 season, with scoring connections to Rob Gronkowski and Danny Woodhead. At the of four, Brady attended the 1981 NFC Championship Game with his dad. This is the game when 49ers quarterback Joe Montana hooked up with wide receiver Dwight Clark for a late game touchdown, known as "The Catch." Wonder if Montana or Clark witnessed Brady's version of "The Drive", in Super Bowl XXXVI? (Photo courtesy of the New England Patriots/Photo by David Silverman)

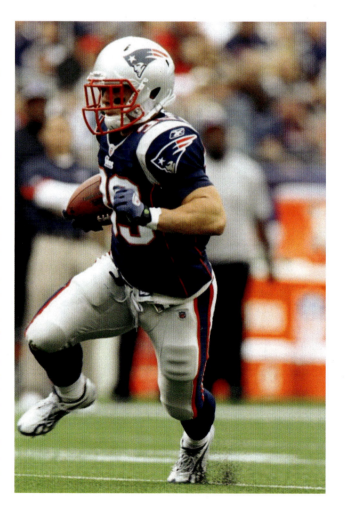

After winning the Harlon Hill Trophy (Most Valuable Player in NCAA Division II) in 2006 and 2007, Danny Woodhead (*right*) became just the third individual to capture this version of the Heisman Trophy in college football history. Attending Chadron State (Nebraska), Woodhead was the first recipient of a full athletic scholarship at Chadron State in its 96-year history. Four years later he graduated, but not before re-writing the NCAA Division II record books. Among his accomplishments were most consecutive games gaining 100-plus yards (16); most consecutive games scoring a touchdown (38, 2004-07); most yards rushing in a season (2,756, an all-NCAA record); and most yards rushing in a career (7,962, 2004-07, the record at that time). He was selected as the 2007 National Scholar-Athlete, earning an $18,000 post-graduate scholarship from the National Football Foundation and College Football Hall of Fame. Woodhead did not receive an invite to the NFL COMBINE but was able to shine in his pro day performance for NFL coaches/scouts. He ran the 40-yard dash in 4.33 to 4.38 seconds which would have been the second-fastest among all running backs at the NFL Combine. Woodhead also posted the best pro-agility time of 4.03 seconds, the second-best vertical jump (38½") and the best 60-yard shuttle time (11.2 seconds). After signing with the New York Jets as a free agent, Woodhead rushed for two touchdowns and 158 yards in a September 3, 2009 preseason game and against the Philadelphia Eagles, the NFL's second-highest preseason total since 1992. The Jets cut Woodhead on September 14, 2010, and the Patriots signed the 5'9", 200-pound all-purpose back four days later. After running 22 yards for a touchdown in his first Patriots game vs. Buffalo, then hooking up with Tom Brady for an 11-yard touchdown pass play in his next game vs. Miami, it looks like the New York Jets' loss is the New England Patriots' gain. (Photo courtesy of the New England Patriots/Photo by David Silverman)

THIRTEEN
AROUND PRO FOOTBALL

The Yanks Playing Home Games At Fenway Park

Before the Patriots arrived on the local scene in the fall of 1960, the last professional football game played in Boston was December 5, 1948 at Fenway Park. The Boston Yanks of the National Football League, after defeating the Philadelphia Eagles, 37-14, planned significant off-season changes. The Yanks waved goodbye to Beantown and traveled south to The Big Apple. Owning just a one-way ticket, the Yanks settled down in the big city and became the New York Bulldogs for the 1949 season. The team changed its name back to the Yanks for 1950 and 1951 before the team folded never to play pro football again.

Highway Robbery, AFL Style

Ron Burton (1960-65) is one of a half-dozen American Football League players remembered as being a true pioneer for the new league. He was one of six players coming out of college in 1960 selected in the first round of the 1960 NFL Draft who elected to play with the upstart AFL instead. The six individuals represented 50 percent of the first round selections of the draft. With the 9th overall pick in the NFL draft, the Philadelphia Eagles selected Burton, out of Northwestern, to only be left standing on the sidelines as the running back inked a deal with the Patriots. The Detroit Lions tabbed Louisiana State University running back Johnny Robinson with the 3rd overall pick; however, the versatile player signed with the Dallas Texans. Converted to a defensive back, Robinson was voted All-Pro eight times during his 12-year career and won a Super Bowl ring (with the Chiefs in Super Bowl IV). Quarterback Richie Lucas from Penn State, drafted 4th overall by the Washington Redskins, decided to head to Buffalo and donned #11 for the Bills. Jack Spikes, a fullback from Texas Christian University, was chosen by the Pittsburgh Steelers 6th overall but decided to stay near his Big Springs, TX home and joined Robinson with the Texans. The Baltimore Colts plucked University of Southern California's mammoth offensive tackle Ron Mix, who was raised and played college football in Los Angeles, with the 10th overall selection. Mix wanted to stay near home; and although the Patriots drafted him in their initial 1960 draft, Boston owner Billy Sullivan, wanting to see the AFL succeed, transferred Mix's rights to the Chargers free of charge. Signing with the hometown Chargers, Mix is the only player selected in the 1960 NFL draft who was also voted into the Pro Football Hall of Fame (see next story for Billy Cannon, the sixth player to spur the NFL for the AFL).

What A Big Catch

Billy Cannon, the 1959 Heisman Trophy winner, was the overall number one pick of the 1960 NFL draft by the Los Angeles Rams. The upstart AFL assigned each club territorial rights to one player and Cannon's rights were assigned to the Houston Oilers. Raised in Baton Rouge and playing his college football at Louisiana State University, the Heisman Trophy winning running back decided to forgo living in Los Angeles and stayed in the south signing with the Oilers.

In the seven years, before the AFL and NFL drafts merged, the upstart AFL outbid the established NFL four times for the services of the current Heisman Trophy winner. Joe Bellino, the 1960 Heisman Trophy winner from Navy, was drafted by the Washington Redskins in the 17th round of the 1961 NFL draft while Boston selected this award-winning running back as its 19th round selection. After a four-year commitment to the United States Navy, in 1965, this Winchester, MA native joined the Patriots. Quarterback John Huarte, 1964 Heisman Trophy winner from Notre Dame, signed with the New York Jets rather than ink an NFL contract with the Philadelphia Eagles. Two weeks after Huarte signed his contract, the Jets signed quarterback Joe

Namath to a $400,000 record contract. Mike Garrett, a running back from University of Southern California, won the 1965 Heisman Trophy and was expected to stay in the Los Angeles area where he grew up. His NFL rights belonged to the Rams who selected Garrett as their 2nd-round pick (18th overall) of the 1966 NFL draft. The Heisman Trophy winner was also drafted by the Kansas City Chiefs in the 1966 AFL draft in the 20th (and last) round with the 177th (a total of 181 players were selected in the draft) Just about everyone in the football world believed Garrett would stay locally and sign with the Rams. Thanks to Chiefs owner Lamar Hunt's wallet, Garrett decided not to stick around, bid adieu to the sunny beaches of California, and headed to the plains of mid-America to play football in Kansas City, MO. The three Heisman Trophy winners to choose the established league over the upstart league during the AFL-NFL bidding wars were Ernie Davis, the 1961 winner – Syracuse running back who signed with the Cleveland Browns over the Buffalo Bills; Terry Baker the 1962 winner – Oregon State quarterback who inked a deal with the Rams rather than the San Diego Chargers; and Roger Staubach, the 1963 winner – Navy quarterback who, after filling his four-year commitment to Uncle Sam, joined the Dallas Cowboys rather than give it a go with the Chiefs.

Once An All-Star Always An All-Star

In the 1935 College All-Star Game, the Chicago Bears defeated the All-Stars, 5-0. Playing for the All-Stars from the University of Michigan wearing #48 was center/linebacker Gerald Ford who one day would become the 38th President of the United States.

Matching Bookend Ties In The Rocky Mountains

The first tie game to take place in the American Football League was played on November 27, 1960 when the Denver Broncos scored the last 31 points of the game in 18 minutes to tie the Buffalo Bills, 38-38. The last AFL game to finish in a deadlock was on November 16, 1969 when the Broncos allowed the Houston Oilers to score the last 17 points of the game, all in the last 10 minutes of the game, to earn a 20-20 tie. Both games were played in Denver at Bears Stadium which was renamed Mile High Stadium before the 1969 season.

Big East Football In Providence

The New Orleans Saints, with the 445th and last selection of the 1967 NFL Draft chose Jimmy Walker, a "wide receiver" out of Providence College. Walker, a standout guard for the Friars basketball team was also the overall number one selection by the Detroit Pistons in the 1967 NBA Draft. There you have it, number one in the NBA and Mr. Irrelevant in the NFL, one player in one year.

A New Secret Weapon Unveiled

At 6'10", Morris Stroud of the Kansas City Chiefs became both a significant physical and psychological weapon (specifically at blocking field goals in an unconventional style) for head coach Hank Stram. On many opponents' field goal attempts, Stroud lined up under the goalpost and would attempt to deflect the ball as its downward flight headed toward its destination. Later, rule changes led to the adoption of Rule 12, Section 3, Article 1 (informally known as the "Stroud Rule"): *"Goal tending by any player leaping up to deflect a kick as it passes above the crossbar of a goal post is prohibited. The referee could award three points for a palpably unfair act"*.

Let's Stick To The Script

Dating back to the beginning of the 1970 season (AFL-NFL merger) through the 2008 season, the Chicago Bears, Dallas Cowboys, Green Bay Packers, and Pittsburgh Steelers are the only clubs of the 26 merger teams to not yet make any mid-season head coach changes. In 1961, Boston replaced Lou Saban (2-3) with Mike

Holovak (7-1-1); in 1970, the Patriots sent Clive Rush packing (1-6) and replaced him with John Mazur (1-6); in 1972, New England booted Mazur (2-7) out the door and Phil Bengtson (1-4) finished the year running the team; in 1978, owner Billy Sullivan relieved Chuck Fairbanks (11-4) of his head coaching duties due to his recent commitment to the University of Colorado for the next season and elevated assistant coaches Ron Erhardt (0-1) and Hank Bullough (0-1) to co-head coaches for the last regular-season game (Fairbanks returned to coach the Patriots for their first 1978 playoff game and New England lost, 31-14, to the Houston Oilers); and in 1984, Ron Meyer (4-4) was let go, Raymond Berry (5-3) took over the helm, and before the end of the next season, the New England Patriots and coach Berry were playing in Super Bowl XX – the franchise's first appearance in the Big Game.

AFL Big Wigs

Sid Gilliam was the individual to suggest AFL players wear their names on the back of the uniform. Although Gillman did not have an opportunity to coach in a Super Bowl, two of his original Chargers assistant coaches won a total of seven Super Bowl rings. His offensive end coach, Al Davis went on to win three Super Bowl rings as the owner of the Oakland/Los Angeles Raiders. His defensive assistant coach, Chuck Noll collected four Super Bowl rings as the head coach of the Pittsburgh Steelers. In the extended Sid Gillman coaching family tree, a total of 22 Super Bowl victories reside. In addition to Noll's four and Davis' three, Bill Walsh has three titles; Tom Flores and George Seifert have collected two Super Bowl rings; and Brian Billick, Tony Dungy, Jon Gruden, Mike Holmgren, John Madden, Mike Shanahan, Mike Tomlin, and Dick Vermeil own one Super Bowl victory each as head coach.

Al Davis was born on July 4, 1929 in Brockton, MA. For just two months in 1966, he served as the last American Football League commissioner. When the AFL-NFL merger was approved and announced, Davis was not happy with the impending marriage of the leagues and bolted back to the Raiders. The AFL owners named Milt Woodward president and he presided over the league's affairs until March 1970 when the American Football League officially closed its doors.

You'll Get A Boot About This One

When Redskins kicker Mark Mosley retired after the 1986 season, he became the last full-time straight-on placekicker to play in the NFL.

No Wonder His Nose Isn't Straight

Quarterback Billy Kilmer (49ers/Saints/Redskins) began his NFL career in 1961 playing in San Francisco. When he retired after the 1978 season, pro football lost a rare breed. Kilmer was the last NFL player to wear the single bar face mask.

Three League Players

In 1960, the Los Angeles Chargers placekicker was Ben Agajanian, "The Toeless Wonder", a native of Southern California. While attending the University of New Mexico, Agajanian lost four toes on his kicking foot while working on campus. Overcoming his injury, after college, Ben joined the Philadelphia Eagles in 1945 as pro football's first kicking specialist. Agajanian kicked for five teams in the National Football League (Philadelphia, Pittsburgh Steelers, New York Giants, Los Angeles Rams, Green Bay Packers), one team in the All-American Football Conference (Los Angeles Dons) and three teams in the American Football League (Chargers, Dallas Texans, Oakland Raiders). Along with linebacker Hardy Brown (NFL – Baltimore Colts, Washington Redskins, San Francisco 49ers, Chicago Cardinals; AAFC – Brooklyn Dodgers, Chicago Hornets;

AFL – Denver Broncos), they are the only two players in professional football history to wear a game uniform and play in the NFL, AAFC and AFL.

From One Winner To Another Winner

From 1977-79, quarterback Roger Staubach and running back Tony Dorsett both played for the Dallas Cowboys. Staubach won the 1963 Heisman Trophy while playing for the Naval Academy, and Dorsett won the 1976 Heisman Trophy while attending the University of Pittsburgh. On December 12, 1977, Staubach hooked up with Dorsett for a 20-yard touchdown pass for the first Heisman Trophy to Heisman Trophy touchdown-pass play in NFL history. The two players teamed up for four career-touchdown passes.

From 1982-86, quarterback Jim Plunkett and running back Marcus Allen both wore uniforms for the Oakland/Los Angeles Raiders. Plunkett won the 1970 Heisman Trophy while at Stanford, and Allen won the 1981 Heisman Trophy while playing at the University of Southern California. In his second pro football game, September 19, 1982, Allen caught a 14-yard touchdown pass from Plunkett – the first of six times the two former Heisman Trophy winners hooked up on a pass for a touchdown all in Raiders uniforms.

At Least Someone Might Remember Me

Wilbur "Weeb" Ewbank was the winning head coach in two of the most memorable professional football games ever played. On December 28, 1958, his Baltimore Colts defeated the New York Giants, 23-17, for the NFL championship in a contest widely remembered as *The Greatest Game Ever Played.* Ewbank was fired by the Colts after the 1962 season. On January 12, 1969, his New York Jets defeated the Baltimore Colts, 16-7, in the third AFL-NFL World Championship Game. This was also the first game officially referred to as a Super Bowl – Super Bowl III. Thanks to Joe Namath, this game is also remembered as *"The Guarantee"*.

Big Apple Football

In 1960, when selecting his team's name in the brand-new American Football League, New York owner Harry Wismer, referring to his now cross-town rival New York Football Giants, told the press, *"The only thing I know bigger than a Giant is a Titan!"* The New York Titans, on shaky financial ground, were sold to a group headed by Sonny Werblin for $1 million. In 1964, the club switched playing fields from the old Polo Grounds to a brand new Shea Stadium. Searching for a new identity, and considering the new stadium was next to LaGuardia Airport with planes constantly flying over the ballpark (the baseball tenants were the Mets), New York's AFL entry became the Jets. The Jets also hired a new head coach, Weeb Ewbank who had been fired by the Baltimore Colts at the conclusion of the 1962 season.

Hollywood Comes Calling

For movie buffs, War Memorial Stadium, the original home for the Buffalo Bills, was the site of a famous 1983 film. The stadium, nicknamed "The Rockpile" due to its weathered, worn-down look, was selected by director Barry Levinson and TriStar Pictures to fill the need for a professional baseball park. The movie, starring Robert Redford and Glenn Close, was *The Natural*. Redford graduated from Van Nuys High School, CA, Class of 1954. As a high school pitcher, he earned a baseball scholarship to Colorado University. His classmate and fellow pitcher in the Van Nuys rotation was famed Los Angeles Dodgers pitcher and Hall of Famer Don Drysdale. To take this even one step further, another student in his graduating class was actress Natalie Wood.

From The NBA To The Super Bowl

Bud Grant served as head coach for the Minnesota Vikings in Super Bowls IV, XIII, IX, and XI. He is the first coach to lose four Super Bowl games. Buffalo head coach Marv Levy failed to lead the Bills to victory in Super Bowls XXV, XXVI, XXVII and XXVIII to tie Grant for the most Super Bowl losses as a head coach. Grant was a member of the 1949-50 National Basketball Association champions Minneapolis Lakers making him the only person to win an NBA championship ring as a player and lose a Super Bowl as a head coach.

He Should Have Called Offensive Pass Interference

Adrian Burk, a former NFL back judge is still entrenched in NFL lore. Burk, of the Philadelphia Eagles vs. Washington Redskins in 1954, along with Sid Luckman of the Chicago Bears vs. New York Giants in 1943, George Blanda of the Houston Oilers vs. New York Titans in 1961, Y.A. Tittle of the New York Giants vs. Washington Redskins in 1962, and Joe Kapp of the Minnesota Vikings vs. Baltimore Colts in 1969, all share a spot in the NFL record books. Each player tossed seven touchdown passes during one game. Burk was also the back judge in the game in 1969 when Joe Kapp tied the record.

They Played Inside, And It Wasn't Even Raining

The first regular-season AFL touchdown ever scored in the Astrodome belongs to Houston Oilers running back Hoyle Granger with a 5-yard run against the Kansas City Chiefs on Monday, September 9, 1968. For the record, the first regular-season home run hit at the "Eighth Wonder of the World" on April 12, 1965 was by Richie Allen of the Philadelphia Phillies, a two-run blast off Astros pitcher Bob Bruce. The first home run ever at the Astrodome was hit on April 9, 1965 in an exhibition game between the Astros and the New York Yankees. The pitcher was Houston's Turk Farrell and the batter was the Yankees' Mickey Mantle.

More Versatile Than A Swiss Army Knife

Denver Broncos defensive back Goldie Sellers has a unique claim to fame unanswered by any other AFL player during the league's 10 years. He is the only AFL player to return a kickoff for a touchdown (twice in 1966 for 88 and 100 yards), return an interception for a touchdown (1966 for 29 yards), return a punt for a touchdown (1967 for 76 yards), and a fumble for a touchdown (1969 for 21 yards). Sellers also won a Super Bowl ring with the Kansas City Chiefs in Super Bowl IV.

Running Back University

During the 1950s and 1960s the Syracuse University football program, under the guidance of head coach Ben Schwartzwalder, spawned more than their fair share of top-class running backs. The Orangemen produced Jimmy Brown (1954-56) who played for Cleveland Browns; Ernie Davis (1959-61), Heisman Trophy winner in 1961, drafted by the Washington Redskins, traded to Cleveland Browns, and never played pro football; Jim Nance (1962-64) who played for the Boston Patriots and New York Jets; Floyd Little (1964-66), played for Denver Broncos; and Larry Csonka (1965-67) who played for the Miami Dolphins and New York Giants. These five running backs' total college rushing yardage was over 12,000 with an average carry of 5.5 yards.

Ten-Pin, Candlepin, Or Duck-Pin

Running back Don Nottingham (Baltimore Colts, Miami Dolphins) stood 5'10", weighed 210 pounds, and was nicknamed "The Human Bowling Ball." From Kent State, he scored five touchdowns against the Patriots during his seven-year NFL career (1971-77). His teams were 4-0 against New England when he scored a touchdown.

Running back Charlie Tolar played seven years for the Houston Oilers (1960-66) after attending Northwest State (LA). Tolar rushed for four touchdowns against Boston and his team's record was 2-1-1 in the game. Tolar was 5'6", weighed 199 pounds, and was also nicknamed "The Human Bowling Ball."

Three Heads Are Better Than One

The only time during the pro football expansion era that a team was officially coached by three individuals in one game was during the 1961 NFL season. With two games left in the season, after posting a 5-7 record, the St. Louis Cardinals fired head coach Pop Ivy and promoted three assistant coaches to guide the team. Chuck Drulis, Ray Prochaska, and Ray Willsey shared head coach duties and closed the season with two victories. None of the three would move on to serve as a head coach in the NFL again. After the 1961 season, Wally Lemm was hired as head coach. Lemm had taken over at the helm for the Houston Oilers early in the 1961 season and finished the year with a perfect 10-0 record and an AFL Championship title.

Did He Get His Coach's Autograph?

Edward "Wahoo" McDaniel was of Choctaw-Chickasaw Native American heritage and a fan favorite throughout a majority of the 10 years of AFL football. Playing linebacker for the Houston Oilers, Denver Broncos, New York Jets, and Miami Dolphins, after retiring in 1968, McDaniel turned to the professional wrestling circuit. He spent close to 25 years on the wrestling circuit and entered the "square circle" to battle "Superstar" Billy Graham, Ivan Koloff, Greg Valentine, Roddy Piper, Curt Henning, Larry Zbyszko, Tully Blanchard, and Sgt. Slaughter to name a few. In 2003, one year after he passed away, Pro Wrestling Illustrated ranked McDaniel 97th on the list of the *Top 500 Wrestlers Ever*. While in middle school, his family moved from Bernice, OK to Midland, TX and McDaniel played baseball. One of his baseball coaches once captained the Yale University baseball team, played in the first two years of the College World Series, and as senior, once met Babe Ruth. His coach was George H. W. Bush – 41st President of the United States.

What About Commissioner Gordon?

The Continental Football League was formed in 1965; and on St. Patrick's Day, the league hired its first commissioner. Albert Benjamin "Happy" Chandler, former Kentucky Governor, U.S. Senator (D-Kentucky), and retired Commissioner of Major League Baseball, was named the first Commissioner of the Continental Football League. Chandler is still the only individual to serve as commissioner for two different professional sports leagues.

From Red Sox Baseball To The Networks And The Patriots – Conflict Of Interest?

NBC purchased the rights to broadcast the 1963 American Football League Championship Game for $926,000 and placed Curt Gowdy behind the mike with Paul Christman serving as his color commentator. At this time, Gowdy was still the Red Sox play-by-play broadcaster.

A True One-Of-A-Kind Player

Billy Shaw was the prototypical pulling guard any running back would love to have as a teammate and blazing a trail. After playing college ball at Georgia Tech, Shaw was drafted in 1961 by the Dallas Cowboys in the 14th round and the Buffalo Bills in the 2nd round. Electing to sign with the Bills, he spent nine years as the mainstay of Buffalo's offensive line. Shaw was a first-team All-American Football League selection four times (1963 through 1966) and second team All-AFL in 1968 and 1969. He played in the first eight American Football League All-Star Games and was named to the All-Time All-AFL team. He played his entire career with the Bills and retired after the 1969 season. In 1999, along with Eric Dickerson, Tom Mack, Ozzie Newsome and

Lawrence Taylor, Shaw was enshrined in the Pro Football Hall of Fame. Shaw remains the only player ever inducted into the Hall of Fame never to play in the National Football League.

And He Also Played For The Packers

Quarterback Tobin Rote is the only player to lead his team to a National Football League Championship victory (Detroit Lions – 1957) and an American Football League Championship game (San Diego Chargers – 1963) as the starting signal-caller.

Not Only Could He Coach, He Also Could Play

In the very first National Football League draft (1936), Paul "Bear" Bryant, an end from the University of Alabama, was drafted in the 4th round/31st overall by the Brooklyn Dodgers.

Would You Believe I Didn't Get The Memo?

After former Colts/Hall of Fame quarterback Johnny Unitas passed away on September 11, 2005, Payton Manning told the media he would wear a pair of black cleats in the next game as a tribute to Johnny U's signature black high-top cleats the legend always wore. The NFL caught wind of this idea and notified Manning there would be a $25,000 fine if he followed through with his promise. Although Manning backed off, Baltimore Ravens quarterback Chris Redman wore high top black cleats in Unitas' honor not being aware of the NFL ruling toward Manning. Redman was fined $5,000.

Is She Still Using Her Lifetime Pass?

In 1965, a contest was held to name the new AFL expansion team to play in Miami, FL and 19,843 entries were submitted. The names were culled down to seven and a seven-member committee made up of local media constituents made the final choice. Names considered were the Dolphins, Mariners, Marauders, Mustangs, Missiles, Moons, Sharks, and Suns. The winning entry (Dolphins) was submitted by 622 entrants, and Mrs. Robert Swanson won two lifetime passes to Dolphins home games when her entry successfully predicted the score of the 1965 Notre Dame/Miami contest which ended in a scoreless tie.

Doug Flutie and Boston College Fans Love This Nickname

In the 1975 NFC divisional playoffs, Dallas defeated Minnesota, 17-14, with a 50-yard touchdown pass from Roger Staubach to Drew Pearson on the last play of the game. When asked to recall the last play, Staubach told reporters he closed his eyes, threw the ball as hard and as far as he could, and said a Hail Mary prayer – hence, the nickname for a last-ditch long pass for a touchdown.

All That – For Nothing

As the 20th century came to a close, Vikings wide receiver Ahmad Rashād had the distinction of being the ball-carrier in the longest NFL play from scrimmage who did not score a touchdown. On November 19, 1972, against the Los Angeles Rams at the LA Coliseum, Rashād caught a pass from quarterback Fran Tarkenton and covered 98 yards without scoring; then, during a Patriots playoff game (2005/game 18) in Denver, Broncos defensive back Champ Bailey ran the entire length of the field, 100 yards, yet still did not post any points on the scoreboard. Trailing, 10-6, in an AFC Divisional Playoff game, Tom Brady was on the verge of leading the Patriots to a go-ahead touchdown. New England covered 73 yards in just over 3:36 and faced a third-and-goal from the Denver 5-yard line. Brady, facing a blitz from the Broncos defense, tossed a pass in the direction of the end zone and Troy Brown. The pass ended up a jump ball between Bailey and Brown with the defender winning out. The All-Pro defensive back picked off the pass and bolted down the left sideline with his sights set on the Patriots end zone – a 101-yard adventure. New England tight end Benjamin Watson covered the entire length of the field beginning from the opposite side of the play and chased down the would-be touchdown scorer before crossing the goal line. Watson knocked the ball carrier out of bounds at the Patriots 1-yard line spoiling any plans of Bailey scoring a touchdown. – a 100-yard return but no paydirt. Not expecting anyone to catch him from the right, not hearing any footsteps behind, it looked as if Bailey eased up at about the 4-yard line to cruise into the end zone. Watson (like Bailey, a former Georgia Bulldog) came out of nowhere like a streaking comet to become an important footnote in a sudden NFL-record-breaking play.

Showed Up For One Thing, Left With Something Else

Before the 1979 NFL Draft, 49ers head coach Joe Walsh traveled to Clemson, SC to scout quarterback Steve Fuller. The Kansas City Chiefs selected Fuller in the 1st round (23rd overall) and San Francisco picked Notre Dame quarterback Joe Montana in the 3rd round (82nd overall). While watching Fuller throw during his workout, Walsh noticed the receiver catching the quarterback's passes and made note of his good hands. Remembering back to this workout on draft day, Walsh and the 49ers selected this Clemson wide receiver in the 10th round (249th overall). The person in question, the player on the receiving end of the famous San Francisco/NFL play, "The Catch", was Dwight Clark.

FOURTEEN
GAME BY GAME FROM DAY ONE

1960 (5-9), fourth in the AFL East
Head Coach – Lou Saban

1st round pick – Ron Burton, RB, Northwestern
Territorial pick – Gerhard Schwedes, RB, Syracuse

Game #1 – Friday, September 9, 1960

@ Nickerson Field	1	2	3	4	Final
Denver Broncos (1-0)	0	7	6	0	13
Boston Patriots (0-1)	3	0	7	0	10

Attendance: 21,597

Game #2 – Saturday, September 16, 1960

@ Polo Grounds	1	2	3	4	Final
Boston Patriots (1-1)	7	0	0	21	28
NY Titans (1-1)	3	14	7	0	24

Attendance: 19,200

Game #3 – Friday, September 23, 1960

@ Nickerson Field	1	2	3	4	Final
Buffalo Bills (1-2)	6	7	0	0	13
Boston Patriots (1-2)	0	0	0	0	0

Attendance: 20,732

Game #4 – Saturday, October 8, 1960

@ LA Memorial Coliseum	1	2	3	4	Final
Boston Patriots (2-2)	18	7	10	0	35
LA Chargers (2-3)	0	0	0	0	0

Attendance: 18,226

Game #5 – Sunday, October 16, 1960

@ Kezar Stadium	1	2	3	4	Final
Boston Patriots (2-3)	6	0	8	0	14
Oakland Raiders (3-3)	7	14	0	6	27

Attendance: 11,500

Game #6 – Sunday, October 23, 1960

@ Bears Stadium	1	2	3	4	Final
Boston Patriots (2-4)	10	7	7	0	24
Denver Broncos (4-2)	0	0	14	17	31

Attendance: 12,683

Game #7 – Friday, October 28, 1960

@ Nickerson Field	1	2	3	4	Final
LA Chargers (4-3)	7	21	7	10	45
Boston Patriots (2-5)	0	0	14	2	16

Attendance: 13,988

Game #8 – Friday, November 4, 1960

@ Nickerson Field	1	2	3	4	Final
Oakland Raiders (4-5)	0	7	7	14	28
Boston Patriots (3-5)	14	7	7	6	34

Attendance: 8,446

Game #9 – Friday, November 11, 1960

@ Nickerson Field	1	2	3	4	Final
NY Titans (4-6)	0	14	7	0	21
Boston Patriots (4-5)	7	10	7	14	38

Attendance: 11,653

Game #10 – Friday, November 18, 1960

@ Nickerson Field	1	2	3	4	Final
Dallas Texans (5-5)	0	7	0	7	14
Boston Patriots (5-5)	13	7	22	0	42

Attendance: 14,721

GAME BY GAME FROM DAY ONE

Game #11 – Friday, November 25, 1960

@ Nickerson Field	1	2	3	4	Final
Houston Oilers (8-3)	0	7	7	10	24
Boston Patriots (5-6)	0	3	7	0	10

Attendance: 27,123

Game #12 – Sunday, December 4, 1960

@ War Memorial Stadium	1	2	3	4	Final
Boston Patriots (5-7)	7	7	0	0	14
Buffalo Bills (5-6-1)	7	7	10	14	38

Attendance: 14,335

Game #13 – Sunday, December 11, 1960

@ Cotton Bowl	1	2	3	4	Final
Boston Patriots (5-8)	0	0	0	0	0
Dallas Texans (7-6)	3	7	14	10	34

Attendance: 12,000

Game #14 – Sunday, December 18, 1960

@ Jeppesen Stadium	1	2	3	4	Final
Boston Patriots (5-9)	0	0	21	0	21
Houston Oilers (10-4)	3	7	10	17	37

Attendance: 22,352

Win-Loss (W-L) record	5-9
Coin toss record	8-6

1961 (9-4-1), second in the AFL East

Head Coaches – Lou Saban (2-3), Mike Holovak (7-7-1)

1st round pick – Tommy Mason, RB, Tulane (2nd overall)

Game #1 – Saturday, September 9, 1961

@ Nickerson Field	1	2	3	4	Final
NY Titans (1-0)	7	7	0	7	21
Boston Patriots (0-1)	0	7	10	3	20

Attendance: 16,683

Game #2 – Saturday, September 16, 1961

@ Nickerson Field	1	2	3	4	Final
Denver Broncos (1-1)	3	0	7	7	17
Boston Patriots (1-1)	3	7	21	14	45

Attendance: 14,479

Game #3 – Saturday, September 23, 1961

@ War Memorial Stadium	1	2	3	4	Final
Boston Patriots (2-1)	3	3	14	3	23
Buffalo Bills (1-2)	7	0	7	7	21

Attendance: 21,504

Game #4 – Sunday, October 1, 1961

@ Polo Grounds	1	2	3	4	Final
Boston Patriots (2-2)	9	0	14	7	30
NY Titans (3-1)	0	20	3	14	37

Attendance: 15,189

Game #5 – Saturday, October 7, 1961

@ Nickerson Field	1	2	3	4	Final
SD Chargers (5-0)	7	24	0	7	38
Boston Patriots (2-3)	0	14	7	6	27

Attendance: 17,748

Game #6 – Friday, October 13, 1961

@ Nickerson Field	1	2	3	4	Final
Houston Oilers (1-3-1)	0	14	7	10	31
Boston Patriots (2-3-1)	7	3	14	7	31

Attendance: 15,070

PATRIOTS PASSION

Game #7 – Sunday, October 22, 1961

@ Nickerson Field	1	2	3	4	Final
Buffalo Bills (3-4)	0	0	0	21	21
Boston Patriots (3-3-1)	17	21	7	7	52

Attendance: 9,398

Game #8 – Sunday, October 29, 1961

@ Cotton Bowl	1	2	3	4	Final
Boston Patriots (4-3-1)	0	7	0	11	18
Dallas Texans (3-4)	0	3	7	7	17

Attendance: 20,055

Game #9 – Friday, November 3, 1961

@ Nickerson Field	1	2	3	4	Final
Dallas Texans (3-5)	7	7	7	0	21
Boston Patriots (5-3-1)	14	0	14	0	28

Attendance: 25,063

Game #10 – Sunday, November 12, 1961

@ Jeppesen Stadium	1	2	3	4	Final
Boston Patriots (5-4-1)	0	6	3	6	15
Houston Oilers (5-3-1)	7	13	0	7	27

Attendance: 35,469

Game #11 – Friday, November 17, 1961

@ Nickerson Field	1	2	3	4	Final
Oakland Raiders (2-8)	0	14	3	0	17
Boston Patriots (6-4-1)	7	6	0	7	20

Attendance: 17,169

Game #12 – Sunday, December 3, 1961

@ Bears Field	1	2	3	4	Final
Boston Patriots (7-4-1)	14	0	0	14	28
Denver Broncos (3-10)	0	7	3	14	24

Attendance: 9,303

Game #13 – Saturday, December 9, 1961

@ Candlestick Park	1	2	3	4	Final
Boston Patriots (8-4-1)	7	14	7	7	35
Oakland Raiders (2-11)	7	0	7	7	21

Attendance: 6,500

Game #14 – Sunday, December 17, 1961

@ Balboa Stadium	1	2	3	4	Final
Boston Patriots (9-4-1)	17	10	7	7	41
SD Chargers (12-2)	0	0	0	0	0

Attendance: 21,339

Lifetime W-L record   14-13-1
Lifetime coin toss record   15-13

1962 (9-4-1), second in AFL East
Head Coach – Mike Holovak

1st round pick – Gary Collins, WR-P, Maryland (6th overall)

Game #1 – Saturday, September 8, 1962

@ Cotton Bowl	1	2	3	4	Final
Boston Patriots (0-1)	0	14	0	14	28
Dallas Texans (1-0)	0	21	7	14	42

Attendance: 32,000

Game #2 – Sunday, September 16, 1962

@ Harvard Stadium	1	2	3	4	Final
Houston Oilers (1-1)	7	14	0	0	21
Boston Patriots (1-1)	7	17	0	10	34

Attendance: 32,276

GAME BY GAME FROM DAY ONE

Game #3 – Friday, September 21, 1962

@ Nickerson Field	1	2	3	4	Final
Denver Broncos (2-1)	0	3	0	13	16
Boston Patriots (2-1)	3	14	10	14	41

Attendance: 21,038

Game #4 – Saturday, October 6, 1962

@ Polo Grounds	1	2	3	4	Final
Boston Patriots (3-1)	3	21	13	6	43
NY Titans (2-3)	0	7	7	0	14

Attendance: 14,412

Game #5 – Friday, October 12, 1962

@ Nickerson Field	1	2	3	4	Final
Dallas Texans (4-1)	3	7	0	17	27
Boston Patriots (3-2)	0	0	7	0	7

Attendance: 23,874

Game #6 – Friday, October 19, 1962

@ Nickerson Field	1	2	3	4	Final
SD Chargers (2-3)	10	10	0	0	20
Boston Patriots (4-2)	3	0	14	7	24

Attendance: 20,088

Game #7 – Friday, October 26, 1962

@ Nickerson Field	1	2	3	4	Final
Oakland Raiders (0-7)	7	6	0	3	16
Boston Patriots (5-2)	3	3	10	10	26

Attendance: 12,514

Game #8 – Saturday, November 3, 1962

@ War Memorial Stadium	1	2	3	4	Final
Boston Patriots (5-2-1)	14	0	7	7	28
Buffalo Bills (3-5-1)	14	7	7	0	28

Attendance: 33,247

Game #9 – Sunday, November 11, 1962

@ Bears Stadium	1	2	3	4	Final
Boston Patriots (6-2-1)	3	17	3	10	33
Denver Broncos (7-3)	0	9	7	13	29

Attendance: 28,187

Game #10 – Sunday, November 18, 1962

@ Jeppesen Stadium	1	2	3	4	Final
Boston Patriots (6-3-1)	7	3	7	0	17
Houston Oilers (7-3)	7	7	7	0	21

Attendance: 35,250

Game #11 – Friday, November 23, 1962

@ Nickerson Field	1	2	3	4	Final
Buffalo Bills (5-6-1)	7	0	3	0	10
Boston Patriots (7-3-1)	0	14	0	7	21

Attendance: 20,021

Game #12 – Friday, November 30, 1962

@ Nickerson Field	1	2	3	4	Final
NY Titans (5-7)	7	3	7	0	17
Boston Patriots (8-3-1)	0	3	7	14	24

Attendance: 20,015

Game #13 – Sunday, December 9, 1962

@ Balboa Stadium	1	2	3	4	Final
Boston Patriots (9-3-1)	7	10	0	3	20
SD Chargers (4-9)	0	3	3	8	14

Attendance: 19,887

Game #14 – Sunday, December 16, 1962

@ Frank Youell Field	1	2	3	4	Final
Boston Patriots (9-4-1)	0	0	0	0	0
Oakland Raiders (1-13)	3	7	7	3	20

Attendance: 8,000

Lifetime W-L record	23-17-2
Lifetime coin toss record	23-19

1963 (7-6-1), first in AFL East
Head Coach – Mike Holovak

1st round pick – Art Graham, WR, Boston College (6th overall)
13th round pick – Dave Adams, OT, Arkansas (100th overall)
27th round pick – Dave Adams, OT, Arkansas (215th overall)

Game #1 – Sunday, September 8, 1963

@ Alumni Stadium	1	2	3	4	Final
NY Jets (0-1)	7	7	0	0	14
Boston Patriots (1-0)	7	7	3	21	38

Attendance: 24,120

Game #2 – Saturday, September 14, 1963

@ Balboa Stadium	1	2	3	4	Final
Boston Patriots (1-1)	3	7	0	3	13
SD Chargers (2-0)	0	14	0	3	17

Attendance: 26,097

Game #3 – Sunday, September 22, 1963

@ Frank Youell Field	1	2	3	4	Final
Boston Patriots (2-1)	7	10	3	0	20
Oakland Raiders (2-1)	0	0	0	14	14

Attendance: 17,131

Game #4 – Sunday, September 29, 1963

@ Bears Stadium	1	2	3	4	Final
Boston Patriots (2-2)	3	0	7	0	10
Denver Broncos (1-2)	0	0	7	7	14

Attendance: 18,636

Game #5 – Saturday, October 5, 1963

@ Polo Grounds	1	2	3	4	Final
Boston Patriots (2-3)	0	10	0	14	24
NY Jets (3-1)	14	7	3	7	31

Attendance: 16,769

Game #6 – Friday, October 11, 1963

@ Fenway Park	1	2	3	4	Final
Oakland Raiders (2-4)	7	0	7	0	14
Boston Patriots (3-3)	3	0	10	7	20

Attendance: 26,494

Game #7 – Friday, October 18, 1963

@ Fenway Park	1	2	3	4	Final
Denver Broncos (2-4)	7	7	7	0	21
Boston Patriots (4-3)	10	13	3	14	40

Attendance: 25,418

Game #8 – Saturday, October 26, 1963

@ War Memorial Stadium	1	2	3	4	Final
Boston Patriots (4-4)	0	0	7	14	21
Buffalo Bills (3-4-1)	0	7	7	14	28

Attendance: 29,243

Game #9 – Friday, November 1, 1963

@ Fenway Park	1	2	3	4	Final
Houston Oilers (5-4)	0	3	0	0	3
Boston Patriots (5-4)	14	14	7	10	45

Attendance: 31,185

Game #10 – Sunday, November 10, 1963

@ Fenway Park	1	2	3	4	Final
SD Chargers (7-2)	7	0	0	0	7
Boston Patriots (5-5)	0	0	6	0	6

Attendance: 28,402

Game #11 – Sunday, November 17, 1963

@ Fenway Park	1	2	3	4	Final
KC Chiefs (2-6-2)	7	3	7	7	24
Boston Patriots (5-5-1)	0	15	2	7	24

Attendance: 27,123

PATRIOTS PASSION

The American Football League Wins the Respect of America

On November 22, 1963, John Fitzgerald Kennedy, 35th President of the United States was assassinated in Dallas, Texas. Pete Rozelle, commissioner of the National Football League, against his better judgment decided to go on with the NFL's regularly scheduled games for Sunday, November 24, 1963. Rozelle, a close friend of the Kennedy family conferred with JFK's press secretary Pierre Salinger. The two gentlemen had been classmates at the University of San Francisco and Salinger gave his blessing to play the games. Joe Foss, commissioner of the American Football League, after briefly speaking with some team owners, cancelled all of the league's game for the weekend of November 24, 1963. Foss's decision to cancel the games is often considered a turning point when the nation began to take the AFL seriously. Before he took over the leadership of the AFL in 1959, Joe Ross was awarded a Congressional Medal of Honor from FDR in 1943. He served as governor of South Dakota (R) from 1955-1959 and in 1957 lost an election to gain a seat in the United States House of Representatives, South Dakota, to George McGovern (1972 Democratic candidate for the President of the United State).

Game #12 – Sunday, December 1, 1963

@ Fenway Park	1	2	3	4	Final
Buffalo Bills (5-6-1)	0	7	0	0	7
Boston Patriots (6-5-1)	0	0	14	3	17

Attendance: 16,981

Game #13 – Sunday, December 8, 1963

@ Jeppesen Stadium	1	2	3	4	Final
Boston Patriots (7-5-1)	10	21	10	5	46
Houston Oilers (6-6)	7	7	7	7	28

Attendance: 23,462

Game #14 – Saturday, December 14, 1963

@ Municipal Stadium	1	2	3	4	Final
Boston Patriots (7-6-1)	3	0	0	0	3
KC Chiefs (4-7-2)	0	7	14	14	35

Attendance: 12,598

Game #15 - East Division Play-off Game
Saturday, December 28, 1963

@ War Memorial Stadium	1	2	3	4	Final
Boston Patriots (8-6-1)	10	6	0	10	26
Buffalo Bills (7-7-1)	0	0	8	0	8

Attendance: 33,044

Game #16 – American Football League Championship Game
Sunday, January 5, 1964

@ Balboa Stadium	1	2	3	4	Final
Boston Patriots (8-7-1)	7	3	0	0	10
SD Chargers (12-3)	21	10	7	13	51

Attendance: 30,127

Lifetime W-L record   31-24-3
Lifetime coin toss record   30-28

1964 (10-3-1), second in AFL East
Head Coach – Mike Holovak

1st round pick – Jack Concannon, QB, Boston College (1st overall)

Game #1 – Sunday, September 13, 1964

@ Frank Youell Field	1	2	3	4	Final
Boston Patriots (1-0)	0	7	7	3	17
Oakland Raiders (0-1)	7	0	0	7	14

Attendance: 21,216

Game #2 – Sunday, September 20, 1964

@ Balboa Stadium	1	2	3	4	Final
Boston Patriots (2-0)	10	3	10	10	33
SD Chargers (1-1)	0	10	0	18	28

Attendance: 20,568

Game #3 – Sunday, September 27, 1964

@ Fenway Park	1	2	3	4	Final
NY Jets (1-1)	3	7	0	0	10
Boston Patriots (3-0)	0	13	10	3	26

Attendance: 22,716

Game #4 – Sunday, October 4, 1964

@ Bears Stadium	1	2	3	4	Final
Boston Patriots (4-0)	9	10	6	14	39
Denver Broncos (0-4)	0	0	3	7	10

Attendance: 18,226

Game #5 – Friday, October 9, 1964

@ Fenway Park	1	2	3	4	Final
SD Chargers (2-2-1)	0	10	13	3	26
Boston Patriots (4-1)	3	0	7	7	17

Attendance: 35,096

Game #6 – Friday, October 16, 1964

@ Fenway Park	1	2	3	4	Final
Oakland Raiders (0-5-1)	3	21	10	9	43
Boston Patriots (4-1-1)	0	14	7	22	43

Attendance: 23,279

Game #7 – Friday, October 23, 1964

@ Fenway Park	1	2	3	4	Final
KC Chiefs (2-4)	0	0	0	7	7
Boston Patriots (5-1-1)	7	0	10	7	24

Attendance: 27,400

Game #8 – Saturday, October 31, 1964

@ Shea Stadium	1	2	3	4	Final
Boston Patriots (5-2-1)	0	0	7	7	14
NY Jets (4-2-1)	7	14	7	7	35

Attendance: 45,003

Game #9 – Friday, November 6, 1964

@ Fenway Park	1	2	3	4	Final
Houston Oilers (2-7)	7	0	7	10	24
Boston Patriots (6-2-1)	7	6	3	9	25

Attendance: 28,161

Game #10 – Sunday, November 15, 1964

@ War Memorial Stadium	1	2	3	4	Final
Boston Patriots (7-2-1)	0	14	7	15	36
Buffalo Bills (9-1)	10	3	15	0	28

Attendance: 42,308

Game #11 – Friday, November 20, 1964

@ Fenway Park	1	2	3	4	Final
Denver Broncos (2-9)	7	0	0	10	7
Boston Patriots (8-2-1)	2	7	3	0	12

Attendance: 24,979

Game #12 – Sunday, November 29, 1964

@ Jeppesen Stadium	1	2	3	4	Final
Boston Patriots (9-2-1)	7	10	14	3	34
Houston Oilers (2-10)	7	3	7	0	17

Attendance: 17,560

GAME BY GAME FROM DAY ONE

Game #13 – Sunday, December 6, 1964

@ Municipal Stadium	1	2	3	4	Final
Boston Patriots (10-2-1)	10	0	7	14	31
KC Chiefs (5-7)	7	3	7	7	24

Attendance: 13,166

Game #14 – Sunday, December 20, 1964

@ Fenway Park	1	2	3	4	Final
Buffalo Bills (12-2)	7	10	0	7	24
Boston Patriots (10-3-1)	6	0	0	8	14

Attendance: 38,021

Lifetime W-L record   41-27-4
Lifetime coin toss record   36-36

1965 (4-8-2), third in AFL East
Head Coach – Mike Holovak

1st round pick – Jerry Rush DT Michigan State (7th overall)

Game #1 – Saturday, September 11, 1965

@ War Memorial Stadium	1	2	3	4	Final
Boston Patriots (0-1)	0	7	0	0	7
Buffalo Bills (1-0)	0	7	10	7	24

Attendance: 45,502

Game #2 – Sunday, September 19, 1965

@ Rice Stadium	1	2	3	4	Final
Boston Patriots (0-2)	0	10	0	0	10
Houston Oilers (2-0)	7	7	7	10	31

Attendance: 32,445

Game #3 – Friday, September 24, 1965

@ Fenway Park	1	2	3	4	Final
Denver Broncos (1-2)	7	3	14	3	27
Boston Patriots (0-3)	7	3	0	0	10

Attendance: 26,782

Game #4 – Sunday, October 3, 1965

@ Municipal Stadium	1	2	3	4	Final
Boston Patriots (0-4)	3	7	0	7	17
KC Chiefs (2-1-1)	7	13	0	7	27

Attendance: 26,773

Game #5 – Friday, October 8, 1965

@ Fenway Park	1	2	3	4	Final
Oakland Raiders (3-2)	7	3	7	7	24
Boston Patriots (0-5)	0	7	3	0	10

Attendance: 24,824

Game #6 – Sunday, October 17, 1965

@ Fenway Park	1	2	3	4	Final
SD Chargers (4-0-2)	3	10	0	0	13
Boston Patriots (0-5-1)	0	7	3	3	13

Attendance: 20,924

Game #7 – Sunday, October 24, 1965

@ Frank Youell Field	1	2	3	4	Final
Boston Patriots (0-6-1)	0	0	7	14	21
Oakland Raiders (4-2-1)	3	3	10	14	30

Attendance: 20,858

Game #8 – Sunday, October 31, 1965

@ Balboa Stadium	1	2	3	4	Final
Boston Patriots (1-6-1)	9	0	3	10	22
SD Chargers (5-1-2)	0	0	0	6	6

Attendance: 33,336

123

Game #9 – Sunday, November 7, 1965

@ Fenway Park	1	2	3	4	Final
Buffalo Bills (7-2)	3	17	3	0	23
Boston Patriots (1-7-1)	0	7	0	0	7

Attendance: 24,415

Game #10 – Sunday, November 14, 1965

@ Fenway Park	1	2	3	4	Final
NY Jets (3-5-1)	17	7	3	3	30
Boston Patriots (1-8-1)	0	17	3	0	20

Attendance: 18,589

Game #11 – Sunday, November 21, 1965

@ Fenway Park	1	2	3	4	Final
KC Chiefs (5-4-2)	0	7	0	3	10
Boston Patriots (1-8-2)	0	3	0	7	10

Attendance: 13,056

Game #12 – Sunday, November 28, 1965

@ Shea Stadium	1	2	3	4	Final
Boston Patriots (2-8-2)	3	0	17	7	27
NY Jets (4-6-1)	0	10	0	13	23

Attendance: 59,334

Game #13 – Sunday, December 12, 1965

@ Bears Stadium	1	2	3	4	Final
Boston Patriots (3-8-2)	7	14	7	0	28
Denver Broncos (4-9)	6	0	0	14	20

Attendance: 27,207

Game #14 – Saturday, December 18, 1965

@ Fenway Park	1	2	3	4	Final
Houston Oilers (4-10)	0	0	8	6	14
Boston Patriots (4-8-2)	10	16	3	13	42

Attendance: 14,508

Lifetime W-L record 45-35-6
Lifetime coin toss record 45-41

1966 (8-4-2), second in AFL East

Head Coach – Mike Holovak

1st round pick – Karl Singer, T, Purdue (3rd overall)

Game #1 – Saturday, September 10, 1966

@ Balboa Stadium	1	2	3	4	Final
Boston Patriots (0-1)	0	0	0	0	0
SD Chargers (1-0)	3	14	0	7	24

Attendance: 29,539

Game #2 – Sunday, September 18, 1966

@ Bears Stadium	1	2	3	4	Final
Boston Patriots (1-1)	3	6	0	15	24
Denver Broncos (0-2)	3	7	0	0	10

Attendance: 25,337

Game #3 – Sunday, September 25, 1966

@ Fenway Park	1	2	3	4	Final
KC Chiefs (3-0)	17	6	0	20	43
Boston Patriots (1-2)	0	14	7	3	24

Attendance: 22,641

Game #4 – Sunday, October 2, 1966

@ Fenway Park	1	2	3	4	Final
NY Jets (3-0-1)	0	7	0	17	24
Boston Patriots (1-2-1)	7	3	14	0	24

Attendance: 27,225

GAME BY GAME FROM DAY ONE

Game #5 – Saturday, October 8, 1966

@War Memorial Stadium	1	2	3	4	Final
Boston Patriots (2-2-1)	10	3	7	0	20
Buffalo Bills (3-3)	0	0	3	7	10

Attendance: 45,542

Game #6 – Sunday, October 23, 1966

@ Fenway Park	1	2	3	4	Final
SD Chargers (4-2-1)	7	3	7	0	17
Boston Patriots (3-2-1)	0	14	7	14	35

Attendance: 32,371

Game #7 – Sunday, October 30, 1966

@ Fenway Park	1	2	3	4	Final
Oakland Raiders (4-4)	0	7	0	14	21
Boston Patriots (4-2-1)	14	3	7	0	24

Attendance: 26,491

Game #8 – Sunday, November 6, 1966

@ Fenway Park	1	2	3	4	Final
Denver Broncos (2-7)	0	3	7	7	17
Boston Patriots (4-3-1)	0	7	3	0	10

Attendance: 18,154

Game #9 – Sunday, November 13, 1966

@ Fenway Park	1	2	3	4	Final
Houston Oilers (3-7)	7	7	0	7	21
Boston Patriots (5-3-1)	7	13	7	0	27

Attendance: 23,426

Game #10 – Sunday, November 20, 1966

@ Municipal Stadium	1	2	3	4	Final
Boston Patriots (5-3-2)	0	17	7	3	27
KC Chiefs (8-2-1)	17	0	10	0	27

Attendance: 41,475

Game #11 – Sunday, November 27, 1966

@ Orange Bowl	1	2	3	4	Final
Boston Patriots (6-3-2)	0	10	10	0	20
Miami Dolphins (2-9)	0	0	7	7	14

Attendance: 22,754

Game #12 – Sunday, December 4, 1966

@ Fenway Park	1	2	3	4	Final
Buffalo Bills (8-4-1)	3	0	0	0	3
Boston Patriots (7-3-2)	7	0	7	0	14

Attendance: 39,350

Game #13 – Sunday, December 11, 1966

@ Rice Stadium	1	2	3	4	Final
Boston Patriots (8-3-2)	3	21	7	7	38
Houston Oilers (3-10)	7	0	0	7	14

Attendance: 17,100

Game #14 – Saturday, December 17, 1966

@ Shea Stadium	1	2	3	4	Final
Boston Patriots (8-4-2)	7	0	6	15	28
NY Jets (6-6-2)	7	10	14	7	38

Attendance: 58,921

Lifetime W-L record	53-39-8
Lifetime coin toss record	51-49

1967 (3-10-1), fifth in AFL East
Head Coach – Mike Holovak

1st round pick – John Charles, DB, Purdue (21st overall)

Game #1 – Sunday, September 3, 1967

@ Bears Stadium	1	2	3	4	Final
Boston Patriots (0-1)	7	0	14	0	21
Denver Broncos (1-0)	7	3	6	10	26

Attendance: 35,488

Game #2 – Saturday, September 9, 1967

@ San Diego Stadium	1	2	3	4	Final
Boston Patriots (0-2)	7	7	0	0	14
SD Chargers (1-0)	7	7	0	14	28

Attendance: 39,227

Game #3 – Sunday, September 17, 1967

@ Oakland-Alameda Col.	1	2	3	4	Final
Boston Patriots (0-3)	7	0	0	0	7
Oakland Raiders (2-0)	7	14	14	0	35

Attendance: 26,289

Game #4 – Sunday, September 24, 1967

@War Memorial Stadium	1	2	3	4	Final
Boston Patriots (1-3)	6	7	0	10	23
Buffalo Bills (1-2)	0	0	0	0	0

Attendance: 45,748

Game #5 – Sunday, October 8, 1967

@ San Diego Stadium	1	2	3	4	Final
SD Chargers (3-0-1)	7	10	0	14	31
Boston Patriots (1-3-1)	7	14	10	0	31

Attendance: 23,620

Game #6 – Sunday, October 15, 1967

@ Alumni Stadium	1	2	3	4	Final
Miami Dolphins (1-4)	3	0	7	0	10
Boston Patriots (2-3-1)	7	20	7	7	41

Attendance: 23,955

Game #7 – Sunday, October 22, 1967

@ Fenway Park	1	2	3	4	Final
Oakland Raiders (5-1)	14	6	7	21	48
Boston Patriots (2-4-1)	0	0	7	7	14

Attendance: 25,057

Game #8 – Sunday, October 29, 1967

@ Shea Stadium	1	2	3	4	Final
Boston Patriots (2-5-1)	10	10	3	0	23
NY Jets (5-1-1)	0	14	9	7	30

Attendance: 62,784

Game #9 – Sunday, November 5, 1967

@ Fenway Park	1	2	3	4	Final
Houston Oilers (4-3-1)	0	0	0	7	7
Boston Patriots (3-5-1)	3	3	5	7	18

Attendance: 19,422

Game #10 – Sunday, November 12, 1967

@ Fenway Park	1	2	3	4	Final
KC Chiefs (6-3)	7	23	0	3	33
Boston Patriots (3-6-1)	3	7	0	0	10

Attendance: 23,010

Game #11 – Sunday, November 19, 1967

@ Fenway Park	1	2	3	4	Final
NY Jets (7-2-1)	3	13	7	6	29
Boston Patriots (3-7-1)	0	3	0	21	24

Attendance: 26,790

Game #12 – Sunday, November 26, 1967

@ Rice Stadium	1	2	3	4	Final
Boston Patriots (3-8-1)	3	0	3	0	6
Houston Oilers (6-3-1)	0	3	7	17	27

Attendance: 28,044

Game #13 – Saturday, December 9, 1967

@ Fenway Park	1	2	3	4	Final
Buffalo Bills (4-9)	14	14	10	6	44
Boston Patriots (3-9-1)	0	7	2	7	16

Attendance: 20,627

Game #14 – Sunday, December 17, 1967

@ Orange Bowl	1	2	3	4	Final
Boston Patriots (3-10-1)	14	3	9	6	32
Miami Dolphins (4-9)	7	28	3	3	41

Attendance: 25,969

Lifetime W-L record   56-49-9
Lifetime coin toss record   59-55

1968 (4-10), fourth in AFL East
Head Coach– Mike Holovak

1st round pick – Dennis Byrd, DE, North Carolina State (6th overall)

Game #1 – Sunday, September 8, 1968

@ War Memorial Stad.	1	2	3	4	Final
Boston Patriots (1-0)	0	3	10	3	16
Buffalo Bills (0-1)	7	0	0	0	7

Attendance: 38,865

Game #2 – Sunday, September 22, 1968

@ Legion Field	1	2	3	4	Final
NY Jets (2-0)	14	6	17	10	47
Boston Patriots (1-1)	3	7	7	14	31

Attendance: 29,192

Game #3 – Sunday, September 29, 1968

@ Bears Stadium	1	2	3	4	Final
Boston Patriots (2-1)	7	3	7	3	20
Denver Broncos (0-3)	3	7	0	7	17

Attendance: 37,024

Game #4 – Sunday, October 6, 1968

@ Oakland-Alameda	1	2	3	4	Final
Boston Patriots (2-2)	7	3	0	0	10
Oakland Raiders (4-0)	0	7	21	13	41

Attendance: 44,253

Game #5 – Sunday, October 13, 1968

@ Fenway Park	1	2	3	4	Final
Houston Oilers (2-4)	0	10	3	3	16
Boston Patriots (2-3)	0	0	0	0	0

Attendance: 32,502

Game #6 – Sunday, October 20, 1968

@ Fenway Park	1	2	3	4	Final
Buffalo Bills (1-5-1)	3	3	0	0	6
Boston Patriots (3-3)	3	3	17	0	23

Attendance: 21,082

Game #7 – Sunday, October 27, 1968

@ Shea Stadium	1	2	3	4	Final
Boston Patriots (3-4)	0	0	0	14	14
NY Jets (5-2)	7	3	10	28	48

Attendance: 62,351

Game #8 – Sunday, November 3, 1968

@ Fenway Park	1	2	3	4	Final
Denver Broncos (4-4)	14	7	7	7	35
Boston Patriots (3-5)	0	0	7	7	14

Attendance: 18,304

PATRIOTS PASSION

Game #9 – Sunday, November 10, 1968

@ Fenway Park	1	2	3	4	Final
San Diego Chargers (7-2)	7	10	10	0	27
Boston Patriots (3-6)	3	0	0	14	17

Attendance: 19,278

Game #10 – Sunday, November 17, 1968

@ Municipal Stadium	1	2	3	4	Final
Boston Patriots (3-7)	10	0	7	0	17
KC Chiefs (9-2)	14	10	0	7	31

Attendance: 48,271

Game #11 – Sunday, November 24, 1968

@ Fenway Park	1	2	3	4	Final
Miami Dolphins (4-6-1)	0	13	7	14	34
Boston Patriots (3-8)	10	0	0	0	10

Attendance: 18,305

Game #12 – Sunday, December 1, 1968

@ Fenway Park	1	2	3	4	Final
Cincinnati Bengals (3-10)	0	0	7	7	14
Boston Patriots (4-8)	2	24	0	7	33

Attendance: 17,796

Game #13 – Sunday, December 8, 1968

@ Orange Bowl	1	2	3	4	Final
Boston Patriots (4-9)	0	7	0	0	7
Miami Dolphins (5-7-1)	7	21	0	10	38

Attendance: 24,242

Game #14 – Sunday, December 15, 1968

@ Astrodome	1	2	3	4	Final
Boston Patriots (4-10)	0	7	10	0	17
Houston Oilers (7-7)	7	14	7	17	45

Attendance: 34,198

Lifetime W-L record   60-59-9
Lifetime coin toss record   65-63

1969 (4-10), tied third in AFL East
Head Coach – Clive Rush

1st round pick – Ron Sellers, WR, Florida State (6th overall)

Game #1 – Sunday, September 14, 1969

@ Mile High Stadium	1	2	3	4	Final
Boston Patriots (0-1)	0	0	0	7	7
Denver Broncos (1-0)	14	14	7	0	35

Attendance: 43,679

Game #2 – Sunday, September 21, 1969

@ Alumni Stadium	1	2	3	4	Final
KC Chiefs (2-0)	14	7	10	0	31
Boston Patriots (0-2)	0	0	0	0	0

Attendance: 22,002

Game #3 – Sunday, September 28, 1969

@ Alumni Stadium	1	2	3	4	Final
Oakland Raiders (3-0)	7	3	21	7	38
Boston Patriots (0-3)	13	0	0	10	23

Attendance: 19,609

Game #4 – Sunday, October 5, 1969

@ Alumni Stadium	1	2	3	4	Final
NY Jets (2-2)	3	7	10	3	23
Boston Patriots (0-4)	0	7	0	7	14

Attendance: 25,584

GAME BY GAME FROM DAY ONE

Game #5 – Saturday, October 11, 1969

@ War Memorial	1	2	3	4	Final
Boston Patriots (0-5)	7	0	6	3	16
Buffalo Bills (2-3)	7	3	3	10	23

Attendance: 46,201

Game #6 – Sunday, October 19, 1969

@ Alumni Stadium	1	2	3	4	Final
SD Chargers (4-2)	0	3	3	7	13
Boston Patriots (0-6)	7	0	0	3	10

Attendance: 18,346

Game #7 – Sunday, October 26, 1969

@ Shea Stadium	1	2	3	4	Final
Boston Patriots (0-7)	10	7	0	0	17
NY Jets (5-2)	7	3	3	10	23

Attendance: 62,351

Game #8 – Sunday, November 2, 1969

@ Alumni Stadium	1	2	3	4	Final
Houston Oilers (4-4)	0	0	0	0	0
Boston Patriots (1-7)	0	17	7	0	24

Attendance: 19,006

Game #9 – Sunday, November 9, 1969

@ Alumni Stadium	1	2	3	4	Final
Miami Dolphins (2-6-1)	3	7	0	7	17
Boston Patriots (1-8)	0	0	0	16	16

Attendance: 19,821

Game #10 – Sunday, November 16, 1969

@ Nippert Stadium	1	2	3	4	Final
Boston Patriots (2-8)	19	3	3	0	25
Cincinnati Bengals (4-5-1)	0	7	0	7	14

Attendance: 27,927

Game #11 – Sunday, November 23, 1969

@ Alumni Stadium	1	2	3	4	Final
Buffalo Bills (3-8)	7	7	7	0	21
Boston Patriots (3-8)	14	7	0	14	35

Attendance: 25,584

Game #12 – Sunday, November 30, 1969

@ Orange Bowl	1	2	3	4	Final
Boston Patriots (4-8)	6	16	0	16	38
Miami Dolphins (2-9-1)	9	7	7	0	23

Attendance: 32,121

Game #13 – Sunday, December 7, 1969

@ San Diego Stadium	1	2	3	4	Final
Boston Patriots (4-9)	0	3	0	15	18
SD Chargers (7-6)	7	7	14	0	28

Attendance: 33,146

Game #14 – Sunday, December 14, 1969

@ Astrodome	1	2	3	4	Final
Boston Patriots (4-10)	13	3	7	0	23
Houston Oilers (6-6-2)	0	7	7	13	27

Attendance: 39,215

Lifetime W-L record   64-69-9
Lifetime coin toss record   72-70

1970 (2-12) fifth in AFL East

Head Coaches – Clive Rush (1-6), John Mazur (1-6)

1st round pick – Phil Olsen DT Utah State (4th overall)

Game #1 – Sunday, September 20, 1970

@ Harvard Stadium	1	2	3	4	Final
Miami Dolphins (0-1)	7	7	0	0	14
Boston Patriots (1-0)	3	17	0	7	27

Attendance: 36,040

Game #2 – Sunday, September 27, 1970

@ Harvard Stadium	1	2	3	4	Final
NY Jets (1-1)	7	14	7	3	31
Boston Patriots (1-1)	0	7	14	0	21

Attendance: 36,040

Game #3 – Sunday, October 4, 1970

@ Harvard Stadium	1	2	3	4	Final
Baltimore Colts (2-1)	0	7	0	7	14
Boston Patriots (1-2)	0	3	0	3	6

Attendance: 38,235

Game #4 – Sunday, October 11, 1970

@ Municipal Stadium	1	2	3	4	Final
Boston Patriots (1-3)	3	0	0	7	10
KC Chiefs (2-2)	0	10	0	13	23

Attendance: 50,698

Game #5 – Sunday, October 18, 1970

@ Harvard Stadium	1	2	3	4	Final
NY Giants (2-3)	3	7	0	6	16
Boston Patriots (1-4)	0	0	0	0	0

Attendance: 39,091

Game #6 – Sunday, October 25, 1970

@ Memorial Stadium	1	2	3	4	Final
Boston Patriots (1-5)	0	3	0	0	3
Baltimore Colts (5-1)	3	14	3	7	27

Attendance: 60,240

Game #7 – Sunday, November 1, 1970

@ Harvard Stadium	1	2	3	4	Final
Buffalo Bills (3-4)	10	21	0	14	45
Boston Patriots (1-6)	0	0	3	7	10

Attendance: 31,148

Game #8 – Sunday, November 8, 1970

@ Busch Stadium	1	2	3	4	Final
Boston Patriots (1-7)	0	0	0	0	0
St. Louis Cardinals (6-2)	14	7	3	7	31

Attendance: 46,466

Game #9 – Sunday, November 15, 1970

@ Harvard Stadium	1	2	3	4	Final
SD Chargers (4-3-2)	0	0	7	9	16
Boston Patriots (1-8)	7	0	0	7	14

Attendance: 30,597

Game #10 – Sunday, November 22, 1970

@ Shea Stadium	1	2	3	4	Final
Boston Patriots (2-8)	0	0	3	0	3
NY Jets (4-5-1)	3	0	7	7	17

Attendance: 61,882

Game #11 – Sunday, November 29, 1970

@ War Memorial	1	2	3	4	Final
Boston Patriots (2-9)	0	7	7	0	14
Buffalo Bills (3-7-1)	0	3	0	7	10

Attendance: 31,427

Game #12 – Sunday, December 6, 1970

@ Orange Bowl	1	2	3	4	Final
Boston Patriots (2-10)	0	6	7	7	20
Miami Dolphins (8-4)	17	10	7	3	37

Attendance: 51,032

Game #13 – Sunday, December 13, 1970

@ Harvard Stadium	1	2	3	4	Final
Minnesota Vikings (11-2)	14	7	14	0	35
Boston Patriots (2-11)	0	7	7	0	14

Attendance: 37,819

Game #14 – Sunday, December 20, 1970

@ Riverfront Stadium	1	2	3	4	Final
Boston Patriots (2-12)	0	0	0	7	7
Cincinnati Bengals (8-6)	14	24	7	0	45

Attendance: 37,819

Lifetime W-L record   66-81-9
Lifetime coin toss record   79-77

1971 (6-8), tied for third in AFL East
Head Coach – John Mazur

1st round pick – Jim Plunkett, QB, Stanford (1st overall)

Game #1 – Sunday, September 19, 1971

@ Schaefer Stadium	1	2	3	4	Final
Oakland Raiders (0-1)	0	6	0	0	6
NE Patriots (1-0)	0	0	14	6	20

Attendance: 55,405

Game #2 – Sunday, September 26, 1971

@ Schaefer Stadium	1	2	3	4	Final
Detroit Lions (1-1)	3	14	3	14	34
NE Patriots (1-1)	0	0	7	0	7

Attendance: 61,054

Game #3 – Sunday, October 3, 1971

@ Schaefer Stadium	1	2	3	4	Final
Baltimore Colts (2-1)	14	3	0	6	23
NE Patriots (1-2)	0	3	0	0	3

Attendance: 61,232

Game #4 – Sunday, October 10, 1971

@ Schaefer Stadium	1	2	3	4	Final
NY Jets (1-3)	0	0	0	0	0
NE Patriots (2-2)	0	0	13	7	20

Attendance: 61,357

Game #5 – Sunday, October 17, 1971

@ Orange Bowl	1	2	3	4	Final
NE Patriots (2-3)	0	3	0	0	3
Miami Dolphins (3-1-1)	21	10	7	3	41

Attendance: 58,822

Game #6 – Sunday, October 24, 1971

@ Texas Stadium	1	2	3	4	Final
NE Patriots (2-4)	7	0	0	14	21
Dallas Cowboys (4-2)	10	24	0	10	44

Attendance: 65,708

Game #7 – Sunday, October 31, 1971

@ Candlestick Park	1	2	3	4	Final
NE Patriots (2-5)	0	0	7	3	10
San Francisco 49ers (5-2)	7	6	0	14	27

Attendance: 31,148

Game #8 – Sunday, November 7, 1971

@ Schaefer Stadium	1	2	3	4	Final
Houston Oilers (1-6-1)	0	6	7	7	20
NE Patriots (3-5)	7	7	0	14	28

Attendance: 53,155

PATRIOTS PASSION

Game #9 – Sunday, November 14, 1971

@ Schaefer Stadium	1	2	3	4	Final
Buffalo Bills (0-9)	7	13	10	3	33
NE Patriots (4-5)	7	21	7	3	38

Attendance: 57,446

Game #10 – Sunday, November 21, 1971

@Municipal Stadium	1	2	3	4	Final
NE Patriots (4-6)	0	7	0	0	7
Cleveland Browns (5-5)	10	7	0	10	27

Attendance: 65,238

Game #11 – Sunday, November 28, 1971

@ War Memorial	1	2	3	4	Final
NE Patriots (4-7)	3	3	7	7	20
Buffalo Bills (1-10)	0	17	0	10	27

Attendance: 27,166

Game #12 – Sunday, December 5, 1971

@ Schaefer Stadium	1	2	3	4	Final
Miami Dolphins (9-2-1)	7	3	3	0	13
NE Patriots (5-7)	17	3	14	0	34

Attendance: 61,457

Game #13 – Sunday, December 12, 1971

@ Shea Stadium	1	2	3	4	Final
NE Patriots (5-8)	0	3	0	3	6
NY Jets (5-8)	10	0	3	0	13

Attendance: 63,175

Game #14 – Sunday, December 19, 1971

@ Memorial Stadium	1	2	3	4	Final
NE Patriots (6-8)	0	14	0	7	21
Baltimore Colts (10-4)	0	3	7	7	17

Attendance: 57,942

Lifetime W-L record 72-89-9
Lifetime coin toss record 83-87

1972 (3-11) fifth in AFC East

Head Coaches – John Mazur (2-7), Phil Bengston (1-4)

1st round –Vikings received pick as compensation for Patriots signing Joe Kapp (10th overall)
Vikings selected Jeff Siemon, LB, Stanford
1st round pick – Pick (17th overall) acquired from Rams for Phil Olsen, was sent to Giants for Fred Dwyer who was then traded to Rams for their 1973 first round pick, Sam Cunningham, and Rick Cash.
Giants selected Eldridge Small, DB, Texas A&I (17th overall)
2nd round pick (first Patriots selection of 1972 Draft) – Tom Reynolds, WR, San Diego State (49th overall)

Game #1 – Sunday, September 17, 1972

@ Schaefer Stadium	1	2	3	4	Final
Cincinnati Bengals (1-0)	7	3	7	14	31
NE Patriots (0-1)	0	7	0	0	7

Attendance: 60,999

Game #2 – Sunday, September 24, 1972

@ Schaefer Stadium	1	2	3	4	Final
Atlanta Falcons (1-1)	3	3	14	0	20
NE Patriots (1-1)	0	7	0	14	21

Attendance: 60,999

Game #3 – Sunday, October 1, 1972

@ Schaefer Stadium	1	2	3	4	Final
WDC Redskins (2-1)	0	14	0	9	23
NE Patriots (2-1)	0	7	10	7	24

Attendance: 60,099

Game #4 – Sunday, October 8, 1972

@ War Memorial	1	2	3	4	Final
NE Patriots (2-2)	7	0	0	7	14
Buffalo Bills (2-2)	3	28	7	0	38

Attendance: 41,749

GAME BY GAME FROM DAY ONE

Game #5 – Sunday, October 15, 1972

@ Schaefer Stadium	1	2	3	4	Final
NY Jets (3-2)	7	14	0	20	41
NE Patriots (2-3)	0	6	7	0	13

Attendance: 60,099

Game #6 – Sunday, October 22, 1972

@ Three Rivers Stadium	1	2	3	4	Final
NE Patriots (2-4)	0	0	3	0	3
Pittsburgh Steelers (4-2)	10	7	13	3	33

Attendance: 46,081

Game #7 – Sunday, October 29, 1972

@ Shea Stadium	1	2	3	4	Final
NE Patriots (2-5)	3	0	0	7	10
NY Jets (5-2)	3	14	10	7	34

Attendance: 31,148

Game #8 – Monday, November 6, 1972

@ Schaefer Stadium	1	2	3	4	Final
Baltimore Colts (2-6)	7	3	14	0	24
NE Patriots (2-6)	3	0	7	7	17

Attendance: 60,099

Game #9 – Sunday, November 12, 1972

@ Orange Bowl	1	2	3	4	Final
NE Patriots (2-7)	0	0	0	0	0
Miami Dolphins (9-0)	17	14	7	14	52

Attendance: 80,010

Game #10 – Sunday, November 19, 1972

@ Schaefer Stadium	1	2	3	4	Final
Buffalo Bills (3-7)	0	17	0	10	27
NE Patriots (2-8)	7	0	14	3	24

Attendance: 60,099

Game #11 – Sunday, November 26, 1972

@ Memorial Stadium	1	2	3	4	Final
NE Patriots (2-9)	0	0	0	0	0
Baltimore Colts (4-7)	0	17	14	0	31

Attendance: 54,907

Game #12 – Sunday, December 3, 1972

@ Schaefer Stadium	1	2	3	4	Final
Miami Dolphins (12-0)	3	10	17	7	37
NE Patriots (2-10)	0	7	0	14	21

Attendance: 60,099

Game #13 – Sunday, December 10, 1972

@ Tulane Stadium	1	2	3	4	Final
NE Patriots (3-10)	0	14	3	0	17
NO Saints (2-10-1)	3	0	7	0	10

Attendance: 64,889

Game #14 – Sunday, December 17, 1972

@ Mile High Stadium	1	2	3	4	Final
NE Patriots (3-11)	0	7	0	14	21
Denver Broncos (5-9)	3	21	7	14	45

Attendance: 51,656

Lifetime W-L record	75-100-9
Lifetime coin toss record	90-94

1973 (5-9), third in AFC East
Head Coach – Chuck Fairbanks

1st round pick – John Hannah, T, Alabama (4th overall)
1st round pick – Sam Cunningham, RB, Southern California (11th overall), pick from Rams for Fred Dwyer, DT
1st round pick – Darryl Stingley, WR, Purdue (19th overall), pick from Bears for Carl Garrett, RB

Game #1 – Sunday, September 16, 1973

@ Schaefer Stadium	1	2	3	4	Final
Buffalo Bills (1-0)	7	3	7	14	31
NE Patriots (0-1)	6	0	7	0	13

Attendance: 56,114

Game #2 – Sunday, September 23, 1973

@ Schaefer Stadium	1	2	3	4	Final
KC Chiefs (1-1)	0	10	0	0	10
NE Patriots (0-2)	0	0	0	7	7

Attendance: 57,918

Game #3 – Sunday, September 30, 1973

@ Orange Bowl	1	2	3	4	Final
NE Patriots (0-3)	0	3	13	7	23
Miami Dolphins (2-1)	0	20	3	21	44

Attendance: 80,047

Game #4 – Sunday, October 7, 1973

@ Schaefer Stadium	1	2	3	4	Final
Baltimore Colts (1-3)	3	0	3	10	16
NE Patriots (1-3)	3	7	7	7	24

Attendance: 57,044

Game #5 – Sunday, October 14, 1973

@ Schaefer Stadium	1	2	3	4	Final
NY Jets (2-3)	3	0	3	3	9
NE Patriots (1-4)	0	0	7	0	7

Attendance: 58,659

Game #6 – Sunday, October 21, 1973

@ Soldier Field	1	2	3	4	Final
NE Patriots (2-4)	3	0	3	7	13
Chicago Bears (1-5)	0	7	3	0	10

Attendance: 55,701

Game #7 – Sunday, October 28, 1973

@ Schaefer Stadium	1	2	3	4	Final
Miami Dolphins (6-1)	7	6	10	7	30
NE Patriots (2-5)	7	7	0	0	14

Attendance: 61,279

Game #8 – Sunday, November 4, 1973

@ Veterans Stadium	1	2	3	4	Final
NE Patriots (2-6)	7	3	7	6	23
Phila. Eagles (3-4-1)	0	0	21	3	24

Attendance: 65,070

Game #9 – Sunday, November 11, 1973

@ Shea Stadium	1	2	3	4	Final
NE Patriots (2-7)	6	0	0	7	13
NY Jets (3-6)	7	13	3	10	33

Attendance: 60,737

Game #10 – Sunday, November 18, 1973

@ Schaefer Stadium	1	2	3	4	Final
GB Packers (3-5-2)	14	3	7	0	24
NE Patriots (3-7)	0	9	10	14	33

Attendance: 61, 279

Game #11 – Sunday, November 25, 1973

@ Astrodome	1	2	3	4	Final
NE Patriots (4-7)	10	14	3	5	32
Houston Oilers (1-10)	0	0	0	0	0

Attendance: 27,344

Game #12 – Sunday, December 2, 1973

@ Schaefer Stadium	1	2	3	4	Final
SD Chargers (2-9-1)	0	14	0	0	14
NE Patriots (5-7)s	3	13	7	7	30

Attendance: 58,150

GAME BY GAME FROM DAY ONE

Game #13 – Sunday, December 9, 1973

@ Rich Stadium	1	2	3	4	Final
NE Patriots (5-8)	3	3	7	0	13
Buffalo Bills (8-5)	7	10	17	3	37

Attendance: 75,841

Game #14 – Sunday, December 16, 1973

@ Memorial Stadium	1	2	3	4	Final
NE Patriots (5-9)	0	7	6	0	13
Baltimore Colts (4-10)	9	0	0	9	18

Attendance: 52,065

Lifetime W-L record   80-109-9
Lifetime coin toss record 95-103

1974 (7-7), tied for third in AFC East
Head Coach – Chuck Fairbanks

1st round pick – traded to 49ers for TE Bob Windsor;
49ers selected Wilbur Jackson, RB, Alabama (9th overall)
2nd round pick – Steve Corbett, G, Boston College (30th overall) pick from Bears
2nd round pick – Steve Nelson, LB, North Dakota State (34th overall)

Game #1 – Sunday, September 15, 1974

@ Schaefer Stadium	1	2	3	4	Final
Miami Dolphins (0-1)	0	10	7	7	24
NE Patriots (1-0)	7	17	7	3	34

Attendance: 55,006

Game #2 – Sunday, September 22, 1974

@ Yale Bowl	1	2	3	4	Final
NE Patriots (2-0)	7	7	7	7	28
NY Giants (0-2)	7	7	0	6	20

Attendance: 49,267

Game #3 – Sunday, September 29, 1974

@ Schaefer Stadium	1	2	3	4	Final
LA Rams (2-1)	7	0	0	7	14
NE Patriots (3-0)	0	7	6	7	20

Attendance: 61,279

Game #4 – Sunday, October 6, 1974

@ Schaefer Stadium	1	2	3	4	Final
Baltimore Colts (0-4)	0	3	0	0	3
NE Patriots (4-0)	14	7	14	7	42

Attendance: 59,502

Game #5 – Sunday, October 13, 1974

@ Shea Stadium	1	2	3	4	Final
NE Patriots (5-0)	7	3	0	14	24
NY Jets (1-4)	0	0	0	0	0

Attendance: 61,400

Game #6 – Sunday, October 20, 1974

@ Rich Stadium	1	2	3	4	Final
NE Patriots (5-1)	7	7	7	7	28
Buffalo Bills (1-5)	20	7	0	3	30

Attendance: 80,200

Game #7 – Sunday, October 27, 1974

@ Metropolitan Stadium	1	2	3	4	Final
NE Patriots (6-1)	3	7	0	7	17
Minnesota Vikings (5-2)	0	0	0	14	14

Attendance: 48,497

Game #8 – Sunday, November 3, 1974

@ Schaefer Stadium	1	2	3	4	Final
Buffalo Bills (7-1)	6	13	7	3	29
NE Patriots (6-2)	7	14	7	0	28

Attendance: 61,279

135

Game #9 – Sunday, November 10, 1974

@ Schaefer Stadium	1	2	3	4	Final
Cleveland Browns (3-6)	14	0	0	7	21
NE Patriots (6-3)	0	14	0	0	14

Attendance: 61,279

Game #10 – Sunday, November 17, 1974

@ Schaefer Stadium	1	2	3	4	Final
NY Jets (3-7)	7	7	7	0	21
NE Patriots (6-4)	0	3	10	3	16

Attendance: 61,279

Game #11 – Sunday, November 24, 1974

@ Memorial Stadium	1	2	3	4	Final
NE Patriots (7-4)	0	17	0	10	27
Baltimore Colts (2-9)	0	3	7	7	17

Attendance: 38,971

Game #12 – Sunday, December 1, 1974

@ Oakland-Alameda Col.	1	2	3	4	Final
NE Patriots (7-5)	6	7	6	7	26
Oakland Raiders (10-2)	7	13	7	14	41

Attendance: 54,020

Game #13 – Sunday, December 8, 1974

@ Schaefer Stadium	1	2	3	4	Final
Pitts. Steelers (9-3-1)	0	12	7	2	21
NE Patriots (7-6)	7	3	0	7	17

Attendance: 62,279

Game #14 – Sunday, December 16, 1974

@ Orange Bowl	1	2	3	4	Final
NE Patriots (7-7)	21	3	0	3	27
Miami Dolphins (11-3)	0	17	7	10	34

Attendance: 52,065

Lifetime W-L record	87-116-9
Lifetime coin toss record	104-108

1975 (3-11), tied for fourth in AFC East

Head Coach – Chuck Fairbanks

1st round pick – Russ Francis, TE, University of Oregon (9th overall)

Game #1 – Sunday, September 21, 1975

@ Schaefer Stadium	1	2	3	4	Final
Houston Oilers (1-0)	7	0	0	0	7
NE Patriots (0-1)	0	0	0	0	0

Attendance: 54,212

Game #2 – Sunday, September 28, 1975

@ Schaefer Stadium	1	2	3	4	Final
Miami Dolphins (1-1)	0	0	9	13	22
NE Patriots (0-2)	7	7	0	0	14

Attendance: 61,279

Game #3 – Sunday, October 5, 1975

@ Shea Stadium	1	2	3	4	Final
NE Patriots (0-3)	0	0	0	7	7
NY Jets (2-1)	0	19	10	7	36

Attendance: 61,415

Game #4 – Sunday, October 12, 1975

@ Riverfront Stadium	1	2	3	4	Final
NE Patriots (0-4)	0	7	3	0	10
Cincinnati Bengals (4-0)	0	17	7	3	27

Attendance: 55,856

GAME BY GAME FROM DAY ONE

Game #5 – Sunday, October 19, 1975

@ Schaefer Stadium	1	2	3	4	Final
Baltimore Colts (1-4)	7	0	3	0	10
NE Patriots (1-4)	0	14	0	7	21

Attendance: 56,884

Game #6 – Sunday, October 26, 1975

@ Schaefer Stadium	1	2	3	4	Final
San Francisco 49ers (2-4)	0	0	10	6	16
NE Patriots (2-4)	3	14	0	7	24

Attendance: 60,691

Game #7 – Sunday, November 2, 1975

@ Busch Stadium	1	2	3	4	Final
NE Patriots (2-5)	3	7	7	0	17
St. Louis Cardinals (5-2)	0	7	3	14	24

Attendance: 47,263

Game #8 – Sunday, November 9, 1975

@ San Diego Stadium	1	2	3	4	Final
NE Patriots (3-5)	10	13	7	3	33
SD Chargers (0-8)	3	3	10	3	19

Attendance: 26,090

Game #9 – Sunday, November 16, 1975

@ Schaefer Stadium	1	2	3	4	Final
Dallas Cowboys (6-3)	10	7	7	10	34
NE Patriots (3-6)	0	10	7	14	31

Attendance: 61,279

Game #10 – Sunday, November 23, 1975

@ Rich Stadium	1	2	3	4	Final
NE Patriots (3-7)	7	14	7	3	31
Buffalo Bills (6-4)	14	10	7	14	45

Attendance: 61,279

Game #11 – Monday, December 1, 1975

@ Orange Bowl	1	2	3	4	Final
NE Patriots (3-8)	0	0	0	7	7
Miami Dolphins (8-3)	7	7	3	3	20

Attendance: 68,480

Game #12 – Sunday, December 7, 1975

@ Schaefer Stadium	1	2	3	4	Final
NY Jets (3-9)	6	7	7	10	30
NE Patriots (3-9)	0	7	7	14	28

Attendance: 57,539

Game #13 – Sunday, December 14, 1975

@ Schaefer Stadium	1	2	3	4	Final
Buffalo Bills (8-5)	6	7	14	7	34
NE Patriots (3-10)	0	7	0	7	14

Attendance: 59,646

Game #14 – Sunday, December 21, 1975

@ Memorial Stadium	1	2	3	4	Final
NE Patriots (3-11)	7	7	0	7	21
Baltimore Colts (10-4)	7	3	10	14	34

Attendance: 50,801

Lifetime W-L record	90-127-9
Lifetime coin toss record	110-116

1976 (11-3), second in AFC East
Head Coach – Chuck Fairbanks

1st round pick – Mike Haynes, DB, Arizona State (5th overall)
1st round pick – Pete Brock, C, University of Colorado (12th overall) – pick from 49ers for Jim Plunkett
1st round pick – Tim Fox, DB, Ohio State (21st overall) – pick from Oilers through 49ers for Jim Plunkett

Game #1 – Sunday, September 12, 1976

@ Schaefer Stadium	1	2	3	4	Final
Baltimore Colts (1-0)	3	14	3	7	27
NE Patriots (0-1)s	3	3	0	7	13

Attendance: 43,637

Game #2 – Sunday, September 19, 1976

@ Schaefer Stadium	1	2	3	4	Final
Miami Dolphins (1-1)	0	7	0	7	14
NE Patriots (1-1)	0	13	7	10	30

Attendance: 46,227

Game #3 – Sunday, September 26, 1976

@ Three Rivers Stadium	1	2	3	4	Final
NE Patriots (2-1)	6	3	14	7	30
Pittsburgh Steelers (1-2)	7	6	7	7	27

Attendance: 50,350

Game #4 – Sunday, October 3, 1976

@ Schaefer Stadium	1	2	3	4	Final
Oakland Raiders (3-1)	0	10	0	7	17
NE Patriots (3-1)	7	14	14	13	48

Attendance: 61,279

Game #5 – Sunday, October 10, 1976

@ Pontiac Silverdome	1	2	3	4	Final
NE Patriots (3-2)	0	3	7	0	10
Detroit Lions (2-3)	13	7	0	10	30

Attendance: 63,711

Game #6 – Monday, October 18, 1976

@ Schaefer Stadium	1	2	3	4	Final
NY Jets (1-5)	0	0	7	0	7
NE Patriots (4-2)	7	13	21	0	41

Attendance: 51,236

Game #7 – Sunday, October 24, 1976

@ Rich Stadium	1	2	3	4	Final
NE Patriots (5-2)	0	6	13	7	26
Buffalo Bills (2-5)	0	3	6	13	22

Attendance: 50,383

Game #8 – Sunday, October 31, 1976

@ Orange Bowl	1	2	3	4	Final
NE Patriots (5-3)	0	3	0	3	6
Miami Dolphins (4-4)	0	10	0	0	10

Attendance: 57,984

Game #9 – Sunday, November 7, 1976

@ Schaefer Stadium	1	2	3	4	Final
Buffalo Bills (2-7)	0	3	0	7	10
NE Patriots (6-3)	3	10	7	0	20

Attendance: 61,279

Game #10 – Sunday, November 14, 1976

@ Memorial Stadium	1	2	3	4	Final
NE Patriots (7-3)	7	14	0	0	21
Baltimore Colts (8-2)	7	7	0	0	14

Attendance: 60,020

Game #11 – Sunday, November 21, 1976

@ Shea Stadium	1	2	3	4	Final
NE Patriots (8-3)	14	7	7	10	38
NY Jets (3-8)	10	7	0	7	24

Attendance: 58,509

Game #12 – Sunday, November 28, 1976

@ Schaefer Stadium	1	2	3	4	Final
Denver Broncos (7-5)	0	0	7	7	14
NE Patriots (9-3)	7	24	0	7	38

Attendance: 61,279

Game #13 – Sunday, December 5, 1976

@ Schaefer Stadium	1	2	3	4	Final
NO Saints (4-9)	0	3	0	3	6
NE Patriots (10-3)	0	13	0	14	27

Attendance: 54,057

Game #14 – Sunday, December 12, 1976

@ Tampa Stadium	1	2	3	4	Final
NE Patriots (11-3)	0	7	7	17	31
TB Buccaneers (0-14)	0	14	0	0	14

Attendance: 46,475

Game #15 – AFC Divisional Playoff Game
Saturday, December 18, 1976

@ Oakland-Alameda Col.	1	2	3	4	Final
NE Patriots (11-4)	7	0	14	0	21
Oakland Raiders (14-1)	3	7	0	14	24

Attendance: 54,037

Lifetime W-L record   101-131-9
Lifetime coin toss record   119-122

1977 (9-5), third in AFC East
Head Coach – Chuck Fairbanks

1st round pick – Raymond Clayborn, DB, Texas (16th overall) pick from 49ers for Jim Plunkett, QB
1st round pick – Stanley Morgan, WR, University of Tennessee (25th overall)

Game #1 – Sunday, September 18, 1977

@ Schaefer Stadium	1	2	3	4	Final
KC Chiefs (0-1)	14	0	0	3	17
NE Patriots (1-0)	7	7	7	0	21

Attendance: 58,288

Game #2 – Monday, September 26, 1977

@Municipal Stadium	1	2	3	4	OT	Final
NE Patriots (1-1)	0	17	0	10	0	27
Cleveland Browns (2-0)	7	0	10	10	3	30

Attendance: 77,910

Game #3 – Sunday, October 2, 1977

@ Shea Stadium	1	2	3	4	Final
NE Patriots (1-2)	14	3	3	7	27
NY Jets (1-2)	14	0	0	16	30

Attendance: 49,801

Game #4 – Sunday, October 9, 1977

@ Schaefer Stadium	1	2	3	4	Final
Seattle Seahawks (0-4)	0	0	0	0	0
NE Patriots (2-2)	7	14	10	0	31

Attendance: 54,363

Game #5 – Sunday, October 16, 1977

@ San Diego Stadium	1	2	3	4	Final
NE Patriots (3-2)	7	0	7	10	24
SD Chargers (3-2)	6	0	7	7	20

Attendance: 51,143

Game #6 – Sunday, October 23, 1977

@ Schaefer Stadium	1	2	3	4	Final
Baltimore Colts (5-1)	0	0	3	0	3
NE Patriots (4-2)	7	0	10	0	17

Attendance: 61,279

PATRIOTS PASSION

Game #7 – Sunday, October 30, 1977

@ Schaefer Stadium	1	2	3	4	Final
NY Jets (2-5)	3	7	0	3	13
NE Patriots (5-3)	3	7	14	0	24

Attendance: 61,279

Game #8 – Sunday, November 6, 1977

@ Schaefer Stadium	1	2	3	4	Final
Buffalo Bills (2-6)	14	3	0	7	24
NE Patriots (5-3)	7	0	0	7	14

Attendance: 61,279

Game #9 – Sunday, November 13, 1977

@ Orange Bowl	1	2	3	4	Final
NE Patriots (5-4)	0	0	0	5	5
Miami Dolphins (7-2)	0	7	0	10	17

Attendance: 67,907

Game #10 – Sunday, November 20, 1977

@ Rich Stadium	1	2	3	4	Final
NE Patriots (6-4)	3	0	3	14	20
Buffalo Bills (2-8)	0	0	7	0	7

Attendance: 31,157

Game #11 – Sunday, November 27, 1977

@ Schaefer Stadium	1	2	3	4	Final
Phila. Eagles (3-8)	0	0	0	6	6
NE Patriots (7-4)	7	7	0	0	14

Attendance: 58,192

Game #12 – Sunday, December 4, 1977

@ Fulton Cnty. Stadium	1	2	3	4	Final
NE Patriots (8-4)	3	3	3	7	16
Atlanta Falcons (6-6)	0	0	7	3	10

Attendance: 60,738

Game #13 – Sunday, December 11, 1977

@ Schaefer Stadium	1	2	3	4	Final
Miami Dolphins (9-4)	0	3	7	0	10
NE Patriots (9-4)	14	0	0	0	14

Attendance: 61,279

Game #14 – Sunday, December 18, 1977

@ Memorial Stadium	1	2	3	4	Final
NE Patriots (9-5)	0	14	10	0	24
Baltimore Colts (10-4)	0	3	13	14	30

Attendance: 60,763

Lifetime W-L record	110-136-9
Lifetime coin toss record	123-132
Lifetime OT record	0-1

1978 (11-5), first in AFC East

Head Coaches – Chuck Fairbanks (11-4), Ron Erhardt and Hank Bullough co-head coaches (0-1)

1st round pick – Bob Cryder, G, Alabama (18th overall)

Game #1 – Sunday, September 3, 1978

@ Schaefer Stadium	1	2	3	4	Final
WDC Redskins (1-0)	3	0	6	7	16
NE Patriots (0-1)	0	0	7	7	14

Attendance: 55,063

Game #2 – Sunday, September 10, 1978

@ Busch Stadium	1	2	3	4	Final
NE Patriots (1-1)	3	13	0	0	16
St. Louis Cardinals (0-2)	0	0	6	0	6

Attendance: 49,555

GAME BY GAME FROM DAY ONE

Game #3 – Monday, September 18, 1978

@ Schaefer Stadium	1	2	3	4	Final
Baltimore Colts (1-2)	0	7	0	27	34
NE Patriots (1-2)	6	7	0	14	27

Attendance: 57,503

Game #4 – Sunday, September 24, 1978

@ Oakland-Alameda Col.	1	2	3	4	Final
NE Patriots (2-2)	0	7	7	7	21
Oakland Raiders (2-2)	14	0	0	0	14

Attendance: 53,500

Game #5 – Sunday, October 1, 1978

@ Schaefer Stadium	1	2	3	4	Final
SD Chargers (1-4)	0	13	7	3	23
NE Patriots (3-2)	7	0	7	14	28

Attendance: 61,297

Game #6 – Sunday, October 8, 1978

@ Schaefer Stadium	1	2	3	4	Final
Philadelphia Eagles (3-3)	0	7	7	0	14
NE Patriots (4-2)	10	7	7	0	24

Attendance: 61,297

Game #7 – Sunday, October 15, 1978

@ Riverfront Stadium	1	2	3	4	Final
NE Patriots (5-2)	3	0	0	7	10
Cincinnati Bengals (0-7)	0	3	0	0	3

Attendance: 56,257

Game #8 – Sunday, October 22, 1978

@ Schaefer Stadium	1	2	3	4	Final
Miami Dolphins (5-3)	7	7	3	3	24
NE Patriots (6-2)	0	17	7	9	33

Attendance: 61,297

Game #9 – Sunday, October 29, 1978

@ Schaefer Stadium	1	2	3	4	Final
NY Jets (5-4)	7	0	0	14	21
NE Patriots (7-2)	21	20	7	7	55

Attendance: 61,297

Game #10 – Sunday, November 5, 1978

@ Rich Stadium	1	2	3	4	Final
NE Patriots (8-2)	0	7	7	0	14
Buffalo Bills (3-7)	3	0	0	7	10

Attendance: 46,101

Game #11 – Sunday, November 12, 1978

@ Schaefer Stadium	1	2	3	4	Final
Houston Oilers (7-4)	0	7	7	12	26
NE Patriots (8-3)	6	17	0	0	23

Attendance: 61,297

Game #12 – Sunday, November 19, 1978

@ Shea Stadium	1	2	3	4	Final
NE Patriots (9-3)	0	10	0	9	19
NY Jets (6-6)	7	0	3	7	17

Attendance: 60,372

Game #13 – Sunday, November 26, 1978

@ Memorial Stadium	1	2	3	4	Final
NE Patriots (10-3)	14	7	7	7	35
Baltimore Colts (5-8)	7	0	7	0	14

Attendance: 49,404

Game #14 – Sunday, December 3, 1978

@ Texas Stadium	1	2	3	4	Final
NE Patriots (10-4)	7	3	0	0	10
Dallas Cowboys (10-4)	3	0	7	7	17

Attendance: 65,045

Game #15 – Sunday, December 10, 1978

@ Schaefer Stadium	1	2	3	4	Final
Buffalo Bills (4-11)	0	10	7	7	24
NE Patriots (11-4)	0	7	7	12	26

Attendance: 61,279

Game #16 – Monday, December 18, 1978

@ Orange Bowl	1	2	3	4	Final
NE Patriots (11-5)	0	0	0	3	3
Miami Dolphins (11-5)	7	6	7	3	23

Attendance: 75,445

Game #17 – American Football Conference Divisional Playoff
Sunday, December 31, 1978

@ Schaefer Stadium	1	2	3	4	Final
Houston Oilers (12-6)	0	21	3	7	31
NE Patriots (11-6)	0	0	7	7	14

Attendance: 61,297

Lifetime W-L record	121-142-9
Lifetime coin toss record	130-142
Lifetime OT record	0-1

1979 (9-7), second in AFC East
Head Coach – Ron Erhardt

1st round pick – Rick Sanford, DB, South Carolina (25th overall)

Game #1 – Monday, September 3, 1979

@ Schaefer Stadium	1	2	3	4	OT	Final
Pittsburgh Steelers (1-0)	0	6	0	7	3	16
NE Patriots (0-1)	7	6	0	0	0	13

Attendance: 60,798

Game #2 – Sunday, September 9, 1979

@ Schaefer Stadium	1	2	3	4	Final
NY Jets (0-2)	3	0	0	0	3
NE Patriots (1-1)	14	21	7	14	56

Attendance: 53,115

Game #3 – Sunday, September 18, 1978

@ Riverfront Stadium	1	2	3	4	Final
NE Patriots (2-1)	0	7	7	6	20
Cincinnati Bengals (0-3)	0	0	7	7	14

Attendance: 41,805

Game #4 – Sunday, September 24, 1979

@ Schaefer Stadium	1	2	3	4	Final
SD Chargers (3-1)	0	14	0	7	21
NE Patriots (3-1)	17	3	0	7	27

Attendance: 60,916

Game #5 – Monday, October 1, 1979

@ Lambeau Field	1	2	3	4	Final
NE Patriots (3-2)	7	7	0	0	14
GB Packers (2-3)	7	14	7	0	27

Attendance: 52,842

Game #6 – Sunday, October 7, 1979

@ Schaefer Stadium	1	2	3	4	Final
Detroit Lions (1-5)	0	3	14	0	17
NE Patriots (4-2)	0	14	0	10	24

Attendance: 60,629

Game #7 – Sunday, October 14, 1979

@ Soldier Field	1	2	3	4	Final
NE Patriots (5-2)	14	0	3	10	27
Chicago Bears (3-4)	0	7	0	0	7

Attendance: 54,128

Game #8 – Sunday, October 21, 1979

@ Schaefer Stadium	1	2	3	4	Final
Miami Dolphins (5-3)	10	3	0	0	13
NE Patriots (6-2)	0	7	7	14	28

Attendance: 61,096

GAME BY GAME FROM DAY ONE

Game #9 – Sunday, October 28, 1979

@ Memorial Stadium	1	2	3	4	Final
NE Patriots (6-3)	13	0	6	7	26
Baltimore Colts (3-6)	14	3	7	7	31

Attendance: 41,029

Game #10 – Sunday, November 4, 1979

@ Rich Stadium	1	2	3	4	Final
NE Patriots (7-3)	0	6	10	10	26
Buffalo Bills (4-6)	6	0	0	0	6

Attendance: 67,935

Game #11 – Sunday, November 11, 1979

@ Mile High Stadium	1	2	3	4	Final
NE Patriots (7-4)	0	7	3	0	10
Denver Broncos (8-3)	24	14	0	7	45

Attendance: 74,379

Game #12 – Sunday, November 18, 1979

@ Schaefer Stadium	1	2	3	4	Final
Baltimore Colts (4-8)	7	0	7	7	21
NE Patriots (8-4)	6	27	10	7	50

Attendance: 60,879

Game #13 – Sunday, November 25, 1979

@ Schaefer Stadium	1	2	3	4	OT	Final
Buffalo Bills (7-6)	0	3	3	7	3	16
NE Patriots (8-5)	0	3	0	10	0	13

Attendance: 60,991

Game #14 – Thursday, November 29, 1979

@ Orange Bowl	1	2	3	4	Final
NE Patriots (8-6)	0	17	0	7	24
Miami Dolphins (9-5)	3	10	16	10	39

Attendance: 69,174

Game #15 – Sunday, December 9, 1979

@ Shea Stadium	1	2	3	4	Final
NE Patriots (8-7)	0	12	7	7	26
NY Jets (7-8)	7	10	7	3	27

Attendance: 60,372

Game #16 – Sunday, December 18, 1979

@ Schaefer Stadium	1	2	3	4	Final
Minnesota Vikings (7-9)	6	7	3	7	23
NE Patriots (9-7)	7	0	0	20	27

Attendance: 54,719

Lifetime W-L record	130-149-9
Lifetime coin toss record	140-148
Lifetime OT record	0-3

1980 (10-6), second in AFC East

Head Coach – Ron Erhardt

First round pick – Roland James, DB, Tennessee (14th overall)
1st round pick – Vagas Ferguson, RB, Notre Dame (25th overall) pick from Oilers for Leon Gray, T

Game #1 – Sunday, September 7, 1980

@ Schaefer Stadium	1	2	3	4	Final
Cleveland Browns (0-1)	0	3	0	14	17
NE Patriots (1-0)	3	10	14	7	34

Attendance: 49,222

Game #2 – Sunday, September 14, 1980

@ Schaefer Stadium	1	2	3	4	Final
Atlanta Falcon (1-1)	14	14	3	6	37
NE Patriots (1-1)	7	14	0	0	21

Attendance: 48,321

PATRIOTS PASSION

Game #3 – Sunday, September 21, 1980

@ Kingdome	1	2	3	4	Final
NE Patriots (2-1)	3	17	7	10	37
Seattle Seahawks (1-2)	3	14	0	14	31

Attendance: 61,035

Game #4 – Monday, September 29, 1980

@ Schaefer Stadium	1	2	3	4	Final
Denver Broncos (1-3)	7	0	7	0	14
NE Patriots (3-1)	3	7	7	6	23

Attendance: 59,602

Game #5 – Sunday, October 5, 1980

@ Shea Stadium	1	2	3	4	Final
NE Patriots (4-1)	7	7	7	0	21
NY Jets (0-5)	6	0	0	5	11

Attendance: 53,603

Game #6 – Sunday, October 12, 1980

@ Schaefer Stadium	1	2	3	4	Final
Miami Dolphins (3-3)	0	0	0	0	0
NE Patriots (5-1)	10	7	0	17	34

Attendance: 60,377

Game #7 – Sunday, October 19, 1980

@ Memorial Stadium	1	2	3	4	Final
NE Patriots (6-1)	7	3	17	10	37
Baltimore Colts (4-3)	7	7	7	0	21

Attendance: 53,924

Game #8 – Sunday, October 26, 1980

@ Rich Stadium	1	2	3	4	Final
NE Patriots (6-2)	3	0	10	0	13
Buffalo Bills (6-2)	0	14	0	17	31

Attendance: 75,092

Game #10 – Monday, November 10, 1980

@ Astrodome	1	2	3	4	Final
NE Patriots (7-3)	0	6	14	14	34
Houston Oilers (7-3)	3	21	0	14	38

Attendance: 51,524

Game #11 – Sunday, November 17, 1980

@ Schaefer Stadium	1	2	3	4	Final
LA Rams (7-4)	7	0	10	0	17
NE Patriots (7-4)	0	14	0	0	14

Attendance: 60,609

Game #12 – Sunday, November 23, 1980

@ Schaefer Stadium	1	2	3	4	Final
Baltimore Colts (6-6)	0	0	7	14	21
NE Patriots (8-4)	7	3	10	27	47

Attendance: 60,994

Game #13 – Sunday, November 30, 1980

@ Candlestick Park	1	2	3	4	Final
NE Patriots (8-5)	0	3	7	7	17
San Francisco 49ers (5-8)	7	7	7	0	21

Attendance: 45,254

Game #14 – Monday, December 8, 1980

@ Orange Bowl	1	2	3	4	OT	Final
NE Patriots (8-6)	0	6	0	7	0	13
Miami Dolphins (7-7)	0	0	6	7	3	16

Attendance: 63,292

Game #9 – Sunday, November 2, 1980

@ Schaefer Stadium	1	2	3	4	Final
NY Jets (2-7)	0	14	0	7	21
NE Patriots (7-2)	17	14	3	0	34

Attendance: 60,834

GAME BY GAME FROM DAY ONE

Game #15 – Sunday, December 14, 1980

@ Schaefer Stadium	1	2	3	4	Final
Buffalo Bills (10-5)	0	0	0	2	2
NE Patriots (9-6)	7	7	7	3	24

Attendance: 58,324

Game #16 – Sunday, December 21, 1980

@Superdome	1	2	3	4	Final
NE Patriots (10-6)	3	14	7	14	38
NO Saints (1-15)	10	3	7	7	27

Attendance: 38,277

Lifetime W-L record   140-155-9
Lifetime coin toss record   145-159
Lifetime OT record   0-4

1981 (2-14), fifth in AFC East
Head Coach – Ron Erhardt
1st round pick – Brian Holloway, OT, Stanford (19th overall)

Game #1 – Sunday, September 6, 1981

@ Schaefer Stadium	1	2	3	4	Final
Baltimore Colts (1-0)	10	3	3	13	29
NE Patriots (0-1)	0	14	0	14	28

Attendance: 49,572

Game #2 – Sunday, September 13, 1981

@ Veterans Stadium	1	2	3	4	Final
NE Patriots (0-2)	3	0	0	0	3
Phila. Eagles (2-0)	0	3	10	0	13

Attendance: 71,089

Game #3 – Monday, September 21, 1981

@ Schaefer Stadium	1	2	3	4	Final
Dallas Cowboys (3-0)	7	10	7	11	35
NE Patriots (0-3)	7	7	7	0	21

Attendance: 60,311

Game #4 – Sunday, September 27, 1981

@ Three Rivers Stadium	1	2	3	4	OT	Final
NE Patriots (0-4)	0	7	0	14	0	21
Pittsburgh Steelers (2-2)	7	7	7	0	6	27

Attendance: 53,344

Game #5 – Sunday, October 4, 1981

@ Schaefer Stadium	1	2	3	4	Final
KC Chiefs (2-3)	7	0	3	7	17
NE Patriots (1-4)	7	7	10	9	33

Attendance: 55,931

Game #6 – Sunday, October 11, 1981

@ Shea Stadium	1	2	3	4	Final
NE Patriots (1-5)	0	14	7	3	24
NY Jets (2-3-1)	7	14	7	0	28

Attendance: 55,093

Game #7 – Sunday, October 18, 1981

@ Schaefer Stadium	1	2	3	4	Final
Houston Oilers (4-3)	0	10	0	0	10
NE Patriots (2-5)	7	0	17	14	38

Attendance: 53,924

Game #8 – Sunday, October 25, 1981

@ R.F.K. Stadium	1	2	3	4	Final
NE Patriots (2-6)	6	9	0	7	22
WDC Redskins (2-6)	7	7	10	0	24

Attendance: 50,394

PATRIOTS PASSION

Game #9 – Sunday, November 1, 1981

@ Oakland-Alameda Col.	1	2	3	4	Final
NE Patriots (2-7)	3	7	7	0	17
Oakland Raiders (3-4)	3	10	0	14	27

Attendance: 44,426

Game #10 – Sunday, November 8, 1981

@ Schaefer Stadium	1	2	3	4	OT	Final
Miami Dolphins (7-2-1)	0	6	14	7	3	30
NE Patriots (2-8)	7	10	0	10	0	27

Attendance: 60,436

Game #11 – Sunday, November 15, 1981

@ Schaefer Stadium	1	2	3	4	Final
NY Jets (6-4-1)	0	10	7	0	17
NE Patriots (2-9)	0	3	3	0	6

Attendance: 45,342

Game #12 – Sunday, November 22, 1981

@ Rich Stadium	1	2	3	4	Final
NE Patriots (2-10)	7	0	3	7	17
Buffalo Bills (7-5)	3	10	0	7	20

Attendance: 71,593

Game #13 – Sunday, November 29, 1981

@ Schaefer Stadium	1	2	3	4	Final
St. Louis Cardinals (6-7)	3	3	7	14	27
NE Patriots (2-11)	7	0	6	07	20

Attendance: 39,946

Game #14 – Sunday, December 6, 1981

@ Orange Bowl	1	2	3	4	Final
NE Patriots (2-12)	7	0	7	0	14
Miami Dolphins (9-4-1)	0	14	7	3	24

Attendance: 50,421

Game #15 – Sunday, December 13, 1981

@ Schaefer Stadium	1	2	3	4	Final
Buffalo Bills (10-5)	14	3	2	0	19
NE Patriots (2-13)	0	7	0	3	10

Attendance: 42,549

Game #16 – Sunday, December 20, 1981

@ Memorial Stadium	1	2	3	4	Final
NE Patriots (2-14)	7	7	0	7	21
Baltimore Colts (1-15)	10	7	6	0	23

Attendance: 17,073

Lifetime W-L record	142-169-9
Lifetime coin toss record	151-169
Lifetime OT record	0-6

1982 (5-4), third in AFC East
Head Coach – Ron Meyer

1st round pick – Ken Sims DE Texas (1st overall)
1st round pick – Lester Williams, DT, Miami (FL) (27th overall) pick from 49ers for Russ Francis, TE

Game #1 – Sunday, September 12 1982

@ Memorial Stadium	1	2	3	4	Final
NE Patriots (1-0)	3	7	7	7	24
Baltimore Colts (0-1)	3	7	3	0	13

Attendance: 39,055

Game #2 – Sunday, September 19, 1982

@ Schaefer Stadium	1	2	3	4	Final
NY Jets (1-1)	0	10	7	14	31
NE Patriots (1-1)	0	0	7	0	7

Attendance: 53,515

GAME BY GAME FROM DAY ONE

Players' Strike-Mid Season

The NFL Players Association went out on strike on September 21, 1982 over a dispute about the percentage of gross revenues the league was giving to the players' union. The strike lasted 57 days until both sides came to an agreement on November 16, 1982. The season was cut back to a nine-game schedule and a 16-team playoff at the conclusion of the regular season.

Game #3 – Sunday, November 21, 1982

@ Municipal Stadium	1	2	3	4	Final
NE Patriots (1-2)	0	0	0	7	7
Cleveland Browns (2-1)	0	0	0	10	10

Attendance: 47,281

Game #4 – Sunday, November 28, 1982

@ Schaefer Stadium	1	2	3	4	Final
Houston Oilers (1-3)	7	0	0	14	21
NE Patriots (2-2)	14	6	0	9	29

Attendance: 33,602

Game #5 – Sunday, December 5, 1982

@ Soldier Field	1	2	3	4	Final
NE Patriots (2-3)	0	6	7	0	13
Chicago Bears (2-3)	14	9	0	3	26

Attendance: 36,973

Game #6 – Sunday, December 12, 1982

@ Schaefer Stadium	1	2	3	4	Final
Miami Dolphins (4-2)	0	0	0	0	0
NE Patriots (3-3)	0	0	0	3	3

Attendance: 25,716

Game #7 – Sunday, December 19, 1982

@ Kingdome	1	2	3	4	Final
NE Patriots (4-3)	3	7	3	3	16
Seattle Seahawks (3-4)	0	0	0	0	0

Attendance: 53,457

Game #8 – Sunday, December 26, 1982

@ Three Rivers Stadium	1	2	3	4	Final
NE Patriots (4-4)	0	0	7	7	14
Pittsburgh Steelers (5-3)	10	10	0	17	37

Attendance: 50,515

Game #9 – Sunday, January 3, 1983

@ Schaefer Stadium	1	2	3	4	Final
Buffalo Bills (4-5)	0	13	3	3	19
NE Patriots (5-4)	3	7	6	14	30

Attendance: 36,218

Game #10 – American Football Conference Wild Card Playoff Game
Saturday, January 8, 1983

@ Orange Bowl	1	2	3	4	Final
NE Patriots (5-5)	0	3	3	7	13
Miami Dolphins (8-2)	0	14	7	7	28

Attendance: 68,842

Lifetime W-L record	147-174--9
Lifetime coin toss record	155-175
Lifetime OT record	0-6

1983 (8-8), tied second in AFC East
Head Coach – Ron Meyer

1st round pick – Tony Eason, QB, Illinois (15th overall)

Game #1 – Sunday, September 4, 1983

@ Sullivan Stadium	1	2	3	4	OT	Final
Baltimore Colts (1-0)	3	10	7	3	6	29
NE Patriots (0-1)	0	13	3	7	0	23

Attendance: 45,526

Game #2 – Sunday, September 11, 1983

@ Orange Bowl	1	2	3	4	Final
NE Patriots (0-2)	3	0	0	21	24
Miami Dolphins (2-0)	7	10	10	7	34

Attendance: 59,343

Game #3 – Monday, September 18, 1983

@ Sullivan Stadium	1	2	3	4	Final
NY Jets (1-2)	0	13	0	0	13
NE Patriots (1-2)	13	3	7	0	23

Attendance: 43,182

Game #4 – Sunday, September 25, 1983

@ Three Rivers Stadium	1	2	3	4	Final
NE Patriots (2-2)	7	7	7	7	28
Pittsburgh Steelers (2-2)	7	6	0	10	23

Attendance: 58,282

Game #5 – Sunday, October 2, 1983

@ Sullivan Stadium	1	2	3	4	Final
San Francisco 49ers (4-1)	7	10	13	3	33
NE Patriots (2-3)	6	0	0	7	13

Attendance: 54,293

Game #6 – Sunday, October 9, 1983

@ Memorial Stadium	1	2	3	4	Final
NE Patriots (2-4)	7	0	0	0	7
Baltimore Colts (4-2)	0	0	7	5	12

Attendance: 35,618

Game #7 – Sunday, October 16, 1983

@ Sullivan Stadium	1	2	3	4	Final
SD Chargers (3-4)	7	14	0	0	21
NE Patriots (3-4)	3	7	3	24	37

Attendance: 59,016

Game #8 – Sunday, October 23, 1983

@ Rich Stadium	1	2	3	4	Final
NE Patriots (4-4)	0	7	0	24	31
Buffalo Bills (5-3)	0	0	0	0	0

Attendance: 60,424

Game #9 – Sunday, October 30, 1983

@ Atlanta-Fulton Cty.	1	2	3	4	Final
NE Patriots (4-5)	0	0	0	13	13
Atlanta Falcons (4-5)	3	14	7	0	24

Attendance: 47,546

Game #10 – Sunday, November 6, 1983

@ Sullivan Stadium	1	2	3	4	Final
Buffalo Bills (6-4)	0	0	0	7	7
NE Patriots (5-5)	0	14	7	0	21

Attendance: 42,604

Game #11 – Sunday, November 13, 1983

@ Sullivan Stadium	1	2	3	4	Final
Miami Dolphins (7-4)	0	6	0	0	6
NE Patriots (6-5)	7	7	3	0	17

Attendance: 60,771

Game #12 – Sunday, November 20, 1983

@ Sullivan Stadium	1	2	3	4	Final
Cleveland Browns (7-5)	3	17	3	7	30
NE Patriots (6-6)	0	0	0	0	0

Attendance: 40,987

Game #13 – Sunday, November 27, 1983

@ Shea Stadium	1	2	3	4	Final
NE Patriots (6-7)	0	0	3	0	3
NY Jets (6-7)	0	3	13	10	26

Attendance: 48,620

Game #14 – Sunday, December 4, 1983

@ Sullivan Stadium	1	2	3	4	Final
New Orleans Saints (7-7)	0	0	0	0	0
NE Patriots (7-7)	7	0	0	0	7

Attendance: 24,579

Game #15 – Sunday, December 11, 1983

@ Anaheim Stadium	1	2	3	4	Final
NE Patriots (8-7)	0	7	7	7	21
LA Rams (8-7)	7	0	0	0	7

Attendance: 46,503

Game #16 – Sunday, December 18, 1983

@ Kingdome	1	2	3	4	Final
NE Patriots (8-8)	0	6	0	0	6
Seattle Seahawks (9-7)	3	7	7	7	24

Attendance: 59,688

Lifetime W-L record   155-182-9
Lifetime coin toss record   166-180
Lifetime OT record   0-7

1984 (9-7), second in AFC East

Head Coaches – Ron Meyer (5-3), Raymond Berry (4-4)

1st round pick – Irving Fryar, WR, Nebraska (1st overall)

Game #1 – Sunday, September 2, 1984

@ Rich Stadium	1	2	3	4	Final
NE Patriots (1-0)	14	7	0	0	21
Buffalo Bills (0-1)	0	3	7	7	17

Attendance: 48,528

Game #2 – Sunday, September 9, 1984

@ Orange Bowl	1	2	3	4	Final
NE Patriots (1-1)	0	7	0	0	7
Miami Dolphins (2-0)	0	7	14	7	28

Attendance: 66,083

Game #3 – Sunday, September 16, 1984

@ Sullivan Stadium	1	2	3	4	Final
Seattle Seahawks (2-1)	9	14	0	0	23
NE Patriots (2-1)	0	7	14	17	38

Attendance: 43,140

Game #4 – Sunday, September 23 1984

@ Sullivan Stadium	1	2	3	4	Final
WDC Redskins (2-2)	7	13	3	3	26
NE Patriots (2-2)	0	0	7	3	10

Attendance: 60,503

Game #5 – Sunday, September 30, 1984

@ Giants Stadium	1	2	3	4	Final
NE Patriots (3-2)	7	7	14	0	28
NY Jets (3-2)	7	7	0	7	21

Attendance: 68,978

Game #6 – Sunday, October 7, 1984

@Municipal Stadium	1	2	3	4	Final
NE Patriots (4-2)	3	0	7	7	17
Cleveland Browns (1-5)	0	9	7	0	16

Attendance: 53,036

PATRIOTS PASSION

Game #7 – Sunday, October 14, 1984

@ Sullivan Stadium	1	2	3	4	Final
Cincinnati Bengals (1-6)	7	7	0	0	14
NE Patriots (5-2)	3	0	7	10	20

Attendance: 48,154

Game #8 – Sunday, October 21, 1984

@ Sullivan Stadium	1	2	3	4	Final
Miami Dolphins (8-0)	3	13	14	14	44
NE Patriots (5-3)	3	7	7	7	24

Attendance: 60,711

Game #9 – Sunday, October 28, 1984

@ Sullivan Stadium	1	2	3	4	Final
NY Jets (6-3)	10	10	0	0	20
NE Patriots 6-3)	0	6	10	14	30

Attendance: 60,513

Game #10 – Sunday, November 4, 1984

@ Mile High Stadium	1	2	3	4	Final
NE Patriots (6-4)	03	03	07	06	19
Denver Broncos (9-1)	0	06	6	14	26

Attendance: 74,908

Game #11 – Sunday, November 11, 1984

@ Sullivan Stadium	1	2	3	4	Final
Buffalo Bills (0-11)	7	0	3	0	10
NE Patriots (7-4)	0	10	14	14	38

Attendance: 43,313

Game #12 – Sunday, November 18, 1984

@ Hoosier Dome	1	2	3	4	Final
NE Patriots (8-4)	16	10	7	17	50
Indianapolis Colts (4-8)	0	10	0	7	17

Attendance: 60,009

Game #13 – Thursday, November 22, 1984

@ Texas Stadium	1	2	3	4	Final
NE Patriots (8-5)	3	0	0	14	17
Dallas Cowboys (8-5)	7	3	7	3	20

Attendance: 55,341

Game #14 – Sunday, December 2, 1984

@ Sullivan Stadium	1	2	3	4	Final
St. Louis Cardinals (8-6)	14	13	0	6	33
NE Patriots (8-6)	3	0	7	0	10

Attendance: 53,558

Game #15 – Sunday, December 9, 1984

@ Veterans Stadium	1	2	3	4	Final
NE Patriots (8-7)	10	0	7	0	17
Philadelphia Eagles (8-7)	7	10	3	7	27

Attendance: 41,581

Game #16 – Sunday, December 18, 1984

@ Sullivan Stadium	1	2	3	4	Final
Indianapolis Colts (4-12)	0	0	10	0	10
NE Patriots (9-7)	3	10	0	3	16

Attendance: 22,383

Lifetime W-L record	164-189-9
Lifetime coin toss record	175-187
Lifetime OT record	0-7

1985 (11-5), tied second in AFC East
Head Coach – Raymond Berry

1st round pick – traded to 49ers (16th overall) along with 75th overall
for 49ers 28th overall, 56th overall and 84th overall
1st round pick – Patriots selected Trevor Matich, C, Brigham Young University (28th overall)
With Patriots 16th overall, the 49ers selected Jerry Rice, WR, Mississippi Valley State

Game #1 – Sunday, September 8, 1985

@ Sullivan Stadium	1	2	3	4	Final
GB Packers (0-1)	0	6	0	14	20
NE Patriots (1-0)	7	12	0	7	26

Attendance: 49,488

Game #2 – Sunday, September 15, 1985

@ Soldier Field	1	2	3	4	Final
NE Patriots (1-1)	0	0	0	7	7
Chicago Bears (2-0)	7	3	10	0	20

Attendance: 60,533

Game #3 – Sunday, September 22, 1985

@ Rich Stadium	1	2	3	4	Final
NE Patriots (2-1)	3	7	7	0	17
Buffalo Bills (0-3)	0	7	0	7	14

Attendance: 40,334

Game #4 – Sunday, September 29 1985

@ Sullivan Stadium	1	2	3	4	Final
LA Raiders (2-2)	14	0	14	7	35
NE Patriots (2-2)	10	10	0	0	20

Attendance: 60,686

Game #5 – Sunday, October 6, 1985

@Municipal Stadium	1	2	3	4	Final
NE Patriots (2-3)	7	13	7	0	20
Cleveland Browns (3-2)	7	7	3	7	24

Attendance: 62,139

Game #6 – Sunday, October 13, 1985

@ Sullivan Stadium	1	2	3	4	Final
Buffalo Bills (0-6)	0	3	0	0	3
NE Patriots (3-3)	0	0	7	7	14

Attendance: 40,462

Game #7 – Sunday, October 20, 1985

@ Sullivan Stadium	1	2	3	4	Final
NY Jets (4-3)	0	3	3	7	13
NE Patriots (4-3)	3	3	0	14	20

Attendance: 58,163

Game #8 – Sunday, October 27, 1985

@ Tampa Stadium	1	2	3	4	Final
NE Patriots (5-3)	0	13	3	16	32
TB Buccaneers (0-8)	14	0	0	0	14

Attendance: 34,661

Game #9 – Sunday, November 3, 1985

@ Sullivan Stadium	1	2	3	4	Final
Miami Dolphins (5-4)	7	3	3	00	13
NE Patriots 6-3)	0	3	0	14	17

Attendance: 60,513

Game #10 – Sunday, November 10, 1985

@ Sullivan Stadium	1	2	3	4	Final
Indianapolis Colts (3-7)	0	6	0	9	15
NE Patriots (7-3)	0	7	17	10	34

Attendance: 54,176

Game #11 – Sunday, November 17, 1985

@ Kingdome	1	2	3	4	Final
NE Patriots (8-3)	0	7	0	13	20
Seattle Seahawks (6-5)	0	3	10	0	13

Attendance: 60,345

Game #12 – Sunday, November 24, 1985

@ Giants Stadium	1	2	3	4	OT	Final
NE Patriots (8-4)	0	3	0	10	0	13
NY Jets (9-3)	6	0	7	0	3	16

Attendance: 74,100

Game #13 – Sunday, December 1, 1985

@ Hoosier Dome	1	2	3	4	Final
NE Patriots (9-4)	7	0	17	14	38
Indianapolis Colts (3-10)	7	10	0	14	31

Attendance: 56,740

Game #14 – Sunday, December 8, 1985

@ Sullivan Stadium	1	2	3	4	Final
Detroit Lions (7-7)	3	0	3	0	6
NE Patriots (10-4)	7	10	0	6	23

Attendance: 59,078

Game #15 – Monday, December 16, 1985

@ Orange Bowl	1	2	3	4	Final
NE Patriots (10-5)	7	0	3	17	27
Miami Dolphins (11-4)	7	10	3	10	30

Attendance: 69,489

Game #16 – Sunday, December 22, 1985

@ Sullivan Stadium	1	2	3	4	Final
Cincinnati Bengals (7-9)	3	3	7	10	23
NE Patriots (11-5)	10	10	0	14	34

Attendance: 57,593

Game # 17 – American Football Conference Wild Card Playoff Game
Saturday, December 28, 1985

@ Giant Stadium	1	2	3	4	Final
NE Patriots (12-5)	3	10	10	3	26
NY Jets (11-6)	0	7	7	0	14

Attendance: 55,341

Game # 18 – American Football Conference Divisional Play-off Game
Sunday, January 5, 1986

@ LA Memorial Coliseum	1	2	3	4	Final
NE Patriots (13-5)	7	10	10	0	27
LA Raider (12-5)	3	17	0	0	20

Attendance: 88,939

Game #19 – American Football Conference Championship Game
Sunday, January 12, 1986

@ Orange Bowl	1	2	3	4	Final
NE Patriots (14-5)	3	14	7	7	31
Miami Dolphins (13-5)	0	7	0	7	14

Attendance: 74,978

Game #20 – Super Bowl XX
Sunday, January 26, 1986

@Superdome	1	2	3	4	Final
NE Patriots (15-5)	3	0	0	7	10
Chicago Bears (18-1)	13	10	21	2	46

Attendance: 73,818

Lifetime W-L record	178-195-9
Lifetime coin-toss record	183-199
Lifetime OT record	0-8

1986 (11-5), first in AFC East
Head Coach – Raymond Berry

1st round pick – Reggie Dupard, RB, Southern Methodist University (26th overall

Game #1 – Sunday, September 7, 1986

@ Sullivan Stadium	1	2	3	4	Final
Indianapolis Colts (0-1)	0	3	0	0	3
NE Patriots (1-0)	3	7	10	13	33

Attendance: 55,208

Game #2 – Thursday, September 11, 1986

@ Giant Stadium	1	2	3	4	Final
NE Patriots (2-0)	7	0	10	3	20
NY Jets (1-1)	0	6	0	0	6

Attendance: 72,422

Game #3 – Sunday, September 21, 1986

@ Sullivan Stadium	1	2	3	4	Final
Seattle Seahawks (3-0)	7	0	7	24	38
NE Patriots (2-1)	7	10	0	14	31

Attendance: 58,977

Game #4 – Sunday, September 28, 1986

@ Mile High Stadium	1	2	3	4	Final
NE Patriots (2-2)	0	13	0	7	20
Denver Broncos (4-0)	3	0	14	10	27

Attendance: 75,804

Game #5 – Sunday, October 5, 1986

@ Sullivan Stadium	1	2	3	4	Final
Miami Dolphins (1-4)	7	0	0	7	7
NE Patriots (3-2)	10	17	0	7	34

Attendance: 60,689

Game #6 – Sunday, October 12, 1986

@ Sullivan Stadium	1	2	3	4	Final
NY Jets (5-1)	7	17	0	7	31
NE Patriots (3-3)	0	0	17	7	24

Attendance: 60,342

Game #7 – Sunday, October 19, 1986

@ Three Rivers Stadium	1	2	3	4	Final
NE Patriots (4-3)	10	14	7	3	34
Pittsburgh Steelers (1-6)	0	0	0	0	0

Attendance: 54,743

Game #8 – Sunday, October 26, 1986

@ Rich Stadium	1	2	3	4	Final
NE Patriots (5-3)	7	10	3	3	23
Buffalo Bills (2-6)	0	0	3	0	3

Attendance: 77,808

Game #9 – Sunday, November 2, 1986

@ Sullivan Stadium	1	2	3	4	Final
Atlanta Falcons (5-3-1)	3	7	0	7	17
NE Patriots (6-3)	3	6	10	6	25

Attendance: 60,597

Game #10 – Sunday, November 9, 1986

@ Hoosier Dome	1	2	3	4	Final
NE Patriots (7-3)	3	3	14	10	30
Indianapolis Colts (0-10)	7	7	0	7	21

Attendance: 56,890

Game #11 – Sunday, November 16, 1986

@ Anaheim Stadium	1	2	3	4	Final
NE Patriots (8-3)	6	10	0	14	30
LA Rams (7-4)	0	14	7	7	28

Attendance: 64,339

Game #12 – Sunday, November 23, 1986

@ Sullivan Stadium	1	2	3	4	Final
Buffalo Bills (3-9)	0	3	3	13	19
NE Patriots (9-3)	9	6	0	7	22

Attendance: 60,455

Game #13 – Sunday, November 30, 1986

@ Superdome	1	2	3	4	Final
NE Patriots (10-3)	0	0	7	14	21
NO Saints (6-7)	0	0	10	10	20

Attendance: 58,259

Game #14 – Sunday, December 7, 1986

@ Sullivan Stadium	1	2	3	4	Final
Cincinnati Bengals (9-5)	0	7	10	14	31
NE Patriots (10-4)	0	0	7	0	7

Attendance: 60,633

Game #15 – Sunday, December 14, 1986

@ Sullivan Stadium	1	2	3	4	Final
SF 49ers (9-5-1)	7	9	0	13	29
NE Patriots (10-5)	10	0	7	7	24

Attendance: 60,787

Game #16 – Monday, December 22, 1986

@ Orange Bowl	1	2	3	4	Final
NE Patriots (11-5)	7	6	7	14	34
Miami Dolphins (8-8)	0	10	10	7	27

Attendance: 74,516

Game #17 – American Football Conference Divisional Playoff Game
Monday, January 1, 1987

@ Mile High Stadium	1	2	3	4	Final
NE Patriots (11-6)	0	10	7	0	17
Denver Broncos (12-5)	3	7	10	2	22

Attendance: 76,105

Lifetime W-L record	189-201-9
Lifetime coin-toss record	190-209
Lifetime OT record	0-8

1987 (8-7), tied second in AFC East
Head Coach – Raymond Berry

1st round pick – Bruce Armstrong, OT, University of Louisville (23rd overall)

Game #1 – Sunday, September 13, 1987

@ Sullivan Stadium	1	2	3	4	Final
Miami Dolphins (0-1)	07	14	0	0	21
NE Patriots (1-0)	7	7	14	0	28

Attendance: 54,642

Game #2 – Monday, September 21, 1987

@ Giant Stadium	1	2	3	4	Final
NE Patriots (1-1)	0	3	7	14	24
NY Jets (2-0)	6	0	21	16	43

Attendance: 70,487

Players' Strike – Mid-Season

The NFL Players Association, looking for a better contract agreement with the owners, decided to go on strike after the second week of the season. After one week (#3) of cancelled games, the owners quickly assembled replacement teams. For the next three weeks (#4, #5, #6), the games continued, using the patchwork teams. Beginning with the games of October 25, 1987, the NFLPA resumed their roles as the gladiators of Sunday afternoons, reestablishing the authentic NFL product for the American public. The league decided to play out the balance of the schedule, not make-up the games missed from week #3, thus making the 1987 regular season a 15-game schedule for all teams.

Game #3 – Sunday, September 27, 1987

@ R.F.K. Stadium	1	2	3	4	Final
NE Patriots (1-1)					
WDC Redskins (1-1)					

Cancelled due to NFLPA strike

Game #4 – Sunday, October 4, 1987

@ Sullivan Stadium	1	2	3	4	Final
Cleveland Browns (2-1)	0	0	6	14	20
NE Patriots (1-2)	0	10	0	0	10

Attendance: 14,830

Game #5 – Sunday, October 11, 1987

@ Sullivan Stadium	1	2	3	4	Final
Buffalo Bills (1-3)	7	0	0	7	7
NE Patriots (2-2)	7	0	7	0	14

Attendance: 11,878

Game #6 – Sunday, October 18, 1987

@ Astrodome	1	2	3	4	Final
NE Patriots (3-2)	14	7	0	0	21
Houston Oilers (3-2)	7	0	0	0	7

Attendance: 26,294

Game #7 – Sunday, October 25, 1987

@ Hoosier Dome	1	2	3	4	Final
NE Patriots (3-3)	3	3	7	3	16
Indianapolis Colts (3-3)	0	10	13	7	30

Attendance: 48,850

Game #8 – Sunday, November 1, 1987

@ Sullivan Stadium	1	2	3	4	Final
LA Raiders (3-4)	3	3	0	17	23
NE Patriots (4-3)	3	7	6	10	26

Attendance: 60,664

Game #9 – Sunday, November 8, 1987

@ Giant Stadium	1	2	3	4	Final
NE Patriots (4-4)	0	0	7	3	10
NY Giants (2-6)	0	14	3	0	17

Attendance: 73,817

Game #10 – Sunday, November 15, 1987

@ Sullivan Stadium	1	2	3	4	OT	Final
Dallas Cowboys (5-4)	7	7	0	3	6	23
NE Patriots (4-5)	0	7	0	10	0	17

Attendance: 60,567

Game #11 – Sunday, November 22, 1987

@ Sullivan Stadium	1	2	3	4	Final
Indianapolis Colts (5-5)	0	0	0	0	0
NE Patriots (5-5)	0	10	14	0	24

Attendance: 56,906

Game #12 – Sunday, November 29, 1987

@ Sullivan Stadium	1	2	3	4	OT	Final
Philadelphia Eagles (5-6)	3	14	7	7	3	34
NE Patriots (5-6)	0	10	0	21	0	31

Attendance: 54,198

Game #13 – Sunday, December 6, 1987

@ Mile High Stadium	1	2	3	4	Final
NE Patriots (5-7)	7	10	3	0	20
Denver Broncos (8-3-1)	0	3	14	14	31

Attendance: 75,794

Game #14 – Sunday, December 13, 1987

@ Sullivan Stadium	1	2	3	4	Final
NY Jets (6-7)	3	3	0	14	20
NE Patriots (6-7)	14	21	7	0	42

Attendance: 60,617

PATRIOTS PASSION

Game #15 – Sunday, December 20, 1987

@ Rich Stadium	1	2	3	4	Final
NE Patriots (7-7)	7	6	0	0	13
Buffalo Bills (7-7)	0	0	7	0	7

Attendance: 74,945

Game #16 – Monday, December 28, 1987

@ Joe Robbie Stadium	1	2	3	4	Final
NE Patriots (8-7)	14	10	0	0	24
Miami Dolphins (8-7)	3	0	0	7	10

Attendance: 61,192

Lifetime W-L record   197-208-9
Lifetime coin-toss record   200-214
Lifetime OT record   0-10

1988 (9-7), tied second in AFC East
Head Coach – Raymond Berry
1st round pick – John Stephens, RB, Northwestern (LA) State (17th overall)

Game #1 – Sunday, September 4, 1988

@ Sullivan Stadium	1	2	3	4	Final
NY Jets (0-1)	3	0	0	0	3
NE Patriots (1-0)	3	3	10	12	28

Attendance: 44,027

Game #2 – Sunday, September 11, 1988

@Humphrey Metrodome	1	2	3	4	Final
NE Patriots (1-1)	3	3	0	0	6
Minnesota Vikings (1-1)	10	14	2	10	36

Attendance: 55,545

Game #3 – Sunday, September 18, 1988

@ Sullivan Stadium	1	2	3	4	Final
Buffalo Bills (3-0)	0	3	3	10	16
NE Patriots (1-2)	0	14	0	0	14

Attendance: 55,945

Game #4 – Sunday, September 25, 1988

@ Astrodome	1	2	3	4	Final
NE Patriots (1-3)	6	0	0	0	6
Houston Oilers (3-1)	7	7	7	10	31

Attendance: 38,646

Game #5 – Sunday, October 2, 1988

@ Sullivan Stadium	1	2	3	4	Final
Indianapolis Colts (1-4)	7	7	0	10	17
NE Patriots (2-3)	0	7	0	14	21

Attendance: 58,050

Game #6 – Sunday, October 9, 1988

@Milwaukee Cty. Stadium	1	2	3	4	Final
NE Patriots (2-4)	3	0	0	0	3
GB Packers (1-5)	0	17	7	21	45

Attendance: 51,932

Game #7 – Sunday, October 16, 1988

@ Sullivan Stadium	1	2	3	4	Final
Cincinnati Bengals (6-1)	0	0	14	7	21
NE Patriots (3-4)	7	7	6	7	27

Attendance: 59,969

Game #8 – Sunday, October 23, 1988

@ Rich Stadium	1	2	3	4	Final
NE Patriots (3-5)	7	6	0	7	20
Buffalo Bills (7-1)	7	6	7	3	23

Attendance: 75,824

GAME BY GAME FROM DAY ONE

Game #9 – Sunday, October 30, 1988

@ Sullivan Stadium	1	2	3	4	Final
Chicago Bears (7-2)	7	0	0	0	7
NE Patriots (4-5)	6	14	3	7	30

Attendance: 60,821

Game #10 – Sunday, November 6, 1988

@ Sullivan Stadium	1	2	3	4	Final
Miami Dolphins (5-5)	0	3	7	0	10
NE Patriots (5-5)	0	14	7	0	21

Attendance: 60,840

Game #11 – Sunday, November 13, 1988

@ Giants Stadium	1	2	3	4	Final
NE Patriots (6-5)	0	0	7	7	14
NY Jets (5-5-1)	0	3	3	7	13

Attendance: 48,385

Game #12 – Sunday, November 20, 1988

@ Joe Robbie Stadium	1	2	3	4	Final
NE Patriots (7-5)	0	3	3	0	6
Miami Dolphins (5-7)	0	3	0	0	3

Attendance: 53,526

Game #13 – Sunday, November 27, 1988

@ Hoosier Dome	1	2	3	4	Final
NE Patriots (7-6)	7	7	0	7	21
Indianapolis Colts (7-6)	7	7	0	10	24

Attendance: 58,157

Game #14 – Sunday, December 4, 1988

@ Sullivan Stadium	1	2	3	4	Final
Seattle Seahawks (7-7)	0	0	7	0	7
NE Patriots (8-6)	0	6	7	0	13

Attendance: 59,068

Game #15 – Sunday, December 11, 1988

@ Sullivan Stadium	1	2	3	4	OT	Final
TB Buccaneers (4-11)	0	0	0	7	0	7
NE Patriots (9-6)	0	0	7	0	3	10

Attendance: 39,889

Game #16 – Saturday, December 17, 1988

@ Mile High Stadium	1	2	3	4	Final
NE Patriots (9-7)	7	3	0	0	10
Denver Broncos (8-8)	7	7	0	7	21

Attendance: 70,910

Lifetime W-L record	206 – 215 – 9
Lifetime coin-toss record	208 – 222
Lifetime OT record	1-10

1989 (5-11), fourth in AFC East

Head Coach – Raymond Berry

1st round pick – Hart Lee Dykes, WR, Oklahoma State (16th overall)

Game #1 – Sunday, September 10, 1989

@ Giants Stadium	1	2	3	4	Final
NE Patriots (1-0)	7	14	0	6	27
NY Jets (0-1)	0	0	7	17	24

Attendance: 64,541

Game #2 – Sunday, September 17, 1989

@ Sullivan Stadium	1	2	3	4	Final
Miami Dolphins (1-1)	17	7	0	0	24
NE Patriots (1-1)	0	0	3	7	10

Attendance: 57,043

PATRIOTS PASSION

Game #3 – Sunday, September 24, 1989

@ Sullivan Stadium	1	2	3	4	Final
Seattle Seahawks (1-2)	0	21	3	10	24
NE Patriots (1-2)	3	0	0	0	3

Attendance: 48,025

Game #4 – Sunday, October 1, 1989

@ Rich Stadium	1	2	3	4	Final
NE Patriots (1-3)	3	0	7	00	10
Buffalo Bills (3-1)	17	7	0	7	31

Attendance: 78,921

Game #5 – Sunday, October 8, 1989

@ Sullivan Stadium	1	2	3	4	Final
Houston Oilers (2-3)	7	3	0	10	13
NE Patriots (2-3)	10	0	10	3	23

Attendance: 59,828

Game #6 – Sunday, October 15, 1989

@ Fulton County Stadium	1	2	3	4	Final
NE Patriots (2-4)	6	9	0	0	15
Atlanta Falcons (1-5)	3	3	7	3	16

Attendance: 39,697

Game #7 – Sunday, October 22, 1989

@ Stanford Stadium	1	2	3	4	Final
NE Patriots (2-5)	0	10	7	3	20
San Francisco 49ers (6-1)	0	17	7	13	37

Attendance: 70,000

Game #8 – Sunday, October 29, 1989

@ Hoosier Dome	1	2	3	4	OT	Final
NE Patriots (3-5)	3	0	7	10	3	23
Indianapolis Colts (4-4)	10	0	0	10	0	20

Attendance: 59,356

Game #9 – Sunday, November 5, 1989

@ Sullivan Stadium	1	2	3	4	Final
NY Jets (2-7)	7	7	3	10	27
NE Patriots (3-6)	3	0	6	17	26

Attendance: 53,366

Game #10 – Sunday, November 12, 1989

@ Sullivan Stadium	1	2	3	4	Final
NO Saints (5-5)	7	21	0	0	28
NE Patriots (3-7)	0	10	7	7	24

Attendance: 47,680

Game #11 – Sunday, November 19, 1989

@ Sullivan Stadium	1	2	3	4	Final
Buffalo Bills (7-4)	7	3	14	0	24
NE Patriots (4-7)	0	6	7	20	33

Attendance: 49,663

Game #12 – Sunday, November 26, 1989

@ LA Memorial Coliseum	1	2	3	4	Final
NE Patriots (4-8)	0	14	7	0	21
LA Raiders (8-4)	7	7	7	3	24

Attendance: 38,747

Game #13 – Sunday, December 3, 1989

@ Sullivan Stadium	1	2	3	4	Final
Indianapolis Colts (6-7)	0	3	7	6	16
NE Patriots (5-8)	6	0	3	13	22

Attendance: 32,234

Game #14 – Sunday, December 10, 1989

@ Joe Robbie Stadium	1	2	3	4	Final
NE Patriots (5-9)	3	0	7	0	10
Miami Dolphins (8-6)	7	14	0	10	31

Attendance: 55,913

GAME BY GAME FROM DAY ONE

Game #15 – Sunday, December 17, 1989

@ Three Rivers Stadium	1	2	3	4	Final
NE Patriots (5-10)	3	0	0	7	10
Pittsburgh Steelers (8-7)	17	7	7	7	28

Attendance: 26,594

Game #16 – Saturday December 24, 1989

@ Sullivan Stadium	1	2	3	4	Final
LA Rams (11-5)	3	7	7	7	24
NE Patriots (5-11)	0	3	7	10	20

Attendance: 37,940

Lifetime W-L record   211-226-9
Lifetime coin-toss record   214-232
Lifetime OT record   2-10

1990 (1-15), fifth in AFC East
Head Coach – Rod Rust

1st round pick – traded 3rd and 29th overall to Seattle for Seahawks (8th, 10th, 59th overall)
1st round pick – Patriots selected Chris Singleton, LB, Arizona (8th overall)
1st round pick – Patriots select Ray Agnew, DE, North Carolina State (10th overall)
Seahawks selected Cortez Kennedy, DT, Miami (FL) with Patriots (3rd overall)

Game #1 – Sunday, September 9, 1990

@Foxboro Stadium	1	2	3	4	Final
Miami Dolphins (1-0)	3	10	7	7	27
NE Patriots (0-1)	7	14	3	0	24

Attendance: 45,305

Game #2 – Sunday, September 16, 1990

@ Hoosier Dome	1	2	3	4	Final
NE Patriots (1-1)	0	7	3	6	16
Indianapolis Colts (0-2)	7	0	0	7	14

Attendance: 49,256

Game #3 – Sunday, September 23, 1990

@ Riverfront Stadium	1	2	3	4	Final
NE Patriots (1-2)	0	7	0	10	7
Cincinnati Bengals (3-0)	17	14	3	7	41

Attendance: 56,470

Game #4 – Sunday, September 30, 1990

@ Foxboro Stadium	1	2	3	4	Final
NY Jets (2-2)	7	17	10	3	37
NE Patriots (1-3)	3	3	0	7	13

Attendance: 36,724

Game #5 – Sunday, October 7, 1990

@ Foxboro Stadium	1	2	3	4	Final
Seattle Seahawks (2-3)	13	6	0	14	33
NE Patriots (1-4)	3	7	7	3	20

Attendance: 39,735

Game #6 – Thursday, October 18, 1990

@ Joe Robbie Stadium	1	2	3	4	Final
NE Patriots (1-5)	0	3	0	7	10
Miami Dolphins (5-1)	0	10	7	0	17

Attendance: 62,630

Game #7 – Sunday, October 28, 1990

@ Foxboro Stadium	1	2	3	4	Final
Buffalo Bills (6-1)	7	7	13	0	27
NE Patriots (1-6)	0	3	0	7	10

Attendance: 51,959

Game #8 – Sunday, November 4, 1990

@ Veterans Stadium	1	2	3	4	Final
NE Patriots (1-7)	3	7	3	7	20
Philadelphia Eagles (4-4)	10	10	7	21	48

Attendance: 65,514

Game #9 – Sunday, November 11, 1990

@ Foxboro Stadium	1	2	3	4	Final
Indianapolis Colts (3-6)	0	3	3	7	13
NE Patriots (1-8)	7	3	0	0	10

Attendance: 28,924

Game #10 – Sunday, November 18, 1990

@ Rich Stadium	1	2	3	4	Final
NE Patriots (1-9)	0	0	0	0	0
Buffalo Bills (9-1)	7	0	0	7	14

Attendance: 74,720

Game #11 – Sunday, November 25, 1990

@ Sun Devil Stadium	1	2	3	4	Final
NE Patriots (1-10)	7	7	0	0	14
Phoenix Cardinals (3-8)	7	7	10	10	34

Attendance: 30,110

Game #12 – Sunday, December 2, 1990

@ Foxboro Stadium	1	2	3	4	Final
KC Chiefs (8-4)	13	10	7	7	37
NE Patriots (1-11)	0	0	7	0	7

Attendance: 26,280

Game #13 – Sunday, December 9, 1990

@ Three Rivers Stadium	1	2	3	4	Final
NE Patriots (1-12)	0	3	0	0	3
Pittsburgh Steelers (8-7)	3	7	7	7	24

Attendance: 48,354

Game #14 – Saturday, December 15, 1990

@ Foxboro Stadium	1	2	3	4	Final
WDC Redskins (9-5)	9	10	0	6	25
NE Patriots (1-13)	0	0	7	3	10

Attendance: 22,286

Game #15 – Sunday, December 23, 1990

@ Giants Stadium	1	2	3	4	Final
NE Patriots (1-14)	0	7	0	0	7
NY Jets (5-10)	17	14	14	7	42

Attendance: 30,250

Game #16 – Saturday, December 30, 1990

@ Foxboro Stadium	1	2	3	4	Final
NY Giants (13-3)	10	3	0	0	13
NE Patriots (1-15)	0	10	0	0	10

Attendance: 60,410

Lifetime W-L record	212-241-9
Lifetime coin-toss record	223-239
Lifetime OT record	2-10

1991 (6-10), fourth in AFC East
Head Coach – Dick MacPherson

1st round pick – traded 1st, 17th and 110th overall to Dallas for Cowboys 11th, 14th, and 41st overall
1st round pick – Patriots select Pat Harlow, T, Southern California (11th overall)
1st round pick – Patriots select Leonard Russell, RB, Arizona State (14th overall)
Cowboys selected Russell Maryland, DT, Miami (FL) with Patriots 1st overall and traded 17th overall to Redskins who selected Bobby Wilson, DT, Michigan State

Game #1 – Sunday, September 1, 1991

@ Hoosier Dome	1	2	3	4	Final
NE Patriots (1-0)	7	3	3	3	16
Indianapolis Colts (0-1)	7	0	0	0	7

Attendance: 49,961

Game #2 – Sunday, September 9, 1991

@ Foxboro Stadium	1	2	3	4	Final
Cleveland Browns (1-1)	0	7	3	10	20
NE Patriots (1-1)	0	0	0	0	0

Attendance: 35,377

Game #3 – Sunday, September 15, 1991

@ Three Rivers Stadium	1	2	3	4	Final
NE Patriots (1-2)	0	6	0	10	6
Pittsburgh Steelers (2-1)	3	3	0	14	20

Attendance: 53,703

Game #4 – Sunday, September 22, 1991

@ Foxboro Stadium	1	2	3	4	Final
Houston Oilers (3-1)	3	3	0	14	20
NE Patriots (2-2)	3	14	0	7	24

Attendance: 30,702

Game #5 – Sunday, September 29, 1991

@ Sun Devil Stadium	1	2	3	4	Final
NE Patriots (2-3)	0	7	0	3	10
Phoenix Cardinals (3-2)	0	14	0	10	24

Attendance: 26,043

Game #6 – Sunday, October 6, 1991

@ Foxboro Stadium	1	2	3	4	Final
Miami Dolphins (3-3)	0	17	0	3	10
NE Patriots (2-4)	7	0	3	3	20

Attendance: 49,749

Game #7 – Sunday, October 20, 1991

@ Foxboro Stadium	1	2	3	4	OT	Final
Minnesota Vikings (3-5)	0	10	3	10	0	23
NE Patriots (3-4)	7	7	0	9	3	26

Attendance: 45,367

Game #8 – Sunday, October 27, 1991

@ Foxboro Stadium	1	2	3	4	Final
Denver Broncos (6-2)	3	3	0	3	9
NE Patriots (3-5)	0	3	0	3	6

Attendance: 43,994

Game #9 – Sunday, November 3, 1991

@ Rich Stadium	1	2	3	4	Final
NE Patriots (3-6)	0	3	7	7	17
Buffalo Bills (8-1)	3	3	7	9	22

Attendance: 78,278

Game #10 – Sunday, November 10, 1991

@ Joe Robbie Stadium	1	2	3	4	Final
NE Patriots (3-7)	3	3	7	7	20
Miami Dolphins (5-5)	7	10	3	10	30

Attendance: 56,065

PATRIOTS PASSION

Game #11 – Sunday, November 17, 1991

@ Foxboro Stadium	1	2	3	4	Final
NY Jets (6-5)	7	7	7	7	28
NE Patriots (3-8)	0	0	0	21	21

Attendance: 30,743

Game #12 – Sunday, November 24, 1991

@ Foxboro Stadium	1	2	3	4	Final
Buffalo Bills (10-2)	3	7	3	0	13
NE Patriots (4-8)	0	9	0	7	16

Attendance: 47,053

Game #13 – Sunday, December 1, 1991

@ Mile High Stadium	1	2	3	4	Final
NE Patriots (4-9)	0	0	3	0	3
Denver Broncos (9-4)	10	7	3	0	20

Attendance: 67,116

Game #14 – Saturday, December 8, 1991

@ Foxboro Stadium	1	2	3	4	OT	Final
Indianapolis Colts (1-13)	0	14	3	0	0	17
NE Patriots (5-9)	3	0	0	14	6	23

Attendance: 20,131

Game #15 – Sunday, December 15, 1991

@ Giants Stadium	1	2	3	4	Final
NE Patriots (6-9)	3	0	3	0	6
NY Jets (7-8)	10	3	0	0	3

Attendance: 55,689

Game #16 – Saturday, December 22, 1991

@ Riverfront Stadium	1	2	3	4	Final
NE Patriots (6-10)	7	0	0	0	7
Cincinnati Bengals (3-13)	7	14	0	8	29

Attendance: 46,394

Lifetime W-L record	218-251-9
Lifetime coin-toss record	230-248
Lifetime OT record	4-10

1992 (2-14), fifth in AFC East
Head Coach – Dick MacPherson

1st round pick – traded 19th, 37th, and 104th overall to Dallas for the Cowboys 13th and 64th overall
1st round pick – Patriots selected Eugene Chung, T, Virginia Tech (13th overall)
Cowboys traded 19th overall to Falcons who selected Tony Smith, RB, Southern Mississippi

Game #1 – Sunday, September 13, 1992

@ Anaheim Stadium	1	2	3	4	Final
NE Patriots (0-1)	0	0	0	0	0
LA Rams (1-0)	0	0	7	7	14

Attendance: 40,402

Game #2 – Sunday, September 20, 1992

@ Foxboro Stadium	1	2	3	4	Final
Seattle Seahawks (1-2)	7	0	0	3	10
NE Patriots (0-2)	0	0	6	0	6

Attendance: 42,327

Game #3 – Sunday, September 27, 1992

@ Foxboro Stadium	1	2	3	4	Final
Buffalo Bills (4-0)	3	3	21	14	41
NE Patriots (0-3)	0	0	0	7	7

Attendance: 52,527

Game #4 – Sunday, October 4, 1992

@ Giants Stadium	1	2	3	4	Final
NE Patriots (0-4)	0	0	7	14	21
NY Jets (1-4)	3	14	0	13	30

Attendance: 60,108

GAME BY GAME FROM DAY ONE

Game #5 – Sunday, October 11, 1992

@ Foxboro Stadium	1	2	3	4	Final
San Francisco 49ers (5-1)	0	10	0	14	24
NE Patriots (0-5)	0	3	9	0	12

Attendance: 54,126

Game #6 – Sunday, October 18, 1992

@ Joe Robbie Stadium	1	2	3	4	Final
NE Patriots (0-6)	10	0	0	7	17
Miami Dolphins (6-0)	0	17	21	0	38

Attendance: 57,282

Game #7 – Sunday, October 25, 1992

@ Foxboro Stadium	1	2	3	4	Final
Cleveland Browns (4-3)	6	3	0	10	19
NE Patriots (0-7)	0	7	10	0	17

Attendance: 32,219

Game #8 – Sunday, November 1, 1992

@ Rich Stadium	1	2	3	4	Final
NE Patriots (0-8)	0	7	0	0	7
Buffalo Bills (6-2)	0	0	9	07	16

Attendance: 78,268

Game #9 – Sunday, November 8, 1992

@ Foxboro Stadium	1	2	3	4	Final
New Orleans Saints (7-2)	14	7	7	3	31
NE Patriots (0-9)	0	7	0	7	14

Attendance: 45,413

Game #10 – Sunday, November 15, 1992

@ Hoosier Dome	1	2	3	4	OT	Final
NE Patriots (1-9)	14	7	0	13	3	37
Indianapolis Colts (4-6)	14	7	3	10	0	34

Attendance: 42,631

Game #11 – Sunday, November 22, 1992

@ Foxboro Stadium	1	2	3	4	Final
NY Jets (3-8)	0	3	0	0	3
NE Patriots (2-9)	10	14	0	0	24

Attendance: 27,642

Game #12 – Sunday, November 29, 1992

@ Georgia Dome	1	2	3	4	Final
NE Patriots (2-10)	0	0	0	0	0
Atlanta Falcons (5-7)	14	10	7	3	34

Attendance: 54,494

Game #13 – Sunday, December 6, 1992

@ Foxboro Stadium	1	2	3	4	Final
Indianapolis Colts (6-7)	3	3	0	0	6
NE Patriots (2-11)	0	0	0	0	0

Attendance: 19,424

Game #14 – Saturday, December 13, 1992

@ Arrowhead Stadium	1	2	3	4	Final
NE Patriots (2-12)	13	0	0	7	20
KC Chiefs (9-5)	3	3	7	14	27

Attendance: 52,208

Game #15 – Sunday, December 20, 1992

@ Riverfront Stadium	1	2	3	4	Final
NE Patriots (2-13)	7	0	0	3	10
Cincinnati Bengals (5-10)	14	0	3	3	20

Attendance: 45,335

Game #16 – Saturday, December 27, 1992

@ Foxboro Stadium	1	2	3	4	OT	Final
Miami Dolphins (11-5)	3	0	3	7	3	16
NE Patriots (2-14)	7	6	0	0	0	13

Attendance: 34,726

Lifetime W-L record	220-265-9
Lifetime coin-toss record	240-254
Lifetime OT record	5-11

1993 (5-11), fourth in AFC East
Head Coach – Bill Parcells

1st round pick – Drew Bledsoe, QB, Washington State (1st overall)

Game #1 – Sunday, September 5, 1993

@ Rich Stadium	1	2	3	4	Final
NE Patriots (0-1)	0	7	7	0	14
Buffalo Bills (1-0)	0	17	0	21	38

Attendance: 79,751

Game #2 – Sunday, September 12, 1993

@ Foxboro Stadium	1	2	3	4	OT	Final
Detroit Lions (2-0)	7	0	3	6	3	19
NE Patriots (0-2)	6	3	0	7	0	16

Attendance: 54,151

Game #3 – Sunday, September 19, 1993

@ Foxboro Stadium	1	2	3	4	Final
Seattle Seahawks (1-2)	7	0	10	0	17
NE Patriots (0-3)	0	0	0	14	14

Attendance: 50,392

Game #4 – Sunday, September 26, 1993

@ Giants Stadium	1	2	3	4	Final
NE Patriots (0-4)	0	0	0	7	7
NY Jets (2-1)	14	21	0	10	45

Attendance: 64,836

Game #5 – Sunday, October 10, 1993

@ Sun Devil Stadium	1	2	3	4	Final
NE Patriots (1-4)	0	13	3	7	23
Phoenix Cardinals (1-4)	0	14	0	7	21

Attendance: 36,115

Game #6 – Sunday, October 17, 1993

@ Foxboro Stadium	1	2	3	4	Final
Houston Oilers (2-4)	0	14	7	7	28
NE Patriots (1-5)	0	0	7	7	14

Attendance: 51,037

Game #7 – Sunday, October 24, 1993

@ Kingdome	1	2	3	4	Final
NE Patriots (1-6)	0	0	3	6	9
Seattle Seahawks (4-3)	0	3	0	7	10

Attendance: 56,526

Game #8 – Sunday, October 31, 1993

@ Hoosier Dome	1	2	3	4	Final
NE Patriots (1-7)	0	3	0	3	6
Indianapolis Colts (6-2)	3	0	0	6	9

Attendance: 46,552

Game #9 – Sunday, November 7, 1993

@ Foxboro Stadium	1	2	3	4	OT	Final
Buffalo Bills (7-1)	0	0	0	10	3	13
NE Patriots (1-8)	0	0	7	3	0	10

Attendance: 54,326

Game #10 – Sunday, November 21, 1993

@ Joe Robbie Stadium	1	2	3	4	Final
NE Patriots (1-9)	3	0	3	7	13
Miami Dolphins (8-2)	0	0	3	14	17

Attendance: 59,982

Game #11 – Sunday, November 28, 1993

@ Foxboro Stadium	1	2	3	4	Final
NY Jets (7-4)	3	3	0	0	6
NE Patriots (1-10)	0	0	0	0	0

Attendance: 42,810

Game #12 – Sunday, December 5, 1993

@ Three Rivers Stadium	1	2	3	4	Final
NE Patriots (1-11)	14	0	0	0	14
Pittsburgh Steelers (7-5)	0	17	0	0	17

Attendance: 51,358

Game #13 – Sunday, December 12, 1993

@ Foxboro Stadium	1	2	3	4	Final
Cincinnati Bengals (1-12)	0	0	0	2	2
NE Patriots (2-11)	0	7	0	0	7

Attendance: 29,794

Game #14 – Saturday, December 19, 1993

@Municipal Stadium	1	2	3	4	Final
NE Patriots (3-11)	0	10	3	7	20
Cleveland Browns (6-8)	7	7	0	3	17

Attendance: 48,618

Game #15 – Sunday, December 26, 1993

@ Foxboro Stadium	1	2	3	4	Final
Indianapolis Colts (4-11)	0	0	0	0	0
NE Patriots (4-11)	7	10	14	7	38

Attendance: 26,571

Game #16 – Saturday, January 2, 1993

@ Foxboro Stadium	1	2	3	4	OT	Final
Miami Dolphins (9-7)	0	7	3	17	0	27
NE Patriots (5-11)	3	7	7	10	6	33

Attendance: 53,883

Lifetime W-L record   225-276-9
Lifetime coin-toss record   249-261
Lifetime OT record   6-13

1994 (10-6), second in AFC East
Head Coach – Bill Parcells

1st round pick – Willie McGinest LB Southern California (4th overall)

Game #1 – Sunday, September 4, 1994

@ Joe Robbie Stadium	1	2	3	4	Final
NE Patriots (0-1)	7	7	14	7	35
Miami Dolphins (1-0)	0	10	15	14	39

Attendance: 69,613

Game #2 – Sunday, September 11, 1994

@ Foxboro Stadium	1	2	3	4	Final
Buffalo Bills (1-1)	14	14	0	10	38
NE Patriots (0-2)	7	7	7	14	35

Attendance: 60,274

Game #3 – Sunday, September 18, 1994

@ Riverfront Stadium	1	2	3	4	Final
NE Patriots (1-2)	7	6	12	6	31
Cincinnati Bengals (0-3)	6	7	7	8	28

Attendance: 46,640

Game #4 – Sunday, September 25, 1994

@ Pontiac Silverdome	1	2	3	4	Final
NE Patriots (2-2)	3	14	3	3	23
Detroit Lions (2-2)	0	7	7	3	17

Attendance: 59,618

Game #5 – Sunday, October 2, 1994

@ Foxboro Stadium	1	2	3	4	Final
GB Packers (2-3)	3	7	0	6	16
NE Patriots (3-2)	0	0	10	7	17

Attendance: 57,522

Game #6 – Sunday, October 9, 1994

@ Foxboro Stadium	1	2	3	4	Final
LA Raiders (2-3)	0	14	7	0	21
NE Patriots (3-3)	0	17	0	0	17

Attendance: 59,889

PATRIOTS PASSION

Game #7 – Sunday, October 16, 1994

@ Giant Stadium	1	2	3	4	Final
NE Patriots (3-4)	0	7	0	10	17
NY Jets (4-3)	7	14	0	3	24

Attendance: 71,123

Game #8 – Sunday, October 30, 1994

@ Foxboro Stadium	1	2	3	4	Final
Miami Dolphins (6-2)	0	13	7	3	23
NE Patriots (3-5)	3	0	0	0	3

Attendance: 59,167

Game #9 – Sunday, November 6, 1994

@ Cleveland Stadium	1	2	3	4	Final
NE Patriots (3-6)	0	0	3	3	6
Cleveland Browns (7-2)	0	3	0	10	13

Attendance: 73,878

Game #10 – Sunday, November 13, 1994

@ Foxboro Stadium	1	2	3	4	OT	Final
Minnesota Vikings (7-3)	10	10	0	0	0	20
NE Patriots (4-6)	0	3	7	10	6	26

Attendance: 58,382

Game #11 – Sunday, November 20, 1994

@ Foxboro Stadium	1	2	3	4	Final
San Diego Chargers (8-3)	0	0	10	7	17
NE Patriots (5-6)	7	3	3	10	23

Attendance: 59,690

Game #12 – Sunday, November 27, 1994

@ RCA Dome	1	2	3	4	Final
NE Patriots (6-6)	3	0	3	6	12
Indianapolis Colts (5-7)	0	7	0	3	10

Attendance: 43,839

Game #13 – Sunday, December 4, 1994

@ Foxboro Stadium	1	2	3	4	Final
NY Jets (6-7)	0	10	3	0	13
NE Patriots (7-6)	3	7	7	7	24

Attendance: 60,138

Game #14 – Saturday, December 11, 1994

@ Foxboro Stadium	1	2	3	4	Final
Indianapolis Colts (6-8)	0	10	0	3	13
NE Patriots (8-6)	0	7	14	7	28

Attendance: 57,656

Game #15 – Sunday, December 18, 1994

@ Rich Stadium	1	2	3	4	Final
NE Patriots (9-6)	3	14	14	10	41
Buffalo Bills (7-8)	10	7	0	0	17

Attendance: 56,784

Game #16 – Saturday, December 24, 1994

@ Soldier Field	1	2	3	4	Final
NE Patriots (10-6)	3	3	0	7	13
Chicago Bears (9-7)	3	0	0	0	3

Attendance: 60,178

Game #17 – American Football Conference Wild Card Game
Sunday, January 1, 1995

@ Cleveland Stadium	1	2	3	4	Final
NE Patriots (10-7)	0	10	0	3	13
Cleveland Browns (12-5)	3	7	7	3	20

Attendance: 77,452

Lifetime W-L record	235-283-9
Lifetime coin-toss record	259-268
Lifetime OT record	7-13

GAME BY GAME FROM DAY ONE

1995 (6-10), fourth in AFC East
Head Coach – Bill Parcells

1st round pick – Ty Law, CB, Michigan (23rd overall)

Game #1 – Sunday, September 3, 1995

@ Foxboro Stadium	1	2	3	4	Final
Cleveland Browns (0-1)	7	7	0	0	14
NE Patriots (1-0)	6	0	0	11	17

Attendance: 60,126

Game #2 – Sunday, September 10, 1995

@ Foxboro Stadium	1	2	3	4	Final
Miami Dolphins (2-0)	10	7	0	3	20
NE Patriots (1-1)	0	3	0	0	3

Attendance: 60,239

Game #3 – Sunday, September 17, 1995

@ 3-COM Park	1	2	3	4	Final
NE Patriots (1-2)	0	3	0	0	3
San Francisco 49ers (3-0)	0	7	7	14	28

Attendance: 66,179

Game #4 – Sunday, October 1, 1995

@ Georgia Dome	1	2	3	4	Final
NE Patriots (1-3)	7	7	3	0	17
Atlanta Falcons (4-1)	3	14	0	13	30

Attendance: 47,114

Game #5 – Sunday, October 8, 1995

@ Foxboro Stadium	1	2	3	4	Final
Denver Broncos (3-3)	14	9	14	0	37
NE Patriots (1-4)	3	0	0	0	3

Attendance: 60,074

Game #6 – Sunday, October 15, 1995

@ Arrowhead Stadium	1	2	3	4	Final
NE Patriots (1-5)	7	3	9	7	26
KC Chiefs (6-1)	3	21	0	7	31

Attendance: 77,992

Game #7 – Monday, October 23, 1995

@ Foxboro Stadium	1	2	3	4	Final
Buffalo Bills (5-2)	6	8	0	0	14
NE Patriots (2-5)	7	14	3	3	27

Attendance: 60,203

Game #8 – Sunday, October 29, 1995

@ Foxboro Stadium	1	2	3	4	OT	Final
Carolina Panthers (3-5)	0	0	17	0	3	20
NE Patriots (2-6)	0	3	0	14	0	17

Attendance: 60,064

Game #9 – Sunday, November 5, 1995

@ Giants Stadium	1	2	3	4	Final
NE Patriots (3-6)	3	10	7	0	20
NY Jets (2-8)	0	0	0	7	7

Attendance: 61,462

Game #10 – Sunday, November 12, 1995

@ Joe Robbie Stadium	1	2	3	4	Final
NE Patriots (4-6)	0	10	14	10	34
Miami Dolphins (6-4)	0	10	7	0	17

Attendance: 70,339

Game #11 – Sunday, November 19, 1995

@ Foxboro Stadium	1	2	3	4	Final
Indianapolis Colts (6-5)	0	17	0	7	24
NE Patriots (4-7)	3	0	7	0	10

Attendance: 59,544

Game #12 – Sunday, November 26, 1995

@ Rich Stadium	1	2	3	4	Final
NE Patriots (5-7)	3	7	3	22	35
Buffalo Bills (8-4)	3	16	6	0	25

Attendance: 69,384

PATRIOTS PASSION

Game #13 – Sunday, December 3, 1995

@ Foxboro Stadium	1	2	3	4	Final
New Orleans Saints (6-7)	14	3	0	14	31
NE Patriots (5-8)	7	7	0	3	17

Attendance: 59,876

Game #14 – Sunday, December 10, 1995

@ Foxboro Stadium	1	2	3	4	Final
NY Jets (3-11)	0	7	7	14	28
NE Patriots (6-8)	0	7	7	17	31

Attendance: 46,617

Game #15 – Saturday, December 18, 1995

@ Three Rivers Stadium	1	2	3	4	Final
NE Patriots (6-9)	3	3	6	15	27
Pittsburgh Steelers (11-4)	0	17	7	17	41

Attendance: 57,158

Game #16 – Saturday, December 24, 1995

@ RCA Dome	1	2	3	4	Final
NE Patriots (6-10)	0	7	0	0	7
Indianapolis Colts (9-7)	0	0	7	3	10

Attendance: 54,685

Lifetime W-L record   241-293-9
Lifetime coin-toss record   268-275
Lifetime OT record   7-14

1996 (11-5), first in AFC East
Head Coach – Bill Parcells

1st round pick – Terry Glenn, WR, Ohio State (7th overall)

Game #1 – Sunday, September 1, 1996

@ Pro Player Park	1	2	3	4	Final
NE Patriots (0-1)	0	3	7	0	10
Miami Dolphins (1-0)	10	7	7	0	24

Attendance: 71,542

Game #2 – Sunday, September 8, 1996

@ Rich Stadium	1	2	3	4	Final
NE Patriots (0-2)	3	0	7	0	10
Buffalo Bills (2-0)	3	7	0	7	17

Attendance: 78,104

Game #3 – Sunday, September 15, 1996

@ Foxboro Stadium	1	2	3	4	Final
Arizona Cardinals (0-3)	0	0	0	0	0
NE Patriots (1-2)	7	13	8	3	31

Attendance: 59,118

Game #4 – Sunday, September 22, 1996

@ Foxboro Stadium	1	2	3	4	OT	Final
JAX Jaguars (1-3)	0	7	15	3	0	25
NE Patriots (2-2)	9	13	3	0	3	28

Attendance: 59,446

Game #5 – Sunday, October 6, 1996

@ Memorial Stadium	1	2	3	4	Final
NE Patriots (3-2)	3	17	15	11	46
Baltimore Ravens (2-3)	0	14	0	24	38

Attendance: 63,569

Game #6 – Sunday, October 13, 1996

@ Foxboro Stadium	1	2	3	4	Final
WDC Redskins (5-1)	3	14	7	3	27
NE Patriots (3-3)	6	10	0	6	22

Attendance: 59,638

GAME BY GAME FROM DAY ONE

Game #7 – Sunday, October 20, 1996

@ RCA Dome	1	2	3	4	Final
NE Patriots (4-3)	0	10	14	3	27
Indianapolis Colts (5-2)	3	3	0	3	9

Attendance: 58,725

Game #8 – Sunday, October 27, 1996

@ Foxboro Stadium	1	2	3	4	Final
Buffalo Bills (5-3)	0	0	10	15	25
NE Patriots (5-3)	7	6	2	13	28

Attendance: 58,858

Game #9 – Sunday, November 3, 1996

@ Foxboro Stadium	1	2	3	4	Final
Miami Dolphins (4-5)	7	7	3	6	23
NE Patriots (6-3)	7	7	7	21	42

Attendance: 58,942

Game #10 – Sunday, November 10, 1996

@ Giants Stadium	1	2	3	4	Final
NE Patriots (7-3)	0	7	10	14	31
NY Jets (1-9)	7	14	3	3	27

Attendance: 61,715

Game #11 – Sunday, November 17, 1996

@ Foxboro Stadium	1	2	3	4	Final
Denver Broncos (10-1)	14	10	7	3	34
NE Patriots (7-4)	0	0	8	0	8

Attendance: 59,452

Game #12 – Sunday, November 24, 1996

@ Foxboro Stadium	1	2	3	4	Final
Indianapolis Colts (6-6)	0	3	3	7	13
NE Patriots (8-4)	10	7	3	7	27

Attendance: 58,226

Game #13 – Sunday, December 1, 1996

@ Jack Murphy Stadium	1	2	3	4	Final
NE Patriots (9-4)	14	17	14	0	45
SD Chargers (7-6)	7	0	0	0	7

Attendance: 59,209

Game #14 – Sunday, December 8, 1996

@ Foxboro Stadium	1	2	3	4	Final
NY Jets (1-13)	0	3	7	0	10
NE Patriots (10-4)	7	13	7	7	34

Attendance: 54,621

Game #15 – Sunday, December 15, 1996

@ Texas Stadium	1	2	3	4	Final
NE Patriots (10-5)	6	0	0	0	6
Dallas Cowboys (10-5)	3	3	6	0	12

Attendance: 64,578

Game #16 – Saturday, December 21, 1996

@ Giants Stadium	1	2	3	4	Final
NE Patriots (11-5)	0	0	3	20	23
NY Giants (6-10)	2	20	0	0	22

Attendance: 65,387

Game #17 – American Football Conference Divisional Playoff Game
Sunday, January 5, 1997

@ Foxboro Stadium	1	2	3	4	Final
Pittsburgh Steelers (11-7)	0	0	3	0	3
NE Patriots (12-5)	14	7	0	7	28

Attendance: 60,188

Game #18 – American Football Conference Championship Game
Sunday, January 15, 1997

@ Foxboro Stadium	1	2	3	4	Final
JAX Jaguars (11-8)	0	3	3	0	6
NE Patriots (13-5)	7	6	0	7	20

Attendance: 60,190

Game #19 – Super Bowl XXXI
Sunday, January 26, 1997

@ Superdome	1	2	3	4	Final
NE Patriots (13-6)	14	0	7	0	21
GB Packers (16-3)	10	17	8	0	35

Attendance: 72,301

Lifetime W-L record	254-299-9
Lifetime coin-toss record	280-282
Lifetime OT record	9-14

1997 (10-6), first in AFC East
Head Coach – Pete Carroll

1st round pick – Chris Canty, DB, Kansas State (29th overall)
3rd round pick – Sedrick Shaw, RB, Iowa (61st overall) from Jets compensation for Bill Parcells
4th round pick – Damon Denson, OL, Michigan (97th overall) from Jets compensation for Bill Parcells

Game #1 – Sunday, August 31, 1997

@ Foxboro Stadium	1	2	3	4	Final
San Diego Chargers (0-1)	0	0	7	0	7
NE Patriots (1-0)	14	17	0	10	41

Attendance: 60,190

Game #2 – Sunday, September 7, 1997

@ RCA Dome	1	2	3	4	Final
NE Patriots (2-0)	7	7	7	10	31
Indianapolis Colts (0-2)	3	3	0	0	6

Attendance: 53,632

Game #3 – Sunday, September 14, 1997

@ Foxboro Stadium	1	2	3	4	OT	Final
NY Jets (1-2)	7	3	7	7	0	24
NE Patriots (3-0)	14	3	0	7	3	27

Attendance: 60,072

Game #4 – Sunday, September 21, 1997

@ Foxboro Stadium	1	2	3	4	Final
Chicago Bears (0-4)	0	0	3	0	3
NE Patriots (4-0)	7	7	0	17	31

Attendance: 59,873

GAME BY GAME FROM DAY ONE

Game #5 – Monday, October 6, 1997

@ Mile High Stadium	1	2	3	4	Final
NE Patriots (4-1)	0	13	0	0	13
Denver Broncos (6-0)	14	0	17	3	34

Attendance: 75,821

Game #6 – Sunday, October 12, 1997

@ Foxboro Stadium	1	2	3	4	Final
Buffalo Bills (3-3)	0	0	0	6	6
NE Patriots (5-1)	10	6	17	0	33

Attendance: 59,802

Game #7 – Sunday, October 19, 1997

@ Giants Stadium	1	2	3	4	Final
NE Patriots (5-2)	0	5	14	0	19
NY Jets (5-3)	3	0	14	7	24

Attendance: 71,061

Game #8 – Monday, October 27, 1997

@ Foxboro Stadium	1	2	3	4	Final
GB Packers (6-2)	7	7	7	7	28
NE Patriots (5-3)	0	10	0	0	10

Attendance: 59,972

Game #9 – Sunday, November 2, 1997

@ Humphrey Metrodome	1	2	3	4	Final
NE Patriots (5-4)	0	3	0	15	18
Minnesota Vikings (7-2)	10	3	3	7	23

Attendance: 62,917

Game #10 – Sunday, November 9, 1997

@ Rich Stadium	1	2	3	4	Final
NE Patriots (6-4)	7	10	7	7	31
Buffalo Bills (5-5)	3	0	7	0	10

Attendance: 65,783

Game #11 – Sunday, November 16, 1997

@ Houlihan's Stadium	1	2	3	4	Final
NE Patriots (6-5)	0	0	0	7	7
TB Buccaneers (8-3)	7	3	7	10	27

Attendance: 70,479

Game #12 – Sunday, November 23, 1997

@ Foxboro Stadium	1	2	3	4	Final
Miami Dolphins (7-5)	0	3	7	14	24
NE Patriots (7-5)	3	21	3	0	27

Attendance: 59,002

Game #13 – Sunday, November 30, 1997

@ Foxboro Stadium	1	2	3	4	Final
Indianapolis Colts (1-12)	3	0	7	7	17
NE Patriots (8-5)	7	6	0	7	20

Attendance: 58,507

Game #14 – Sunday, December 7, 1997

@ ALLTEL Stadium	1	2	3	4	Final
NE Patriots (9-5)	13	7	3	3	26
Jacksonville Jaguars (9-5)	0	7	0	13	20

Attendance: 73,446

Game #15 – Saturday, December 13, 1997

@ Foxboro Stadium	1	2	3	4	OT	Final
Pittsburgh Steelers (11-4)	0	7	3	11	3	24
NE Patriots (9-6)	0	14	0	7	0	21

Attendance: 60,013

Game #16 – Monday, December 21, 1997

@ Pro Player Stadium	1	2	3	4	Final
NE Patriots (10-6)	0	0	7	7	14
Miami Dolphins (9-7)	3	3	0	6	12

Attendance: 74,379

Game #17 – American Conference Wild Card Playoff Game
Sunday, December 28, 1997

@ Foxboro Stadium	1	2	3	4	Final
Miami Dolphins (9-8)	0	0	0	3	3
NE Patriots (11-6)	0	7	10	0	17

Attendance: 60,041

Game #18 – American Conference Divisional Playoff Game
Saturday, December 13, 1997

@ Three River Stadium	1	2	3	4	Final
NE Patriots (11-7)	0	3	0	3	6
Pittsburgh Steelers (12-5)	7	0	0	0	7

Attendance: 61,228

Lifetime W-L record	265-306-9
Lifetime coin-toss record	290-290
Lifetime OT record	9-15

1998 (9-7), fourth in AFC East
Head Coach – Pete Carroll

1st round pick – Robert Edwards, RB, Georgia (18th overall) from Jets compensation for Curtis Martin
1st round pick – Tebucky Jones, DB, Syracuse (22nd overall)
2nd round pick – Tony Simmons, WR, Wisconsin (52nd overall) from Jets compensation for Bill Parcells
3rd round pick – Chris Floyd, FB, Michigan (81st overall) from Jets compensation for Curtis Martin

Game #1 – Monday, September 7, 1998

@ Mile High Stadium	1	2	3	4	Final
NE Patriots (0-1)	0	7	7	7	21
Denver Broncos (1-0)	10	7	3	7	27

Attendance: 74,745

Game #2 – Sunday, September 13, 1998

@ Foxboro Stadium	1	2	3	4	Final
Indianapolis Colts (0-2)	0	0	0	6	6
NE Patriots (1-1)	10	6	6	7	29

Attendance: 60,068

Game #3 – Sunday, September 20, 1998

@ Foxboro Stadium	1	2	3	4	Final
Tennessee Oilers (1-2)	3	3	7	3	16
NE Patriots (2-1)	3	3	7	14	27

Attendance: 59,973

Game #4 – Sunday, October 4, 1998

@ Superdome	1	2	3	4	Final
NE Patriots (3-1)	3	14	10	3	30
NO Saints (3-1)	0	14	3	10	27

Attendance: 56,172

GAME BY GAME FROM DAY ONE

Game #5 – Sunday, October 11, 1998

@ Foxboro Stadium	1	2	3	4	Final
KC Chiefs (4-2)	0	0	7	3	10
NE Patriots (4-1)	7	20	10	3	40

Attendance: 59,749

Game #6 – Monday, October 19, 1998

@ Foxboro Stadium	1	2	3	4	Final
NY Jets (3-3)	7	3	0	14	24
NE Patriots (4-2)	7	7	0	0	14

Attendance: 60,062

Game #7 – Sunday, October 25, 1998

@ Pro Player Stadium	1	2	3	4	OT	Final
NE Patriots (4-3)	0	0	3	6	0	9
Miami Dolphins (5-2)	0	3	0	6	3	12

Attendance: 73,973

Game #8 – Sunday, November 1, 1998

@ RCA Dome	1	2	3	4	Final
NE Patriots (5-3)	7	7	0	7	21
Indianapolis Colts (1-7)	7	3	0	6	16

Attendance: 58,056

Game #9 – Sunday, November 8, 1998

@ Foxboro Stadium	1	2	3	4	Final
Atlanta Falcons (7-2) x	14	14	3	10	41
NE Patriots (5-4)	3	0	7	0	10

Attendance: 59,790

Game #10 – Sunday, November 15, 1998

@ Ralph Wilson Stadium	1	2	3	4	Final
NE Patriots (5-5)	0	3	0	7	10
Buffalo Bills (6-4)	3	3	7	0	13

Attendance: 72,020

Game #11 – Monday, November 23, 1998

@ Foxboro Stadium	1	2	3	4	Final
Miami Dolphins (7-4)	7	7	3	6	23
NE Patriots (6-5)	7	3	6	10	26

Attendance: 58,729

Game #12 – Sunday, November 29, 1998

@ Foxboro Stadium	1	2	3	4	Final
Buffalo Bills (7-5)	0	6	9	6	21
NE Patriots (7-5)	0	14	3	8	25

Attendance: 58,304

Game #13 – Sunday, December 6, 1998

@ Three Rivers Stadium	1	2	3	4	Final
NE Patriots (8-5)	3	10	0	10	23
Pittsburgh Steelers (7-6)	0	6	3	0	9

Attendance: 58,632

Game #14 – Sunday, December 13, 1998

@ Trans World Dome	1	2	3	4	Final
NE Patriots (8-6)	3	12	3	0	18
St. Louis Rams (4-10)	10	7	15	0	32

Attendance: 48,946

Game #15 – Sunday, December 20, 1998

@ Foxboro Stadium	1	2	3	4	Final
San Francisco 49ers (11-4)	0	21	0	0	21
NE Patriots (9-6)	7	7	0	10	24

Attendance: 59,153

Game #16 – Sunday, December 27, 1998

@ The Meadowlands	1	2	3	4	Final
NE Patriots (9-7)	0	3	0	7	10
NY Jets (12-4)	3	14	7	7	31

Attendance: 74,302

Game #17 – American Conference Wild Card Play-Off Game
Sunday, January 3, 1999

@ ALLTEL Stadium	1	2	3	4	Final
NE Patriots (9-8)	0	0	7	3	10
JAX Jaguars (12-5)	6	6	0	13	23

Attendance: 72,302

Lifetime W-L record	274-314-9
Lifetime coin-toss record	296-301
Lifetime OT record	9-16

1999 (8-8), fourth in AFC East
Head Coach – Pete Carroll

1st round pick – Damien Woody C Boston College (17th overall), from Seattle for 20th, 82nd and 191st overall
Seahawks traded 20th overall to Dallas, the Cowboys selected Ebenezer Ekuban, LB, North Carolina
1st round pick – Andy Katzenmoyer, LB, Ohio State (28th overall) from Jets compensation for Bill Parcells

Game #1 – Sunday, September 12, 1999

@ The Meadowlands	1	2	3	4	Final
NE Patriots (1-0)	3	7	17	3	30
NY Jets (0-1)	7	9	6	6	28

Attendance: 78,277

Game #2 – Sunday, September 19, 1999

@ Foxboro Stadium	1	2	3	4	Final
Indianapolis Colts (1-1)	14	14	0	0	28
NE Patriots (2-0)	0	7	7	17	31

Attendance: 59,640

Game #3 – Sunday, September 26, 1999

@ Foxboro Stadium	1	2	3	4	Final
NY Giants (1-2)	7	0	0	7	14
NE Patriots (2-1)	0	7	6	3	16

Attendance: 59,169

Game #4 – Sunday, October 3, 1999

@ Browns Stadium	1	2	3	4	Final
NE Patriots (4-0)	0	6	7	6	19
Cleveland Browns (0-4)	7	0	0	0	7

Attendance: 72,368

Game #5 – Sunday, October 10, 1999

@ Arrowhead Stadium	1	2	3	4	Final
NE Patriots (4-1)	7	0	0	7	14
KC Chiefs (3-2)	3	0	10	3	16

Attendance: 78,636

Game #6 – Sunday, October 17, 1999

@ Foxboro Stadium	1	2	3	4	Final
Miami Dolphins (4-1)	3	16	0	12	31
NE Patriots (4-2)	14	10	3	3	30

Attendance: 60,006

GAME BY GAME FROM DAY ONE

Game #7 – Sunday, October 24, 1999

@ Foxboro Stadium	1	2	3	4	Final
Denver Broncos (2-5)	0	10	3	10	23
NE Patriots (5-2)	10	7	7	0	24

Attendance: 60,011

Game #8 – Sunday, October 31, 1999

@ Sun Devil Stadium	1	2	3	4	Final
NE Patriots (6-2)	14	6	0	7	27
Arizona Cardinals (2-5)	0	0	3	0	3

Attendance: 55,830

Game #9 – Monday, November 15, 1999

@ Foxboro Stadium	1	2	3	4	Final
NY Jets (3-6) x	0	21	0	3	24
NE Patriots (6-3)	30	3	0	14	17

Attendance: 59,077

Game #10 – Sunday, November 21, 1999

@ Pro Player Stadium	1	2	3	4	Final
NE Patriots (6-4)	7	3	7	0	17
Miami Dolphins (8-2)	3	7	14	3	27

Attendance: 74,295

Game #11 – Sunday, November 28, 1999

@ Ralph Wilson Stadium	1	2	3	4	Final
NE Patriots (6-5)	0	0	0	7	7
Buffalo Bills (8-4)	3	7	7	0	17

Attendance: 72,111

Game #12 – Sunday, December 5, 1999

@ Foxboro Stadium	1	2	3	4	Final
Dallas Cowboys (6-6)	3	0	0	3	6
NE Patriots (7-5)	3	3	0	7	13

Attendance: 58,444

Game #13 – Sunday, December 12, 1999

@ RCA Dome	1	2	3	4	Final
NE Patriots (7-6)	3	3	3	6	15
Indianapolis Colts (11-2)	7	7	6	0	20

Attendance: 56,975

Game #14 – Sunday, December 19, 1999

@ Veterans Stadium	1	2	3	4	Final
NE Patriots (7-7)	0	6	3	0	9
Phila. Eagles (4-11)	10	7	7	0	24

Attendance: 65,478

Game #15 – Sunday, December 26, 1999

@ Foxboro Stadium	1	2	3	4	OT	Final
Buffalo Bills (10-5)	3	0	0	7	3	13
NE Patriots (7-8)	0	3	0	7	0	10

Attendance: 55,014

Game #16 – Sunday, January 2, 2000

@ Foxboro Stadium	1	2	3	4	Final
Baltimore Ravens (8-8)	0	3	0	0	3
NE Patriots (8-8)	0	13	7	0	20

Attendance: 50,263

Lifetime W-L record	282-322-9
Lifetime coin-toss record	307-306
Lifetime OT record	9-17

2000 (5-11), fifth in AFC East
Head Coach – Bill Belichick

1st round pick – to N.Y. Jets as compensation for Bill Belichick (16th overall)
N.Y. Jets traded pick to 49ers who selected Julian Peterson, LB, Michigan State (16th overall)
2nd round pick – Adrian Klemm, T, Hawaii (46th overall)

Game #1 – Sunday, September 3, 2000

@ Foxboro Stadium	1	2	3	4	Final
TB Buccaneers (1-0)	0	14	7	0	21
NE Patriots (0-1)	3	7	0	6	16

Attendance: 60,292

Game #2 – Monday, September 11, 2000

@ The Meadowlands	1	2	3	4	Final
NE Patriots (0-2)	3	9	0	7	19
NY Jets (2-0)	7	0	0	13	20

Attendance: 77,687

Game #3 – Sunday, September 17, 2000

@ Foxboro Stadium	1	2	3	4	Final
Minnesota Viking (3-0)	7	14	0	0	21
NE Patriots (0-3)	7	0	0	6	13

Attendance: 60,292

Game #4 – Sunday, September 24, 2000

@ Pro Player Stadium	1	2	3	4	Final
NE Patriots (0-4)	0	3	0	0	3
Miami Dolphins (3-1)	0	10	0	0	10

Attendance: 73,344

Game #5 – Sunday, October 1, 2000

@ Mile High Stadium	1	2	3	4	Final
NE Patriots (1-4)	14	7	7	0	28
Denver Broncos (2-3)	0	3	8	8	19

Attendance: 75,684

Game #6 – Sunday, October 8, 2000

@ Foxboro Stadium	1	2	3	4	Final
Indianapolis Colts (3-2)	0	10	3	3	16
NE Patriots (2-4)	3	7	0	14	24

Attendance: 60,292

Game #7 – Sunday, October 15, 2000

@ Foxboro Stadium	1	2	3	4	Final
NY Jets (5-1)	14	10	7	3	34
NE Patriots (2-5)	3	7	0	7	17

Attendance: 60,292

Game #8 – Sunday, October 22, 2000

@ RCA Dome	1	2	3	4	Final
NE Patriots (2-6)	7	6	10	0	23
Indianapolis Colts (5-2)	7	0	7	16	30

Attendance: 56,868

Game #9 – Monday, November 5, 2000

@ Foxboro Stadium	1	2	3	4	OT	Final
Buffalo Bills (5-4)	3	7	0	3	3	16
NE Patriots (2-7)	0	3	0	10	0	13

Attendance: 60,292

Game #10 – Sunday, November 12, 2000

@ Browns Stadium	1	2	3	4	Final
NE Patriots (2-8)	3	0	0	8	11
Cleveland Browns (3-8)	3	10	3	3	19

Attendance: 72,618

Game #11 – Sunday, November 19, 2000

@ Foxboro Stadium	1	2	3	4	Final
Cincinnati Bengals (2-9)	0	10	0	3	13
NE Patriots (3-8)	7	3	0	6	16

Attendance: 62,292

Game #12 – Thursday, November 23, 2000

@ Pontiac Silverdome	1	2	3	4	Final
NE Patriots (3-9)	6	0	3	0	9
Detroit Lions (8-4)	3	3	7	21	34

Attendance: 77,293

Game #13 – Monday, December 4, 2000

@ Foxboro Stadium	1	2	3	4	Final
KC Chief (5-8)	3	7	0	14	24
NE Patriots (4-9)	10	10	7	3	30

Attendance: 60,292

Game #14 – Sunday, December 10, 2000

@ Soldier Field	1	2	3	4	Final
NE Patriots (4-10)	0	10	0	7	17
Chicago Bears (4-10)	3	7	7	7	24

Attendance: 66,944

Game #15 – Sunday, December 17, 2000

@ Ralph Wilson Stadium	1	2	3	4	OT	Final
NE Patriots (5-10)	3	0	0	7	3	13
Buffalo Bills (7-8)	0	3	0	7	0	10

Attendance: 47,230

Game #16 – Sunday, December 24, 2000

@ Foxboro Stadium	1	2	3	4	Final
Miami Dolphins (11-5)	3	14	0	10	27
NE Patriots (5-11)	7	14	3	0	24

Attendance: 60,292

Lifetime W-L record   287-333-9
Lifetime coin-toss record   313-312-4
Lifetime OT record   10-18

2001 (11-5), first in AFC East
Head Coach – Bill Belichick

1st round pick – Richard Seymour, DT, Georgia (6th overall)

Game #1 – Sunday, September 9, 2001

@ Paul Brown Stadium	1	2	3	4	Final
NE Patriots (0-1)	0	10	0	7	17
Cincinnati Bengals (1-0)	0	10	13	0	23

Attendance: 51,521

Game #2 – Sunday, September 23, 2001

@ Foxboro Stadium	1	2	3	4	Final
NY Jets (1-1)	0	3	7	0	10
NE Patriots (0-2)	3	0	0	0	3

Attendance: 60,292

Game #3 – Sunday, September 30, 2001

@ Foxboro Stadium	1	2	3	4	Final
Indianapolis Colts (2-1)	0	0	7	6	13
NE Patriots (1-2)	7	13	3	21	44

Attendance: 60,292

Game #4 – Sunday, October 7, 2001

@ Pro Player Stadium	1	2	3	4	Final
NE Patriots (1-3)	7	3	0	0	10
Miami Dolphins (3-1)	7	10	10	3	30

Attendance: 73,024

Game #5 – Sunday, October 14, 2001

@ Foxboro Stadium	1	2	3	4	OT	Final
SD Chargers (3-2)	3	3	7	13	0	26
NE Patriots (2-3)	3	6	7	10	3	29

Attendance: 60,292

Game #6 – Sunday, October 21, 2001

@ RCA Dome	1	2	3	4	Final
NE Patriots (3-3)	7	21	3	7	38
Indianapolis Colts (2-3)	3	3	11	0	17

Attendance: 56,022

Game #7 – Sunday, October 28, 2001

@ Invesco Field	1	2	3	4	Final
NE Patriots (3-4)	10	7	3	0	20
Denver Broncos (4-3)	7	3	14	7	31

Attendance: 74,750

Game #8 – Sunday, November 4, 2001

@ Georgia Dome	1	2	3	4	Final
NE Patriots (4-4)	0	17	7	0	24
Atlanta Falcons (3-4)	7	0	0	3	10

Attendance: 45,572

Game #9 – Monday, November 11, 2001

@ Foxboro Stadium	1	2	3	4	Final
Buffalo Bills (1-7)	0	3	0	8	11
NE Patriots (5-4)	7	0	7	7	21

Attendance: 60,292

Game #10 – Sunday, November 18, 2001

@ Foxboro Stadium	1	2	3	4	Final
St. Louis Rams (8-1)	7	7	3	7	24
NE Patriots (5-5)	7	3	0	7	17

Attendance: 60,292

Game #11 – Sunday, November 25, 2001

@ Foxboro Stadium	1	2	3	4	Final
NO Saints (5-5)	0	0	10	7	17
NE Patriots (6-5)	7	13	0	14	34

Attendance: 60,292

Game #12 – Sunday, December 2, 2001

@ The Meadowlands	1	2	3	4	Final
NE Patriots (7-5)	0	0	14	3	17
NY Jets (7-4)	10	3	3	0	16

Attendance: 78,712

Game #13 – Sunday, December 9, 2001

@ Foxboro Stadium	1	2	3	4	Final
Cleveland Browns (6-6)	10	0	3	3	16
NE Patriots (8-5)	3	17	0	7	27

Attendance: 60,292

Game #14 – Sunday, December 16, 2001

@ Ralph Wilson Stadium	1	2	3	4	OT	Final
NE Patriots (9-5)	3	3	0	3	3	12
Buffalo Bills (2-11)	0	0	3	6	0	9

Attendance: 45,527

Game #15 – Saturday, December 22, 2001

@ Foxboro Stadium	1	2	3	4	Final
Miami Dolphins (9-5)	0	3	0	10	13
NE Patriots (10-5)	0	20	0	0	20

Attendance: 60,292

Game #16 – Sunday, January 2, 2002

@ Ericsson Stadium	1	2	3	4	Final
NE Patriots (11-5)	10	0	14	14	38
Carolina Panthers (1-15)	0	3	3	0	6

Attendance: 71,907

Game #17 – American Football Conference Divisional Playoff Game
Saturday, January 19, 2002

@ Foxboro Stadium	1	2	3	4	OT	Final
Oakland Raiders (11-7)	0	7	6	0	0	13
NE Patriots (12-5)	0	0	3	10	3	16

Attendance: 60,292

Game #18 – American Football Conference Championship Game
Sunday, January 27, 2002

@ Heinz Field	1	2	3	4	Final
NE Patriots (13-5)	7	7	7	3	24
Pittsburgh Steelers (14-4)	0	3	14	0	17

Attendance: 64,704

Game #19 – Super Bowl XXXVI
Sunday, February 2, 2002

@ Superdome	1	2	3	4	Final
St. Louis Rams (16-3)	3	0	0	14	17
NE Patriots 14-5)	0	14	3	3	20

Attendance: 72,922

Lifetime W-L record	301-338-9
Lifetime coin-toss record	324-324
Lifetime OT record	13-18

2002 (9-7), second in AFC East
Head Coach – Bill Belichick

1st round pick – traded 32nd, 96th and 234th overall to Redskins for 21st overall
Patriots selected Daniel Graham, TE, Colorado (21st overall)
Redskins selected Patrick Ramsey, QB, Tulane (32nd overall)

Game #1 – Monday, September 9, 2002

@ Gillette Stadium	1	2	3	4	Final
Pittsburgh Steelers (0-1)	7	0	0	7	14
NE Patriots (1-0)	7	3	17	3	30

Attendance: 68,436

Game #2 – Sunday, September 15, 2002

@ The Meadowlands	1	2	3	4	Final
NE Patriots (2-0)	0	10	17	17	44
NY Jets (1-1)	0	0	7	0	7

Attendance: 78,726

Game #3 – Sunday, September 22, 2002

@ Gillette Stadium	1	2	3	4	OT	Final
KC Chiefs (1-2)	3	7	7	21	0	38
NE Patriots (3-0)	0	9	8	21	3	41

Attendance: 68,436

Game #4 – Sunday, September 29, 2002

@ Qualcomm Stadium	1	2	3	4	Final
NE Patriots (3-1)	7	7	0	0	14
SD Chargers (4-0)	7	7	7	0	21

Attendance: 66,643

PATRIOTS PASSION

Game #5 – Sunday, October 6, 2002

@ Pro Player Stadium	1	2	3	4	Final
NE Patriots (3-2)	0	0	6	7	13
Miami Dolphins (4-1)	6	10	7	3	26

Attendance: 73,369

Game #6 – Sunday, October 13, 2002

@ Gillette Stadium	1	2	3	4	Final
Green Bay Packers (5-1)	0	14	7	7	28
NE Patriots (3-3)	0	3	0	7	10

Attendance: 68,436

Game #7 – Sunday, October 27, 2002

@ Gillette Stadium	1	2	3	4	Final
Denver Broncos (6-2)	7	14	0	3	24
NE Patriots (3-4)	0	7	3	6	16

Attendance: 68,436

Game #8 – Sunday, November 3, 2002

@ Ralph Wilson Stadium	1	2	3	4	Final
NE Patriots (4-4)	7	10	14	7	38
Buffalo Bills (5-4)	0	7	0	0	7

Attendance: 73,448

Game #9 – Sunday, November 10, 2002

@ Memorial Stadium	1	2	3	4	Final
NE Patriots (5-4)	0	6	10	17	33
Chicago Bears (2-7)	0	6	21	3	30

Attendance: 63,105

Game #10 – Sunday, November 17, 2002

@Network Associates	1	2	3	4	Final
NE Patriots (5-5)	3	3	7	7	20
Oakland Raiders (6-4)	3	14	7	3	27

Attendance: 62,552

Game #11 – Sunday, November 24, 2002

@ Gillette Stadium	1	2	3	4	Final
Minnesota Vikings (3-8)	0	7	7	3	17
NE Patriots (6-5)	7	14	0	3	24

Attendance: 68,436

Game #12 – Thursday, November 28, 2002

@ Ford Field	1	2	3	4	Final
NE Patriots (7-5)	10	7	0	3	20
Detroit Lions (3-9)	3	3	3	3	12

Attendance: 62,109

Game #13 – Sunday, December 8, 2002

@ Gillette Stadium	1	2	3	4	Final
Buffalo Bills (6-7)	0	0	10	7	17
NE Patriots (8-5)	17	3	0	7	27

Attendance: 68,436

Game #14 – Monday, December 16, 2002

@ The Coliseum	1	2	3	4	Final
NE Patriots (8-6)	0	0	7	0	7
Tennessee Titans (9-5)	0	14	7	3	24

Attendance: 68,809

Game #15 – Sunday, December 22, 2002

@ Gillette Stadium	1	2	3	4	Final
NY Jets (8-7)	14	3	3	10	30
NE Patriots (8-7)	7	3	7	0	17

Attendance: 68,436

Game #16 – Sunday, December 29, 2002

@ Gillette Stadium	1	2	3	4	OT	Final
Miami Dolphins (9-7)	7	14	0	3	0	24
NE Patriots (9-7)	0	10	3	11	3	27

Attendance: 68,436

Lifetime W-L record	310-345-9
Lifetime coin-toss record	335-329
Lifetime OT record	15-18

GAME BY GAME FROM DAY ONE

2003 (14-2), first in AFC East
Head Coach – Bill Belichick

1st round pick – traded 14th and 193rd overall to Redskins through Jets and Bears for 13th overall then picked Ty Warren, DT, Texas A&M (13th overall); Bears selected Michael Haynes, DT, Penn State (14th overall) Patriots dealt 19th overall to Ravens for 21st overall in 2004 Draft and 41st overall in 2003, then traded 41st and 75th overall to Texans for 36th and 117th overall and selected Eugene Wilson, DB, Illinois (41st overall) and Dan Klecko, DT, Temple (117th overall); Ravens selected Kyle Boller, QB, California with 19th overall pick

Game #1 – Sunday, September 7, 2003

@ Ralph Wilson Stadium	1	2	3	4	Final
NE Patriots (0-1)	0	0	0	0	0
Buffalo Bills (1-0)	7	14	0	10	31

Attendance: 73,262

Game #2 – Sunday, September 14, 2003

@ Lincoln Financial Field	1	2	3	4	Final
NE Patriots (1-1)	3	14	7	7	31
Phila. Eagles (0-2)	0	7	0	3	10

Attendance: 67,624

Game #3 – Sunday, September 21, 2003

@ Gillette Stadium	1	2	3	4	Final
NY Jets (0-3)	0	3	3	7	16
NE Patriots (2-1)	3	3	10	07	23

Attendance: 68,436

Game #4 – Sunday, September 28, 2003

@ FedEx Field	1	2	3	4	Final
NE Patriots (2-2)	3	0	7	7	17
WDC Redskins (3-1)	3	3	14	0	20

Attendance: 83,632

Game #5 – Sunday, October 5, 2003

@ Gillette Stadium	1	2	3	4	Final
Tennessee Titans (3-2)	6	7	3	14	30
NE Patriots (3-2)	7	0	14	17	38

Attendance: 68,436

Game #6 – Sunday, October 12, 2003

@ Gillette Stadium	1	2	3	4	Final
NY Giants (2-3) x	3	0	0	3	6
NE Patriots (4-2)	7	0	10	0	17

Attendance: 68,436

Game #7 – Sunday, October 19, 2003

@ Pro Player Stadium	1	2	3	4	OT	Final
NE Patriots (5-2)	3	3	7	0	6	19
Miami Dolphins (4-2)	0	10	3	0	0	13

Attendance: 73,650

Game #8 – Sunday, October 26, 2003

@ Gillette Stadium	1	2	3	4	Final
Cleveland Browns (3-5)	0	3	0	0	3
NE Patriots (6-2)	3	0	3	3	9

Attendance: 68,436

Game #9 – Monday, November 3, 2003

@ Invesco Field	1	2	3	4	Final
NE Patriots (7-2)	7	6	7	10	30
Denver Broncos (5-4)	7	10	7	2	26

Attendance: 76,203

Game #10 – Sunday, November 17, 2003

@ Gillette Stadium	1	2	3	4	Final
Dallas Cowboys (7-3)	0	0	0	0	0
NE Patriots (8-2)	3	6	0	3	12

Attendance: 68,436

PATRIOTS PASSION

Game #11 – Sunday, November 24, 2003

@ Reliant Stadium	1	2	3	4	OT	Final
NE Patriots (9-2)	10	0	10	0	3	23
Houston Texans (4-7)	3	0	7	10	0	20

Attendance: 70,719

Game #12 – Sunday, November 30, 2003

@ RCA Dome	1	2	3	4	Final
NE Patriots (10-2)	10	14	7	7	38
Indianapolis Colts (9-3)	0	10	14	10	34

Attendance: 57,102

Game #13 – Sunday, December 7, 2003

@ Gillette Stadium	1	2	3	4	Final
Miami Dolphins (8-5)	0	0	0	0	0
NE Patriots (11-2)	3	0	0	9	12

Attendance: 68,436

Game #14 – Sunday, December 14, 2003

@ Gillette Stadium	1	2	3	4	Final
JAX Jaguars (4-10)	3	3	0	7	13
NE Patriots (12-2)	7	6	0	14	27

Attendance: 68,436

Game #15 – Saturday, December 20, 2003

@ The Meadowlands	1	2	3	4	Final
NE Patriots (13-2)	7	7	7	0	21
NY Jets (6-9)	7	3	0	6	16

Attendance: 77,835

Game #16 – Sunday, December 29, 2003

@ Gillette Stadium	1	2	3	4	Final
Buffalo Bills (6-10)	0	0	0	0	0
NE Patriots (14-2)	14	14	0	3	31

Attendance: 68,436

Game #17 – American Football Conference Divisional Playoff Game
Saturday, January 10, 2004

@ Gillette Stadium	1	2	3	4	Final
Tennessee Titans (13-5)	7	0	7	0	14
NE Patriots (15-2)	7	7	0	3	17

Attendance: 68,436

Game #18 – American Football Conference Championship Game
Sunday, January 18, 2004

@ Gillette Stadium	1	2	3	4	Final
Indianapolis Colts (14-5)	0	0	7	7	14
NE Patriots (16-2)	7	8	6	3	24

Attendance: 68,436

Game # 19 – Super Bowl XXXVIII
Sunday, February 1, 2004

@ Reliant Stadium	1	2	3	4	Final
Carolina Panthers (14-6)	0	10	0	19	29
NE Patriots (17-2)	0	14	0	18	32

Attendance: 71,525

Lifetime W-L record	327-347-9
Lifetime coin-toss record	340-343
Lifetime OT record	17-18

GAME BY GAME FROM DAY ONE

2004 (14-2), first in AFC East
Head Coach – Bill Belichick

Patriots acquired 21st overall in 2004 and 41st overall in 2003 from Ravens for 19th overall in the 2003 Draft
Patriots selected Vince Wolfork, DT, Miami (FL) (21st overall)
1st round pick – Benjamin Watson, TE, Georgia (32nd overall)
Patriots dealt 56th overall to Bengals for RB Corey Dillon; Bengals selected Madieu Williams, DB, Maryland
(56th overall)

Game #1 – Thursday, September 9, 2004

@ Gillette Stadium	1	2	3	4	Final
Indianapolis Colts (0-1)	0	17	0	7	24
NE Patriots (1-0)	3	10	14	0	27

Attendance: 68,756

Game #2 – Sunday, September 19, 2004

@ Sun Devil Stadium	1	2	3	4	Final
NE Patriots (2-0)	7	7	3	6	23
Arizona Cardinals (0-2)	0	6	6	0	12

Attendance: 51,557

Game #3 – Sunday, October 3, 2004

@ Ralph Wilson Stadium	1	2	3	4	Final
NE Patriots (3-0)	10	7	0	14	31
Buffalo Bills (0-3)	10	7	0	0	17

Attendance: 72,698

Game #4 – Sunday, October 10, 2004

@ Gillette Stadium	1	2	3	4	Final
Miami Dolphins (0-5)	0	7	3	0	10
NE Patriots (4-0)	7	10	7	0	24

Attendance: 68,756

Game #5 – Sunday, October 17, 2004

@ Gillette Stadium	1	2	3	4	Final
Seattle Seahawks (3-2)	0	6	3	11	20
NE Patriots (5-0)	10	10	0	10	30

Attendance: 68,756

Game #6 – Sunday, October 24, 2004

@ Gillette Stadium	1	2	3	4	Final
NY Jets (5-1)	0	7	0	0	7
NE Patriots (6-0)	3	10	0	0	13

Attendance: 68,756

Game #7 – Sunday, October 31, 2004

@ Heinz Field	1	2	3	4	Final
NE Patriots (6-1)	3	7	3	7	20
Pittsburgh Steelers (6-1)	21	3	10	0	34

Attendance: 64,737

Game #8 – Sunday, November 7, 2004

@ Edwards Jones Dome	1	2	3	4	Final
NE Patriots (7-1)	6	13	14	7	40
St. Louis Rams (4-4)	0	14	0	8	22

Attendance: 66,107

Game #9 – Sunday, November 14, 2004

@ Gillette Stadium	1	2	3	4	Final
Buffalo Bill (3-6)	0	0	6	0	6
NE Patriots (8-1)	3	17	3	6	29

Attendance: 68,756

Game #10 – Monday, November 22, 2004

@ Arrowhead Stadium	1	2	3	4	Final
NE Patriots (9-1)	7	10	7	3	27
KC Chiefs (3-7)	10	0	3	6	19

Attendance: 78,431

Game #11 – Sunday, November 28, 2004

@ Gillette Stadium	1	2	3	4	Final
Baltimore Ravens (7-4)	0	3	0	0	3
NE Patriots (10-1)	0	3	6	15	24

Attendance: 68,756

Game #12 – Sunday, December 5, 2004

@ Browns Stadium	1	2	3	4	Final
NE Patriots (11-1)	14	7	21	0	42
Cleveland Browns (3-9)	0	7	0	8	15

Attendance: 73,028

Game #13 – Sunday, December 12, 2004

@ Gillette Stadium	1	2	3	4	Final
Cincinnati Bengals (6-7)	0	14	7	7	28
NE Patriots (12-1)	7	21	7	0	35

Attendance: 68,756

Game #14 – Monday, December 20, 2004

@ Pro Player Stadium	1	2	3	4	Final
NE Patriots (12-2)	7	7	7	7	28
Miami Dolphins (3-11)	7	3	7	12	29

Attendance: 73,629

Game #15 – Saturday, December 26, 2004

@ The Meadowlands	1	2	3	4	Final
NE Patriots (13-2)	0	13	3	7	23
NY Jets (10-5)	0	0	0	7	7

Attendance: 77,975

Game #16 – Sunday, January 2, 2005

@ Gillette Stadium	1	2	3	4	Final
San Francisco 49ers (2-14)	7	0	0	0	7
NE Patriots (14-2)	0	7	7	7	21

Attendance: 68,756

Game #17 – American Football Conference Divisional Playoff Game
Sunday, January 16, 2005

@ Gillette Stadium	1	2	3	4	Final
Indianapolis Colts (13-5)	0	3	0	0	3
NE Patriots (15-2)	0	6	7	7	20

Attendance: 68,756

Game #18 – American Football Conference Championship Game
Sunday, January 23, 2005

@ Heinz Field	1	2	3	4	Final
NE Patriots (16-2)	10	14	7	10	41
Pittsburgh Steelers (16-2)	3	0	14	10	27

Attendance: 65,242

Game #19 – Super Bowl XXXVIII
Sunday, February 2, 2005

@ ALLTEL Stadium	1	2	3	4	Final
NE Patriots (17-2)	0	7	7	10	24
Phila. Eagles (15-4)	0	7	7	7	21

Attendance: 78,125

Lifetime W-L record	344-349-9
Lifetime coin-toss record	349-353
Lifetime OT record	17-18

2005 (10-6), first in AFC East

Head Coach – Bill Belichick

1st round pick – Logan Mankins, OG, Fresno State (32nd overall)

Game #1 – Thursday, September 8, 2005

@ Gillette Stadium	1	2	3	4	Final
Oakland Raiders (0-1)	7	7	0	6	20
NE Patriots (1-0)	10	7	6	7	30

Attendance: 68,756

Game #2 – Sunday, September 18, 2005

@ BoA Stadium	1	2	3	4	Final
NE Patriots (1-1)	7	0	10	0	17
Carolina Panthers (1-1)	7	10	3	7	27

Attendance: 73,528

Game #3 – Sunday, September 25, 2005

@ Heinz Field	1	2	3	4	Final
NE Patriots (2-1)	7	0	3	13	23
Pittsburgh Steelers (2-1)	10	0	3	07	20

Attendance: 64,868

Game #4 – Sunday October 2, 2005

@ Gillette Stadium	1	2	3	4	Final
SD Chargers (2-2)	3	14	14	10	41
NE Patriots (2-2)	7	10	0	0	17

Attendance: 68,756

Game #5 – Sunday, October 9, 2005

@ Georgia Dome	1	2	3	4	Final
NE Patriots (3-2)	14	0	14	3	31
Atlanta Falcons (3-2)	0	13	0	15	28

Attendance: 71,079

Game #6 – Sunday, October 16, 2005

@ Invesco Field	1	2	3	4	Final
NE Patriots (3-3)	3	0	3	14	20
Denver Broncos (5-1)	0	21	7	0	28

Attendance: 76,571

Game #7 – Sunday, October 30, 2005

@ Gillette Stadium	1	2	3	4	Final
Buffalo Bills (3-5)	0	3	7	6	16
NE Patriots (4-3)	0	0	7	14	21

Attendance: 68,756

Game #8 – Monday, November 7, 2005

@ Gillette Stadium	1	2	3	4	Final
Indianapolis Colts (8-0)	7	14	10	9	40
NE Patriots (4-4)	7	0	7	7	21

Attendance: 68,756

Game #9 – Sunday, November 13, 2005

@ Dolphins Stadium	1	2	3	4	Final
NE Patriots (5-4)	0	3	9	11	23
Miami Dolphins (3-6)	0	7	0	9	16

Attendance: 73,405

Game #10 – Sunday, November 20, 2005

@ Gillette Stadium	1	2	3	4	Final
NO Saints (2-8)	0	7	0	10	17
NE Patriots (6-4)	7	7	7	3	24

Attendance: 68,756

Game #11 – Sunday, November 27, 2005

@ Arrowhead Stadium	1	2	3	4	Final
NE Patriots (6-5)	0	3	7	6	16
KC Chiefs (7-4)	7	12	7	0	26

Attendance: 78,025

Game #12 – Sunday, December 4, 2005

@ Gillette Stadium	1	2	3	4	Final
NY Jets (2-10)	0	3	0	0	3
NE Patriots (7-5)	0	6	7	3	16

Attendance: 68,756

PATRIOTS PASSION

Game #13 – Sunday, December 11, 2005

@ Ralph Wilson Stadium	1	2	3	4	Final
NE Patriots (8-5)	7	7	7	14	35
Buffalo Bills (4-9)	0	0	0	7	7

Attendance: 71,180

Game #14 – Saturday, December 17, 2005

@ Gillette Stadium	1	2	3	4	Final
TB Buccaneers (9-5)	0	0	0	0	0
NE Patriots (9-5)	7	14	0	7	28

Attendance: 68,756

Game #15 – Monday, December 26, 2005

@ The Meadowlands	1	2	3	4	Final
NE Patriots (10-5)	7	14	7	3	31
NY Jets (3-12)	7	0	0	14	21

Attendance: 77,569

Game #16 – Sunday, January 1, 2006

@ Gillette Stadium	1	2	3	4	Final
Miami Dolphins (9-7)	7	6	5	10	28
NE Patriots (10-6)	7	3	3	13	26

Attendance: 68,756

Game #17 – American Football Conference Wild Card Playoff Game
Saturday, January 7, 2006

@ Gillette Stadium	1	2	3	4	Final
JAX Jaguars (12-5)	0	3	0	0	3
NE Patriots (11-6)	0	7	14	7	28

Attendance: 68,756

Game #18 – American Football Conference Divisional Playoff Game
Saturday, January 14, 2006

@ Invesco Field	1	2	3	4	Final
NE Patriots (11-7)	0	3	3	7	13
Denver Broncos (14-3)	0	10	7	10	27

Attendance: 76,238

Lifetime W-L record	355-356-9
Lifetime coin-toss record	359-361
Lifetime OT record	17-18

2006 (12-4), first in AFC East
Head Coach – Bill Belichick

1st round pick – Laurence Maroney, RB, Minnesota (21st overall)

Game #1 – Sunday, September 10, 2006

@ Gillette Stadium	1	2	3	4	Final
Buffalo Bills (0-1)	10	7	0	0	17
NE Patriots (1-0)	7	0	7	5	19

Attendance: 68,756

Game #2 – Sunday, September 17, 2006

@ The Meadowlands	1	2	3	4	Final
NE Patriots (2-0)	7	10	7	0	24
NY Jets (1-1)	0	0	14	3	17

Attendance: 77,595

Game #3 – Sunday, September 24, 2006

@ Gillette Stadium	1	2	3	4	Final
Denver Broncos (2-1)	0	10	0	7	17
NE Patriots (2-1)	0	0	0	7	7

Attendance: 68,756

Game #4 – Sunday, October 1, 2006

@ Paul Brown Stadium	1	2	3	4	Final
NE Patriots (3-1)	0	14	7	17	38
Cincinnati Bengals (3-1)	6	0	7	0	13

Attendance: 66,035

Game #5 – Sunday, October 8, 2006

@ Gillette Stadium	1	2	3	4	Final
Miami Dolphins (1-4)	0	10	0	0	10
NE Patriots (4-1)	3	10	0	7	20

Attendance: 68,756

Game #6 – Sunday, October 22, 2006

@ Ralph Wilson Stadium	1	2	3	4	Final
NE Patriots (5-1)	14	0	7	7	28
Buffalo Bills (2-5)	3	0	0	3	6

Attendance: 72,180

Game #7 – Monday, October 30, 2006

@ HHH Metrodome	1	2	3	4	Final
NE Patriots (6-1)	7	10	14	0	31
Minnesota Vikings (4-3)	0	0	7	0	7

Attendance: 63,819

Game #8 – Sunday, November 5, 2006

@ Gillette Stadium	1	2	3	4	Final
Indianapolis Colts (8-0)	7	10	7	3	27
NE Patriots (6-2)	0	14	3	3	20

Attendance: 68,756

Game #9 – Sunday, November 12, 2006

@ Gillette Stadium	1	2	3	4	Final
NY Jets (5-4)	0	7	3	7	17
NE Patriots (6-3)	0	6	0	8	14

Attendance: 68,756

Game #10 – Sunday, November 19, 2006

@ Lambeau Field	1	2	3	4	Final
NE Patriots (7-3)	7	14	7	7	35
Green Bay Packers (4-6)	0	0	0	0	0

Attendance: 70,753

Game #11 – Sunday, November 26, 2006

@ Gillette Stadium	1	2	3	4	Final
Chicago Bears (9-2)	0	3	0	10	13
NE Patriots (8-3)	0	10	0	7	17

Attendance: 68,756

Game #12 – Sunday, December 3, 2006

@ Gillette Stadium	1	2	3	4	Final
Detroit Lions (2-10)	0	10	8	3	21
NE Patriots (9-3)	3	10	0	15	28

Attendance: 68,756

Game #13 – Sunday, December 10, 2006

@ Dolphin Stadium	1	2	3	4	Final
NE Patriots (9-4)	0	0	0	0	0
Miami Dolphins (6-7)	3	3	7	8	21

Attendance: 74,033

Game #14 – Sunday, December 17, 2006

@ Gillette Stadium	1	2	3	4	Final
Houston Texans (4-10)	0	0	7	0	7
NE Patriots (10-4)	17	10	7	6	40

Attendance: 68,756

Game #15 – Sunday, December 24, 2006

@ Alltel Stadium	1	2	3	4	Final
NE Patriots (11-4)	0	10	7	7	24
JAX Jaguars (8-7)	0	7	7	7	21

Attendance: 67,164

Game #16 – Sunday, December 31, 2006

@ LP Field	1	2	3	4	Final
NE Patriots (12-4)	9	10	7	14	40
Tennessee Titans (8-8)	3	7	13	0	23

Attendance: 69,143

Game #17 – American Football Conference Wild Card Playoff Game
Sunday, January 7, 2007

@ Gillette Stadium	1	2	3	4	Final
NY Jets (10-7)	3	7	3	3	16
NE Patriots (13-4)	7	10	6	14	37

Attendance: 68,756

Game #18 – American Football Conference Divisional Playoff Game
Saturday, January 14, 2007

@ Qualcomm Stadium	1	2	3	4	Final
NE Patriots (14-4)	3	7	3	11	24
SD Chargers (14-3)	0	14	0	7	21

Attendance: 68,810

Game #19 – American Football Conference Championship Game
Saturday, January 14, 2007

@ RCA Dome	1	2	3	4	Final
NE Patriots (14-5)	7	14	7	6	34
Indianapolis Colts (15-4)	3	3	15	17	38

Attendance: 57,433

Lifetime W-L record	369-361-9
Lifetime coin-toss record	372-367
Lifetime OT record	17-18

2007 (16-0), first in AFC East
Head Coach – Bill Belichick

1st round pick – Brandon Meriweather, DB, Miami (FL) (24th overall)

Game #1 – Sunday, September 9, 2007

@ The Meadowlands	1	2	3	4	Final
NE Patriots (1-0)	7	7	14	10	38
NY Jets (0-1)	0	7	7	0	14

Attendance: 77,900

Game #2 – Sunday, September 16, 2007

@ Gillette Stadium	1	2	3	4	Final
SD Chargers (1-1)	0	0	7	7	14
NE Patriots (2-0)	14	10	7	7	38

Attendance: 68,756

Game #3 – Sunday, September 23, 2007

@ Gillette Stadium	1	2	3	4	Final
Buffalo Bills (0-3)	7	0	0	0	7
NE Patriots (3-0)	3	14	14	7	38

Attendance: 68,756

Game #4 – Monday, October 1, 2007

@ Paul Brown Stadium	1	2	3	4	Final
NE Patriots (4-0)	10	7	7	10	34
Cincinnati Bengals (1-3)	0	7	3	3	13

Attendance: 66,113

GAME BY GAME FROM DAY ONE

Game #5 – Sunday, October 7, 2007

@ Gillette Stadium	1	2	3	4	Final
Cleveland Browns (2-3)	0	0	3	14	17
NE Patriots (5-0)	10	10	0	14	34

Attendance: 68,756

Game #6 – Sunday, October 14, 2007

@ Texas Stadium	1	2	3	4	Final
NE Patriots (6-0)	14	7	10	17	48
Dallas Cowboys (5-1)	0	17	7	3	27

Attendance: 63,984

Game #7 – Sunday, October 21, 2007

@ Dolphin Stadium	1	2	3	4	Final
NE Patriots (7-0)	14	28	0	7	49
Miami Dolphins (0-7)	0	7	0	21	28

Attendance: 71,951

Game #8 – Sunday, October 28, 2007

@ Gillette Stadium	1	2	3	4	Final
WDC Redskins (4-3)	0	0	0	7	7
NE Patriots (8-0)	07	17	14	14	52

Attendance: 68,756

Game #9 – Sunday, November 4, 2007

@ RCA Dome	1	2	3	4	Final
NE Patriots (9-0)	0	7	3	14	24
Indianapolis Colts (7-1)	3	10	0	7	20

Attendance: 57,540

Game #10 – Sunday, November 18, 2007

@ Ralph Wilson Stadium	1	2	3	4	Final
NE Patriots (10-0)	14	21	7	14	56
Buffalo Bills (5-5)	7	0	3	0	10

Attendance: 71,338

Game #11 – Sunday, November 25, 2007

@ Gillette Stadium	1	2	3	4	Final
Phila. Eagles (5-6)	7	14	7	0	28
NE Patriots (11-0)	14	10	0	7	31

Attendance: 68,756

Game #12 – Monday, December 3, 2007

@ M&T Bank Stadium	1	2	3	4	Final
NE Patriots (12-0)	3	7	7	10	27
Baltimore Ravens (4-8)	7	3	7	7	24

Attendance: 71,382

Game #13 – Sunday, December 9, 2007

@ Gillette Stadium	1	2	3	4	Final
Pittsburgh Steelers (9-4)	3	10	0	0	13
NE Patriots (13-0)	7	10	14	3	34

Attendance: 68,756

Game #14 – Sunday, December 16, 2007

@ Gillette Stadium	1	2	3	4	Final
NY Jets (3-11)	0	7	0	3	10
NE Patriots (14-0)	7	10	0	3	20

Attendance: 68,756

Game #15 – Sunday, December 23, 2007

@ Gillette Stadium	1	2	3	4	Final
Miami Dolphins (1-14)	0	0	7	0	7
NE Patriots (15-0)	7	21	0	0	28

Attendance: 68,756

Game #16 – Saturday, December 29, 2007

@ Giant Stadium	1	2	3	4	Final
NE Patriots (16-0)	3	13	7	15	38
NY Giants (10-6)	7	14	7	7	35

Attendance: 79,110

Game # 17 – American Football Conference Divisional Playoff Game
Saturday, January 12, 2008

@ Gillette Stadium	1	2	3	4	Final
JAX Jaguars (12-6)	7	7	3	3	20
NE Patriots (17-0)	7	7	14	3	31

Attendance: 68,756

Game # 18 – American Football Conference Championship Game
Saturday, January 20, 2008

@ Gillette Stadium	1	2	3	4	Final
SD Chargers (13-6)	3	6	3	0	12
NE Patriots (18-0)	0	14	0	7	21

Attendance: 68,756

Game #19 – Super Bowl XLII
Sunday, February 3, 2008

@ U. of Phoenix Stadium	1	2	3	4	Final
NY Giants (14-6)	3	0	0	14	17
NE Patriots (18-1)	0	7	0	7	14

Attendance: 71,101

Lifetime W-L record	387-362-9
Lifetime coin-toss record	379-379
Lifetime OT record	17-18

2008 (11-5), tied for first in AFC East
Head Coach – Bill Belichick

1st round pick – Jerod Mayo, LB, Tennessee (10th overall)

Game #1 – Sunday, September 7, 2008

@ Gillette Stadium	1	2	3	4	Final
KC Chiefs (0-1)	0	3	0	7	10
NE Patriots (1-0)	0	7	7	3	17

Attendance: 68,756

Game #2 – Sunday, September 14, 2008

@ The Meadowlands	1	2	3	4	Final
NE Patriots (2-0)	3	3	10	3	19
NY Jets (1-1)	0	3	0	7	10

Attendance: 78,554

Game #3 – Sunday, September 21, 2008

@ Gillette Stadium	1	2	3	4	Final
Miami Dolphins (1-2)	7	14	17	10	38
NE Patriots (2-1)	0	6	7	0	13

Attendance: 68,756

Game #4 – Sunday, October 5, 2008

@ Candlestick Park	1	2	3	4	Final
NE Patriots (3-1)	7	10	17	6	30
San Francisco 49ers (2-3)	14	0	0	7	21

Attendance: 67,650

GAME BY GAME FROM DAY ONE

Game #5 – Sunday, October 12, 2008

@ Qualcomm Stadium	1	2	3	4	Final
NE Patriots (3-2)	0	3	10	7	10
SD Chargers (3-3)	10	7	10	3	30

Attendance: 68,704

Game #6 – Monday, October 20, 2008

@ Gillette Stadium	1	2	3	4	Final
Denver Broncos (4-3)	0	0	10	7	7
NE Patriots (4-2)	6	14	14	7	41

Attendance: 68,756

Game #7 – Sunday, October 26, 2008

@ Gillette Stadium	1	2	3	4	Final
St. Louis Rams (2-5)	3	7	13	3	26
NE Patriots (5-2)	7	6	0	10	23

Attendance: 68,756

Game #8 – Sunday, November 2, 2008

@ Lucas Oil Stadium	1	2	3	4	Final
NE Patriots (5-3)	0	6	6	3	15
Indianapolis Colts (4-4)	7	0	8	3	18

Attendance: 66,508

Game #9 – Sunday, November 9, 2008

@ Gillette Stadium	1	2	3	4	Final
Buffalo Bills (5-4)	0	3	0	7	10
NE Patriots (6-3)	7	3	3	7	20

Attendance: 68,756

Game #10 – Thursday, November 13, 2008

@ Gillette Stadium	1	2	3	4	OT	Final
NY Jets (7-3)	10	14	0	7	3	34
NE Patriots (6-4)	3	10	8	10	0	31

Attendance: 68,756

Game #11 – Sunday, November 23, 2008

@ Dolphin Stadium	1	2	3	4	Final
NE Patriots (7-4)	3	14	14	17	48
Miami Dolphins (6-5)	7	7	7	7	28

Attendance: 67,146

Game #12 – Sunday, November 30, 2008

@ Gillette Stadium	1	2	3	4	Final
Pittsburgh Steelers (9-3)	3	7	13	10	33
NE Patriots (7-5)	7	3	0	0	10

Attendance: 68,756

Game #13 – Sunday, December 7, 2008

@ Qwest Field	1	2	3	4	Final
NE Patriots (8-5)	3	7	3	11	24
Seattle Seahawks (2-11)	7	7	7	0	21

Attendance: 68,077

Game #14 – Sunday, December 14, 2008

@Oakland-Alameda Col.	1	2	3	4	Final
NE Patriots (9-5)	21	14	17	7	49
Oakland Raiders (3-11)	7	7	6	6	26

Attendance: 62,179

Game #15 – Sunday, December 21, 2008

@ Gillette Stadium	1	2	3	4	Final
Arizona Cardinals (8-7)	0	0	10	7	7
NE Patriots (10-5)	14	17	13	3	47

Attendance: 68,756

Game #16 – Saturday, December 28, 2008

@ Ralph Wilson Stadium	1	2	3	4	Final
NE Patriots (11-5)	3	0	17	3	13
Buffalo Bills (7-9)	0	0	0	0	0

Attendance: 71,282

Lifetime W-L record	398-367-9
Lifetime coin-toss record	387-387
Lifetime OT record	17-19

2009 (10 - 6), second in AFC East
Head Coach – Bill Belichick

Traded 23rd overall pick to Ravens for 26th and 162nd overall picks; then traded the 26th and 162nd overall to Packers for 41st and 73rd overall picks. With the 23rd pick, Ravens selected Michael Oher, OT, Mississippi. With 26th overall selection, the Packers tabbed Clay Matthews, LB, Southern California. The Patriots ended with four 2nd round picks: Patrick Chung, DB, Oregon (34th overall); Ron Brace, DL, Boston College (40th overall); Darius Butler, DB, Connecticut (41st overall); Sebastian Vollmer, OL, Houston (58th overall)

Game #1 – Monday, September 14, 2009

@ Gillette Stadium	1	2	3	4	Final
Buffalo Bills (1-0)	7	7	13	7	24
NE Patriots (1-0)	0	15	0	10	25

Attendance: 68,756

Game #2 – Sunday, September 20, 2009

@ The Meadowlands	1	2	3	4	Final
NE Patriots (1-1)	3	6	0	0	9
NY Jets (2-0)	0	3	10	3	16

Attendance: 78,312

Game #3 – Sunday, September 27, 2009

@ Gillette Stadium	1	2	3	4	Final
Atlanta Falcons (2-1)	3	7	0	0	10
NE Patriots (2-1)	3	10	3	10	26

Attendance: 68,756

Game #4 – Sunday, October 4, 2009

@ Gillette Stadium	1	2	3	4	Final
Baltimore Ravens (3-1)	7	0	7	7	21
NE Patriots (3-1)	3	14	7	3	27

Attendance: 68,756

Game #5 – Sunday, October 11, 2009

@ Invesco Field	1	2	3	4	OT	Final
NE Patriots (3-2)	10	7	0	0	0	17
Denver Broncos (5-0)	0	7	3	7	3	20

Attendance: 76,011

Game #6 – Sunday, October 18, 2009

@ Gillette Stadium	1	2	3	4	Final
Tennessee Titans (0-6)	0	0	10	0	0
NE Patriots (4-2)	10	35	14	0	59

Attendance: 68,756

Game #7 – Sunday, October 25, 2009

@ Wembley Stadium	1	2	3	4	Final
NE Patriots (5-2)	14	7	17	7	35
TB Buccaneers (0-7)	0	7	0	0	7

Attendance: 84,254

Game #8 – Sunday, November 8, 2009

@ Gillette Stadium	1	2	3	4	Final
Miami Dolphins (3-5)	3	7	17	0	17
NE Patriots (6-2)	7	9	8	3	27

Attendance: 68,756

Game #9 – Sunday, November 15, 2009

@ Lucas Oil Stadium	1	2	3	4	Final
NE Patriots (6-3)	7	17	0	10	34
Indianapolis Colts (9-0)	7	7	0	21	35

Attendance:

Game #10 – Sunday, November 22, 2009

@ Gillette Stadium	1	2	3	4	Final
NY Jets (4-6)	0	7	7	0	14
NE Patriots (7-3)	14	10	0	7	31

Attendance: 68,756

GAME BY GAME FROM DAY ONE

Game #11 – Monday, November 30, 2009

@ Louisiana Superdome	1	2	3	4	Final
NE Patriots (7-4)	7	3	7	0	17
NO Saints (11 - 0)	3	21	7	7	38

Attendance: 70,768

Game #12 – Sunday, December 6, 2009

@ Land Shark Stadium	1	2	3	4	Final
NE Patriots (7-5)	7	7	7	0	21
Miami Dolphins (6-6)	0	10	9	3	22

Attendance: 70,102

Game #13 – Sunday, December 13, 2009

@ Gillette Stadium	1	2	3	4	Final
Carolina Panthers (5-8)	7	0	0	3	10
NE Patriots (8-5)	0	7	7	6	20

Attendance: 68,756

Game #14 – Sunday, December 20, 2009

@ Ralph Wilson Stadium	1	2	3	4	Final
NE Patriots (9-5)	0	14	3	0	14
Buffalo Bills (5 -9)	3	0	0	7	10

Attendance: 70,000

Game #15 – Sunday, December 27, 2009

@ Gillette Stadium	1	2	3	4	Final
JAX Jaguars (7-8)	0	0	0	7	7
NE Patriots (10-5)	7	21	0	7	35

Attendance: 68,756

Game #16 – Sunday, January 3, 2010

@ Reliant Stadium	1	2	3	4	Final
NE Patriots (10-6)	7	6	7	7	27
Houston Texans (9-7)	7	6	0	21	34

Attendance: 71,029

Game #17 – American Football Conference Wild Card Playoff Game
Sunday, January 10, 2010

@ Gillette Stadium	1	2	3	4	Final
Baltimore Ravens (10-7)	24	0	3	6	33
NE Patriots (10-7)	0	7	7	0	14

Attendance: 68,756

Lifetime W-L record	408-374-9
Lifetime coin-toss record	396-395
Lifetime OT record	17-20

FIFTEEN
WHO WORE THE JERSEY FIRST?

First Patriots Player to Wear Each Uniform Number

#	Name	Position	College	Year
1	John Smith	K	Southampton (England)	1974
2	Pat Studstill	P	Houston	1972
3	Bruce Barnes	P	UCLA	1973
4	Jerrel Wilson	P	Houston	1978
5	Fred Steinfort	K	Boston College	1983
6	Mike Hubach	P	Kansas	1980
7	John Huarte	QB	Notre Dame	1966
8	Bill Bell	K	Kansas	1973
9	David Posey	K	Florida	1978
10	Harvey White	QB	Clemson	1960
11	Ed "Butch" Songin	QB	Boston College	1960
12	Don Allard	QB	Boston College	1962
13	R.C. Gamble	RB	South Carolina State	1968
14	Tom Greene	QB	Holy Cross	1960
15	Tom Dimitroff	QB	Miami (OH)	1960
16	Jim Plunkett	QB	Stanford	1971
17	Mike Taliaferro	QB	Illinois	1968
18	Randy Vataha	WR	Stanford	1971
19	Mike Kerrigan	QB	Northwestern	1983
20	Gino Cappelletti	WR-K-DB	Minnesota	1960
21	Bob Suci	DB	Michigan State	1963
22	Ron Burton	RB	Northwestern	1960
23	Dick Christy	RB	North Carolina State	1960
24	Walt Livingston	RB	Heidelberg (OH)	1960
25	Ross O'Hanley	DB	Boston College	1960
26	Walter Beach	RB-DB	Central Michigan	1960
27	Joe Bellino	RB	Navy	1965
28	Dave Cloutier	DB	South Carolina	1964
29	Aaron Marsh	WR	Eastern Kentucky	1968
30	Jim Crawford	RB	Wyoming	1960
31	Gerhardt Schwecks	RB	Syracuse	1960
32	Al Miller	RB	Boston College	1960
33	Fred Bruney	DB	Ohio State	1960
34	Joe Bischa	TE	Richmond	1960
35	Jim Nance	FB	Syracuse	1965
36	Tom Neumann	RB	Wisconsin	1963
37	Bill Bailey	RB	Cincinnati	1969
38	Al Snyder	WR	Holy Cross	1964
39	Perry Pruett	DB	North Texas State	1969
40	Larry Garron	RB	Western Illinois	1960

41	Billy Wells	RB	Michigan State	1960
42	Bob Soltis	DB	Minnesota	1960
43	Irvin Mallory	DB	Virginia Union	1971
44	Gerhardt Schwedes	RB	Syracuse	1960
45	Jerry Green	WR	Georgia Tech	1960
46	Larry Garron	RB	Western Illinois	1960
47	Billy Johnson	DB	Nebraska	1966
48	Don Webb	DB	Iowa State	1961
49	Tom Richardson	WR	Jackson State (MS)	1969
50	Bob Yates	C-OT-K	Syracuse	1961
51	Frank Robotti	LB	Boston College	1961
52	Phil Bennett	LB	Miami (FL)	1960
53	Tommy Addison	LB	South Carolina	1960
54	Bill E. Brown	LB	Syracuse	1960
55	Lonnie Farmer	LB	Tennessee-Chattanooga	1964
56	Walt Cudzik	C-LB-K	Purdue	1960
57	John Bramlett	LB	Memphis State	1969
58	Doug Satcher	LB	Southern Mississippi	1966
59	Brian Stenger	LB	Notre Dame	1973
60	Bob Lee	OG	Missouri	1960
61	Bob Yates	C-OT-K	Syracuse	1960
62	Abe Cohen	OG	Tennessee-Chattanooga	1960
63	Charley Leo	OG	Indiana	1960
64	Tony Sardisco	OG-DE-LB	Tulane	1960
65	Jack Davis	OE	Maryland	1960
66	Paul Feldhausen	OT	Northland College (WI)	1968
67	Art Hauser	DT-OT-OG	Xavier (OH)	1960
68	Karl Singer	OT	Purdue	1966
69	Julius Adams	DT-DE	Texas Southern	1971
70	Hal Smith	DT	UCLA	1960
71	Don Oakes	OT-DT	Virginia Tech	1963
72	Al Crow	DT	William & Mary (VA)	1960
73	Harry Jagielski	DT-OT	Indiana	1960
74	Jerry DeLucca	OT-DT	Tennessee	1960
75	George McGee	OT	Southern University (LA)	1960
76	Tony Discenzo	OT-K	Michigan State	1960
77	Bobby Cross	OT-DT	Stephen F. Austin	1960
78	Jim Boudrreaux	DE-OT	Louisiana Tech	1966
79	Al Richardson	DE	Grambling State	1960
80	Jack Rudolph	LB	Georgia Tech	1960
81	Jimmy Colclough	WR	Boston College	1960
82	Jim Whalen	TE	Boston College	1965
83	Harry Jacobs	LB-DE	Bradley	1960
84	Art Graham	WR	Boston College	1964
85	Don McComb	DE	Villanova	1960
86	Oscar Lofton	WR	Southeastern Louisiana	1960
87	Mike Long	WR	Brandeis	1960
88	Ron Berger	DE-DT	Wayne State (MI)	1969
89	Bob Dee	DE	Holy Cross	1960
90	George Webster	LB	Michigan State	1974

91	George Crump	DE	East Carolina	1982
92	Smiley Crewsell	DE	Michigan State	1985
93	Rico Corsetti	LB	Bates	1987
94	Mel Black	LB	Eastern Illinois	1986
95	Ed Reynolds	LB	Virginia	1983
96	Brent Williams	DE	Toledo	1986
97	Milford Hodge	NT-DE	Washington State	1986
98	Dennis Owens	NT	North Carolina State	1982
99	Ben Thomas	NT-DE	Auburn	1985

Sixteen
College Football Coaches' Quotable Quotes

"At Georgia Southern, we don't cheat. That costs money and we don't have any." Erik Russell, Georgia Southern.

"After you retire, there's only one big event left . . . And I ain't ready for that." - Bobby Bowden, Florida State

"The man who complains about the way the ball bounces is likely to be the one who dropped it." - Lou Holtz, Arkansas

"When you win, nothing hurts." - Joe Namath, Alabama

"Motivation is simple. You eliminate those who are not motivated." - Lou Holtz, Arkansas

"If you want to walk the heavenly streets of gold, you gotta know the password, 'Roll, tide, roll!." - Bear Bryant, Alabama

"A school without football is in danger of deteriorating into a medieval study hall." - Frank Leahy, Notre Dame

"There's nothing that cleanses your soul like getting the hell kicked out of you." - Woody Hayes, Ohio State

"I don't expect to win enough games to be put on NCAA probation. I just want to win enough to warrant an investigation." - Bob Devaney, Nebraska

"In Alabama, an atheist is someone who doesn't believe in Bear Bryant." - Wally Butts, Georgia

"You can learn more character on the two-yard line than anywhere else in life." - Paul Dietzel, LSU

"It's kind of hard to rally around a math class." - Bear Bryant, Alabama

When asked if Fayetteville was the end of the world - "No, but you can see it from here." - Lou Holtz, Arkansas

"I make my practices real hard because if a player is a quitter, I want him to quit in practice, not in a game." - Bear Bryant, Alabama

"There's one sure way to stop us from scoring-give us the ball near the goal line." - Matty Bell, SMU

"Lads, you're not to miss practice unless your parents died or you died." - Frank Leahy, Notre Dame

"I never graduated from Iowa, but I was only there for two terms - Truman's and Eisenhower's." - Alex Karras, Iowa

"My advice to defensive players: Take the shortest route to the ball and arrive in a bad humor." - Bowden Wyatt, Tennessee

"I could have been a Rhodes Scholar, except for my grades." - Duffy Daugherty, Michigan State

"Always remember . . . Goliath was a 40-point favorite over David." - Shug Jordan, Auburn

"They cut us up like boarding house pie. And that's real small pieces." - Darrell Royal, Texas

"Show me a good and gracious loser, and I'll show you a failure." - Knute Rockne, Notre Dame

"They whipped us like a tied up goat." - Spike Dykes, Texas Tech

"I asked Darrell Royal, the coach of the Texas Longhorns, why he didn't recruit me and he said: 'Well, Walt, we took a look at you and you weren't any good." - Walt Garrison, Oklahoma State

"Son, you've got a good engine, but your hands aren't on the steering wheel." - Bobby Bowden, Florida State

"Football is not a contact sport - it is a collision sport. Dancing is a contact sport." - Duffy Daugherty, Michigan State

After USC lost 51-0 to Notre Dame, his postgame message to his team: **"All those who need showers, take them."** - John McKay, USC

"If lessons are learned in defeat, our team is getting a great education." - Murray Warmath, Minnesota

"The only qualifications for a lineman are to be big and dumb. To be a back, you only have to be dumb." - Knute Rockne, Notre Dame

"Oh, we played about like three tons of buzzard puke this afternoon." - Spike Dykes, Texas Tech

COLLEGE FOOTBALL COACHES' QUOTABLE QUOTES

'It isn't necessary to see a good tackle. You can hear it.' - Knute Rockne/Notre Dame

'We live one day at a time and scratch where it itches.' - Darrell Royal, Texas

'Football is only a game. Spiritual things are eternal. Nevertheless, Beat Texas ' - Seen on a church sign in Arkansas prior to the 1969 game.

'We didn't tackle well today but we made up for it by not blocking.' - Wilson Matthews, Little Rock Central High School

'Three things can happen when you throw the ball, and two of them are bad.' - Darrell Royal, University of Texas

'I've found that prayers work best when you have big players.' - Knute Rockne, Notre Dame

'Gentlemen, it is better to have died as a small boy than to fumble this football.' - John Heisman

AUTHOR'S NOTE

I did not need a side-line pass, locker room privilege, a seat on the team plane, or a week behind the scenes at training camp to write this book. Give me just over 1,000 Patriot gamebook reports, the internet, almost a photographic memory, a thirst for unique facts/stories/anecdotes, and a life-long love for the New England/Boston Patriots, and voíla – *PATRIOTS PASSION From Day One* is what you get. Of course, there have to be some misstatements, incorrectly recalled numbers, names, and dates; so please drop me a line at mking@readusforfun.com, to share your discoveries. Writing this book for 14 months close to 24/7 was an honor, awesome happening and mostly, just a plain fun time. Thank you to the Patriots, for providing me with the material.

Resources

2008 New England Patriots Media Guide
2009 New England Patriots Media Guide
Boston Herald
Boston Globe
Pro-Football-Reference.com
Wikipedia.com
The American Football League: a year-by-year history, 1960-1969 by Ed Gruver
Remembertheafl.com
My just about photographic memory and my heart

ABOUT THE AUTHOR

PATRIOTS PASSION is Michael A. King's second venture into the literary world. In September 2008, he released *THE HEARTACHE YEARS*, a book about the Red Sox during the 1960s, 1970s and 1980s, focusing on the years 1967, 1975, 1978, and 1986. His ability to uncover the unknown, obscure, and unique within well-known facts and trivia is his specialty and passion. Michael considers himself a sports archeologist. He is able to unearth the most amazing anecdotes, and when unveiled, makes the reader say, *"Oh wow", "How the heck did he find this out?"* His favorite, *"This is a never-to-be-forgotten fact. I have to remember this one!"*

While attending high school in Dover, MA, Michael was a student reporter for *The Dover Reporter, Dover-Sherborn Suburban Press* and *Framingham News* (now the *MetroWest Daily News*) covering football, basketball, and baseball. King attended University of St. Thomas in St. Paul, MN. Despite majoring in journalism in college, after graduation he embarked on 25 years in the retail industry. While in college, he covered football for *The Aquin*, St. Thomas' weekly newspaper.

After recovering from open-heart surgery in 2003, then complications from a double stroke in 2006, King decided to follow his dream and began to dabble in researching and writing a broad array of obscure facts. One thing led to another, and in January 2007, he self-published trivia books to share with friends. He started his own one-man publishing company, Read Us For Fun Publishing (R.U.F.F.) in the summer of 2008 to print his Red Sox book.

After this Patriots book, he is planning to research and write books on the Boston Celtics and Boston Bruins. (He was heard saying, "The Celtics book . . . I could do it in my sleep, but I'm staying up; and it will be the best.")

King lives in Boston's suburban MetroWest area and is planning his wedding as this book goes to print. His son Greg lives just outside Worcester and attends a local college. The dog in the R.U.F.F. logo is modeled after his Yorkie, Tessie. Michael is the play-by-play/color commentator for the Dover-Sherborn Raiders girls basketball team on Dover-Sherborn Cable TV, a role he has enjoyed since January 2002. In Fall 2010, King added both Dovers Sherborn Girls and Boys Varsity soccer to his play-by-play repetoire.

1 First Ave.
Needham MA 02494

Cesar E. Moreno

Tel: 339-225-4558
Fax: 339-225-4562

How May We Help You?

Dover Mobil

2 Walpole St • P.O. Box 145 • Dover, MA 02030
508-785-1304 • 508-785-3365

Mike Sassine

Full mechanic services and state inspections available.